@-trepreneur!

e-trepreneur!

A Radically Simple
and Inexpensive Plan for
a Profitable INTERNET STORE
in 7 DAYS!

Sherry Szydlik
and
Lamont Wood

JOHN WILEY & SONS, INC.
New York • Chichester • Weinheim • Brisbane • Singapore • Toronto

Library of Congress Cataloging-in-Publication Data:

Szydlik, Sherry, 1968–
    E-trepreneur: a radically simple and inexpensive plan for a profitable
Internet store in 7 days / Sherry Szydlik and Lamont Wood.
      p. cm.
    Includes index.
    ISBN 0-471-38075-X (pbk. : alk. paper)
    1. Electronic commerce. 2. Entrepreneurship. I. Wood, Lamont, 1953–
    II. Title.
HF5548.32 .S984 2000
658.8′4—dc21
                                                                        00-36656

Printed in the United States of America.

10 9 8 7 6 5 4 3 2 1

Dedicated to Louise O'Donnell

Contents

Introduction: Is This Book for You?   ix

SECTION ONE: The Promise and Reality of Electronic Commerce   1

Chapter 1   The E-commerce Opportunity   3
Chapter 2   Outsource It!   26
Chapter 3   Reasons You Can Do This   43
Chapter 4   First Things First   51

SECTION TWO: Creating an E-commerce Site, One Day at a Time   55

Chapter 5   Sunday—Drawing Up the Blueprints   57
Chapter 6   Monday—Signing Up   76
Chapter 7   Tuesday—Preproduction, First Steps   85
Chapter 8   Wednesday—Preproduction, Final Steps   98
Chapter 9   Thursday—Site Creation   115
Chapter 10   Friday—Test Drive   143

SECTION THREE: Open for E-business: How to Prosper as an Online Store Owner 153

Chapter 11	Finished.com—Now Comes the Marketing	155
Chapter 12	Won't You Stay for a While?	176
Chapter 13	Love Thy Customer: Customer Service Aspects	181
Chapter 14	Auxiliary E-commerce	187
Chapter 15	The Dark Side	211
Chapter 16	Charting Your Results	236
Chapter 17	Summing Things	246
Appendix A	Sources of Information	251
Appendix B	Representative E-commerce Service Providers	265
Appendix C	Useful HTML Tags	269
Glossary		283
Index		309

Introduction
Is This Book for You?

E-commerce (electronic commerce): the question is not whether you need to know about it. The question is whether this book is for you.

The answer is yes if:

- You're a small operator who sells things. You feel you could sell more of those things online, where countless people from all over the world can visit your shop at any time of the day or night.
- You hope to sell something and figure that getting started on the Web would be faster and cheaper than renting, decorating, equipping, and staffing a shop and then stocking it with inventory. In fact, you suspect that setting up shop on the Web could be cheaper than renting a downtown parking space in certain metropolitan areas.

In both cases, you are correct.

This book is not for you if, say, someone handed it to you between one of the many meetings you've been attending as your corporation gears up for its big e-commerce push, probably through a subsidiary created just for that purpose. Millions are going to be spent on software integration to existing corporate information and accounting systems, and data mining. We wish you lots of luck.

Returning to our target reader: Don't worry. You don't need to do what he is doing. For you, most of the necessary integration can take place inside your head, and we can take *data mining* to mean "deciding what to do next."

In fact, we'd like to call your attention to how thin this book is. We are assuming that you already know most of what you need to know and have the equipment you need to launch into e-commerce. This includes:

- Knowing what the World Wide Web is and how it's organized, with Web sites and search engines.
- Knowing what a Web browser is and how it works.
- Possessing an Internet access account.
- Possessing a personal computer with a modem and browser that you can use to access the Web.
- Having enough computer literacy to know what *file format* means.

Notice that we have not said anything about:

- Servers.
- ISDN, xDSL, or T1 lines.
- Points of presence.
- Domains.
- Multiplexers.
- Routers.
- Shopping-cart software.
- Firewalls.
- Operating systems.

That's because we are going to show you how to find and hire third parties to handle these background details—inexpensively. Just as you already use an Internet service provider (ISP) to handle the many technical details involved in getting you connected to the Web though a phone line, you will learn how to use an E-commerce service provider (ESP)—no psychic jokes allowed—to host your e-commerce site. They'll supply the order-taking and credit card–processing functions. You'll supply (directly from your personal computer) the Web site pages that sell the product—and, of course, whatever manufacturing, shipping, and service is called for by the sale.

So just by being online, you're already well on your way to being an e-commerce merchant—about seven days away, as we'll demonstrate while we walk you through the process.

Meanwhile, the other reason this volume is so thin is that we will not bedevil you with any of the 50-cent terms with which the field of e-commerce—despite its youth—has festooned itself. In case you were wondering what you were missing, here's a rundown:

■ DISINTERMEDIATION

Yes, that's 17 letters long. It means "the state of removing the intermediary." (It seems that *demiddlemanizing* was too sexist to catch on.) Anyway, the word embodies the fear among box pushers that e-commerce will let the consumers buy directly from the manufacturers, leaving them (being no more than intermediaries) no way to justify their existence. As a social trend, it has remained invisible. But if you were already prone to worrying about how to justify your existence, you might as well go on and worry about disintermediation, too.

■ BOTS

That's short for *robot,* but simply using the word would not be with-it enough. It implies Web-browsing software that would shop for you, surfing e-commerce sites until it finds the lowest price for what you want. And it signifies terror to those who depend on marketing hype to move their wares, because a bot won't be pulled in by flashy graphics—typically, pictures of ethereal young models staring wistfully at the camera, perhaps wishing it were a forbidden hamburger.

■ AVATAR

An avatar is a fancy bot, one that will keep your quirks in mind while shopping on-line. Alternately, the word is Sanskrit for "the incarnation of a deity." (Obviously, there are people who take e-commerce far too seriously.)

■ TRADING PARTNER

This term refers to someone with whom you do business, as a customer or supplier or whatever. But somehow you can't just call a customer a customer anymore, or a supplier a supplier.

■ INFRASTRUCTURE

The infrastructure refers to all that stuff around you that you don't miss until it breaks down: roads, bridges, sewers, power lines, the phone system, your computer, and so on. Because you were able to make it to the store and buy this book, we'll assume your infrastructure is adequate.

■ CULTURAL FORCES

Yes, there are people out there who don't like to use computers. And there are people who won't drink Coca-Cola because of its supposed alcohol content. Get over it.

Of course, as we proceed, we will have to use specialized terms that do not amount to gilded jargon. We will highlight their meaning and present timely tips and advice, using these devices:

This is used to introduce new terms (or new uses of old terms) that would probably be unfamiliar to the average reader.

These are mini–case studies highlighting the real-world experiences of e-commerce veterans.

These are snippets of wisdom, encouragement, and advice from e-commerce experts or distilled from multiple sources.

CHEAT SHEET

These are chapter-specific fill-in-the-blank sections to hold names, passwords, notes, numbers, and other important pieces of information the user will have to track during the task of mounting an e-commerce site.

e-trepreneur!

Section One

The Promise and Reality of Electronic Commerce

Chapter 1

The E-commerce Opportunity

Do you like big numbers? Good, because we've got some numbers for you that are big enough to challenge Bill Gates's accountant. Take these projections on the future of e-commerce:

- Jupiter Communications (an Internet market research firm in New York City) said in an August 4, 1999, report that consumer-related e-commerce in the United States is doubling every year and should amount to about $41 billion in 2002.
- International Data Corporation (or IDC, yet another market research firm, this one based in Framingham, Massachusetts) disagrees, saying that consumer e-commerce spending will amount to $56 billion that year. IDC was also bold enough to state (in June 1999) that total worldwide Internet commerce (both consumer and business-to-business) will amount to about $1 trillion in 2003. Six months later, it decided that the world Internet economy would reach $1 trillion a trifle sooner—in 2001. IDC now maintains that by 2003, the volume of trade will have reached $2.8 trillion, thanks to a surge in the numbers of users as well as in the average transaction size.
- Even bolder is a forecast made by Forrester Research, a market research firm in Cambridge, Massachusetts, that no high-tech journalist can go long without quoting. It predicted in December that business-to-business online commerce in the United States alone will amount to $1.3 trillion

in 2003, or more than 9 percent of total business sales. Few industry supply chains will be immune, but e-commerce will be particularly prevalent in fields involving computers, electronics, aerospace, defense, petrochemicals, utilities, and motor vehicles, according to its analysis. Participation will accelerate because of the *network effect*—the more entities that participate, the more gains result from the participation. (This report included a retraction of Forrester's 1997 prediction that U.S. Internet business commerce would amount to $327 billion in 2002. Instead, hypergrowth is at hand, it announced.)

- Analysts at the Gartner Group, a market research firm in Stamford, Connecticut, estimated in January 2000 that by 2004, 7 percent of the globe's business-to-business commerce will take place online. That percent equals $7.3 trillion.

The predictions of the Boston Consulting Group (or BCG, colocated, somehow, in Boston and Toronto) are so remarkable as to deserve special attention. BCG says that by the year 2003, one-fourth of all business-to-business purchasing in the United States will be done online, amounting to a staggering $2.8 trillion. (Financial products, labor, and insurance are not included in this estimate.) Business-to-business e-commerce will be growing by 33 percent yearly in the meantime. Previous attempts to estimate business-to-business e-commerce fell short because they ignored the volume of electronic data interchange (EDI) transactions over private networks, which will amount to $780 million in 2003, explains BCG.

Companies that move aggressively into business-to-business e-commerce report cost reductions of up to 15 percent for materials by using that method, says BCG. Savings on transaction processing alone can reach almost 65 percent, thanks to the simplification of the buyers' internal purchasing and record-keeping processes.

The North American business-to-business e-commerce market is currently twice the size of the rest of the world's business-to-business e-commerce markets combined, and Western Europe lags by about 18 months. But there will be strong growth in all sectors, BCG predicts, as global supply chains go online. By 2003, it expects penetration to include:

- Twenty-four percent in North America, growing from the current 7 percent.
- Eleven percent in Western Europe, growing from the present 3 percent.
- Nine percent in Asia and the Pacific Rim, growing from the present 2 percent.
- Seven percent in Latin America, growing from the present 2 percent.

Back in the United States, by 2003 six industrial sectors will represent 65 percent of all business-to-business e-commerce, adds BCG: retail, motor vehicles, shipping, industrial equipment, high technology, and government. Cost savings (that 15 percent mentioned previously), rather than strategic opportunities, will drive most of the early adoptions.

Now, what conclusions are we to draw from this crescendo of nine-figure numbers? Indeed, as we face an uncertain future, with what wisdom derived from these learned predictions from the finest minds on the East Coast can we arm ourselves? Two insights come to mind:

1. Golly, e-commerce is the wave of the future, a modern gold rush. We have the once-in-a-lifetime opportunity to get aboard on the ground floor, empowering ourselves through socially conscious wealth creation; we should grab what we can, or something in between.

2. Research firms, brokerage houses, and consultancies sure do like to one-up each other by issuing press releases on the latest hot topics.

Congratulations if you were leaning seriously toward number two. But bear in mind that research and predictions such as those we've presented here have some value—much in the way that gold has value, even though it doesn't taste good and is too soft to make into anything useful. Yet everyone assigns it value, and in most situations it lives up to expectations. Likewise, all those predictions must be viewed in light of your own situation, but in doing so, keep these context considerations in mind:

- You can't even define *e-commerce* to everyone's satisfaction.
- This being a new frontier in human experience, the predictions are based more on assumptions than on data.

- The wildest of these assumptions is that as the e-commerce settlers arrive on the frontier, they will behave like the pioneers did, and (to continue the metaphor) the city folk (when they later arrive in serious numbers) will behave like the settlers did. Alas, the only data that have come in so far concerns the behavior of the pioneers, who (as pioneers always do) make a point of acting in nonstandard ways and of not flinching at arrows.
- By the time these near-future predictions arrive, the U.S. gross national product will have grown to something over $10 trillion, if it's not there already. In other words, although some of those numbers we quoted are quite tidy, they don't represent a total takeover of the economy. Offline holdouts will not (in the near future) be relegated to shantytowns along the railroad tracks. Plenty of action will remain offline, especially in the retail arena. (BCG's huge figures represent an accumulation of transactions as items in business-to-business supply chains are resold several times before final consumption.)
- What do you care about these statistics? You have your business to run, and it stands or falls on its own, not as part of some national average.

You'll notice that the pundits did agree on one general trend: e-commerce is headed through the roof. Along the way, they also show general agreement on one nonnumeric fact:

> **In the future there will not be any Internet companies. Because everyone will be doing business on the Internet. Or they won't be in business. (See Chapter 17.)**

Now let's talk about that gold-rush theme. Somehow, the metaphor keeps coming up. Indeed, if you take a look at some of the big names in e-commerce, you do see gold, and it is indeed rushing—out the door. Consider the following cases in point:

■ AMAZON.COM

Doubtless the most visible success story in the consumer e-commerce field, Amazon.com is based in Seattle and sells books online. Millions of them. Plus, it has gotten into CDs, videos, toys, electronics, gifts, and anything else that comes to hand. It has also started an auction service. In its last fiscal year it grossed $1.64 billion—and lost $720 million.

■ CDNOW ONLINE, INC.

Selling music CDs, cassettes, videos, T-shirts, and DVDs, this firm (located in New York City) recently tried unsuccessfully to sell itself to a conglomerate. In its latest fiscal year, it lost $119.2 million on sales of $147.2 million.

■ VALUE AMERICA, INC.

This is a price club located in Charlottesville, Virginia, that sells about one hundred thousand products from about eight hundred different vendors and has no physical stores. In fact, it has no inventory—the vendors drop-ship (a practice defined a little later in this chapter) the orders for Value America from their factories or warehouses. During its latest fiscal year it grossed $182.6 million and lost $143.5 million. The stock price fell from 40 to 2, and the press was reporting "inner turmoil" and "palace coups."

■ BUY.COM

Located in Aliso Viejo, California, buy.com bills itself as an "e-commerce portal" instead of a price club (embracing new buzzwords over the old, as it were) but otherwise operates like Value America in that it processes orders while warehousing and shipping is handled by the vendors. In its latest fiscal year it grossed $125.3 million and lost $17.8 million. (On the day it went public, it nevertheless opened at $13 per share and zoomed to $30. It fell below $5 in about ten weeks.)

These and other firms have bought into the idea that you need to spend money today to be a dominant player tomorrow, when all the world will be buying over the Internet and those who got there early will own the turf. Brand awareness is everything, and because they are starting from scratch, the only thing they can do is buy brand awareness, cost what it may. You can easily see why they have an obsession with brand awareness, because (thanks to a reliance on drop shipping) their brand name is all they have—they don't do any of the things normally associated with commerce. For example, they don't:

- Invent technology.
- Develop products.
- Manufacture products.
- Market products.
- Mine raw materials.
- Process raw materials.
- Produce anything through any method.
- Grow crops.
- Ship anything themselves (typically).

They just put up Web pages and take orders—and spend tons of money on advertising.

At last report, Silicon Valley was said to be bulging at the seams with emulators, frantically pushing and shoving to get office space, clerical employees, technical employees, publicity and advertising representation, and even parking space—everything but money, which they got after dropping by one of the venture capital firms on Sand Hill Road.

Don't go. The opportunity of e-commerce is that you have another channel for doing what businesses must always do to be successful: satisfy the buyer and especially the buyer's perception of quality. And a big part of that perception is the expectation that you can be found on the Web. After all, you might not judge a company by the size of its advertisement in the Yellow Pages, but you would think it a little odd if it were not in the phone book. After that, there is the old foursome of price, convenience, product, and knowledge. Each has its place.

■ PRICE

Yes, the low costs of e-commerce compared with those of having a store may indeed let you offer lower prices online. However, those cost savings can be eaten up by the shipping

department or by your frantic efforts to create brand awareness. Basing your business on having the lowest prices is like
bragging of being the fastest gun in Dodge City. At any moment
someone faster may emerge, with catastrophic results for you.
And online, the latest gunslinger can find you at the speed of
light.

■ CONVENIENCE

Here is where e-commerce shines. Buyers don't have to fight
their way through traffic to reach you. You, meanwhile, don't
even have to be awake to take the call.

■ PRODUCT

It really helps to be selling something of genuine value that's
unique as well. We'll assume you are. But taking quiet satisfaction from that fact is not enough—you need to be touting it
where people expect to see you, and increasingly that means
the Web. If your product or service is not unique, don't despair,
because your Web site can be. It should be well organized so
that everything about your offering is displayed in loving detail
and buying is easy.

■ KNOWLEDGE

People do more shopping online than they do buying. On the
Web, they can gather information: They can see what products
are available, what features those products offer, and what
prices those features involve, and then they can judge whether
the benefits of those features are worth the price—all without
putting up with overbearing, glad-handing, plastic-haired salespeople.

The percentage of lookers that you can turn into buyers is
called your site's *conversion rate*. But although you want to boast
of a high conversion rate, you do not want to do this by spurn-
ing the unconverted surfers at your site. You need to go ahead
and give them the information they are looking for. Some will
find that what you are offering is not what they want, and if

they had made a purchase, they would have been unhappy customers. So you are spared that headache. Others will learn what they sought to know, and even if they don't buy from you, they will thereupon associate you with a positive shopping experience, leaving open the possibility of positive word-of-mouth references. And you were able to provide that positive shopping experience without having to lease, stock, and staff a store or to produce and mail out expensive, full-color catalogs.

Remember that prediction we mentioned earlier: eventually there won't be any Internet companies as distinguished from those that are not online because everyone will be doing business on the Internet—or they won't be in business.

EXPERTS SPEAK

Bargains are not what drive people to shop online, according to a study by Mercer Management Consulting of New York City based on a survey of more than a thousand Internet shoppers. Instead, 82 percent said they liked to use the Internet because they could find the information that helped them make better decisions. Meanwhile, 72 percent cited the Internet's convenience. Only 49 percent cited the Internet's ability to save them money.

EXPERTS SPEAK

Jupiter Communications, mentioned earlier, reports that $7 billion was spent online during the 1999 Christmas shopping season. Ninety percent of surveyed shoppers said they were largely satisfied with their online buying experience, up from 78 percent in 1998. But they were concerned about the same things they had worried about in 1998: security, inventory shortfalls, shipping costs, and slow Web site performance. Half spent less than $200, but 35 percent said they would likely spend more online during the following Christmas shopping season based on their experience, and only 4 percent said they were so discouraged that they would probably spend less.

DEFINE THIS!

Drop Shipping

Drop shipping means that you, the e-commerce merchant, take an order for an item and pass it on to the manufacturer (or, in many cases, distributor) of the item. The manufacturer then ships the item to the buyer with your label, invoice, and so on, and for all the buyer knows, it was sent from your vast warehouse via your fleet of trucks. In reality, all you may have is your Web site and an agreement with the manufacturer. You take orders, pass them on to the manufacturer, and the price differential is your profit. But other challenges may arise.

Drop shipping is a common practice, especially with furniture and large appliances, because it cuts down on shipping—instead of your product being shipped from the manufacturer to a distributor and then to a store and *then* to the consumer, it's sent directly to the consumer.

"If done well, drop shipping does not add any problems," says John Schulte, chairman of the National Mail Order Association in Minneapolis. "But you can go overboard if you are trying to get by with no money and drop shipping everything, down to $9.95 items. What if the buyer is trying to coordinate an ensemble and buying a number of small things from multiple vendors? The buyer will be waiting for several shipments, the supplier will have a hard time coordinating it, and it ends up being a mess.

"In most cases you can't have both 100 percent drop shipping and a high customer satisfaction rate—unless most of the product is coming from one large distributor," Schulte warns.

The problem is especially acute with start-ups by newcomers who have been told—typically in a get-rich seminar or book—that they can start a business with no money by relying on drop shipping, he notes.

"I spend a lot of time telling people not to waste their money buying schemes about setting up a business with $500 in three steps, or something," Schulte adds. "There are so many people out there trying to convince you to start a business without any forethought, to sucker you into thinking you can do it all by drop shipping. Of course, it sounds great, since you don't have to put any money into inventory. We see it all the time since we deal with so many start-ups."

■ THE VIRTUAL BUYERS

Meanwhile, we have to remember that these people whose expectations you need to satisfy are not the same as the ones hanging out at the mall. They're online. True, there is considerable overlap, as mall rats return home and turn on their computers and Web surfers venture out of their houses to check out the face-to-face world. But whoever they are in real life, when online they tend to adopt a set of behaviors and expectations molded by cyberspace. Let's look at their chief characteristics, as determined by recent surveys and polls by market research firms. (As before, their figures do not always agree. This is new territory, after all. Plus, there are disagreements on terms, such as what an adult is—a 16-year-old? an 18-year-old?—and if Mexico is part of North America.)

➤ Their Present Numbers

Based on analyses of published studies, Nua Ltd. (an Internet firm in Dublin, Ireland) estimates that as of March of 2000 there were 304.36 million people online around the world. The breakdown:

Africa	2.58 million
Asia/Pacific	68.9 million
Europe	83.35 million
Middle East	1.9 million
U.S. and Canada	136.86 million
Latin America	10.74 million

According to Nielsen Media Research of New York City, in a June 17, 1999, report, the number of Internet users in North America (defined as the United States and Canada) who were 16 and older reached 92 million in mid-1999. That figure had gone up 16 percent in nine months, which means that 40 percent of the population was online by then.

For the United States alone, other figures (from a May 19, 1999, report by Mediamark Research, Inc., a market research firm in New York City) show that in mid-1999, 64.2 million adults were going online each month. The number of U.S. adults with Internet access stood at 83.7 million, which means that 42.2 percent of Americans over 18 were regular Internet users—a 20 percent increase over the previous year. Other factoids from Mediamark about the U.S. Internet user population:

- A tiny majority was male: 51.4 percent, versus 48.6 percent female.
- Home users led office users by about two to one.
- Asked if they ever used an online service, 28.6 million named America Online (AOL), 7.96 million named Microsoft Network (MSN), 1.96 million named CompuServe, and 1.93 million named Prodigy.

And let's not forget the study in late 1998 by Roper Starch Worldwide, another market research firm in New York City, which found that two-thirds of U.S. Internet users would rather give up their phone and TV than their Internet access. Of those with laptops, 50 percent took them along on vacation.

➤ Their Future Numbers

There will be 545 million users online in 2003, estimates Datamonitor, a market research firm in London. And the *Computer Industry Almanac* (a publication of Computer Industry Almanac, Inc., of Arlington Heights, Illinois, that prefers to render its initials as C-I-A rather than CIA) estimates that there will be over 717 million Internet users worldwide by the end of 2005. It defines *user* as an adult who gets on the Internet at least once a week. Its breakdown for 2005 in a September 9, 1999, press release:

North America	230 million
Western Europe	202 million
Asia/Pacific	171 million
Latin America	43 million
Middle East and Africa	23.6 million

In North America, a little more than a third of all homes were online in 1998, and by 2003 the number is expected to reach 56 percent, says Forrester Research.

➤ E-commerce Becoming Global

According to IDC, non-U.S. e-commerce will grow rapidly, from 26 percent of the global total in 1998 to 46 percent in 2003. In Western Europe it will grow from $5.6 billion in 1998 to $430 billion in 2003—a compounded annual growth rate of 138 percent. Over the same period, Asia/Pacific (including Japan) will see its e-commerce grow from $2.7 billion to $72 billion. IDC figures that worldwide e-commerce will amount to just over $1 trillion in 2003, even assuming that, like today, only 36 percent of online users will buy anything.

➤ Frequency of Online Purchasing

Dataquest, a market research firm in San Jose, Califiornia, reports that in the first half of 1999, there were 37 million U.S. households online. In about a third of the cases, someone in the house bought something or made a reservation online during that period.

Navidec, a market research firm in Englewood, Colorado, got even more favorable results in a phone poll in mid-1999, which showed that 53 percent of U.S. Internet users had made an on-line purchase during the previous year. (That's compared with 26 percent in 1997.)

Nielsen reports that about 30 percent of North American Internet users in 1999 were online consumers according to its criteria and that about 60 percent had used the Internet to compare prices. Of the 28 million people whom Nielsen estimates had made purchases via the Web, 9 million people bought something at least once a month, and 1 million people bought something at least once a week. Of all online buyers, 13 percent had made their first purchase via the Internet in the preceding month.

Other sources put the percent of the online population who buy via the Internet at between 32 and 36 percent.

As for what they are buying online, Greenfield Online, a research firm in Westport, Connccticut, has this breakout of what percentage of the online U.S. population has bought what kind of product:

Computer software	19%
Books	21%
Computer hardware	13%
Music CDs	22%
Clothing	8%

Navidec, meanwhile, reports that the most popular products to buy online are books and publications (52 percent had bought them), computer software (42 percent), and travel products or services (37 percent.)

➤ Buying Online = Not Buying Offline

An August 4, 1999, report by Jupiter Communications forecast that less than 10 percent of online commerce in 2002 would be "incremental," meaning that the sales would not have occurred without the advent of e-commerce. Therefore, about 90 percent of the anticipated growth in e-commerce will be at the expense of offline commerce: Those online sales will take place in lieu of offline sales that would have been otherwise captured by a traditional channel.

The report complains that most traditional merchants' Internet strategies were paralyzed by indecision, allowing newcomers to seize the high ground. The traditional merchants rationalize their inactivity by assuming that any Web sales they achieve would simply cannibalize their traditional channel sales. Hence, there is no point in investing in e-commerce.

But the danger is that buyers will switch to online competitors. Merchants must accept the idea that cannibalized sales are better than no sales at all, said the report.

Navidec reports that 35 percent of online consumers said they were purchasing less from offline stores because of the Internet and that 38 percent said they were purchasing less from mail-order catalogues because of the Internet.

➤ Attitudes toward E-commerce Problems

Dataquest also reports that overall customer satisfaction with the online buying experience was 88 percent, despite the fact that 20 percent of those who bought something experienced some kind of problem. (For the problem cases, 49 percent involved something that did not arrive, and in half of those cases they were billed anyway. For another quarter, the complaint was that they were unable to reach the vendor's customer support department by e-mail.)

Navidec finds that overall satisfaction of Internet users with their online purchases was a whopping 99 percent, with 79 percent describing themselves as "very satisfied." Although 36 percent remained concerned about the security of shopping online, only 21 percent were worried about credit card fraud—half the percentage found in 1997.

➤ Women and E-commerce

A lot of recent growth in Internet use and e-commerce appears to come from a greater participation by women in the online world. Of North American Internet users, the number that were women suddenly rose to 46 percent in 1999, says Nielsen, after several years of staying at 43 percent. Of those who shop via the Internet, 41 percent were women, having risen from 36 percent. Among those who bought something over the Internet, the percentage of women rose from 29 to 38.

Women bought 45 percent of the books sold online during the previous year, reports Nielsen, plus 38 percent of the CDs and videos, 24 percent of the computer hardware, and 53 percent of the clothing.

➤ E-commerce Isn't Small Change

The average value of an online transaction is $4,600, according to a survey by ActivMedia, a market research firm in Peterborough, New Hampshire. But actually this figure is the average for two clusters, one for business-to-business and the other for consumer transactions; the former's average ranged between $1,000 and $10,000, and the latter's ranged between $100 and $500. About 60 percent of consumer transactions were for $500 or less, and a third were for less than $100. Of business-to-business transactions, 1 in 10 were under $100, and a third were between $100 and $500.

In a telephone poll of Internet users, Navidec found that the average online purchase was $206—up 17 percent from 1998.

➤ Age and E-commerce

A survey in 1999 of Americans 50 and older by Charles Schwab & Co., Inc., (the New York City brokerage house) found that 40 percent of them had a computer at home, as opposed to 29 percent three years earlier. Seventy percent of those computer owners had Internet access. Fifteen percent of those were heavy users, defined as people who spent more than 10 hours a week online.

Greenfield, quoted previously concerning what online shoppers buy, has also gathered figures specifically concerning Americans over 55 years of age. Here's what they buy:

Computer software	43%
Books	43%
Computer hardware	24%
Music CDs	29%
Clothing	19%

Notice that the figures are about twice that of the general population. When senior citizens go online, they mean business. Of those who are online, 78 percent had bought something, and 92 percent had window shopped. They tended to be familiar with the technology, as well as the use of peripherals such as scanners and printers. Only 19 percent expressed any discomfort with the complexities of computers, the report found.

➤ Youth and E-commerce

Forrester Research estimates that 47 percent of U.S. citizens between the ages of 16 and 22 are online. That's about 12.4 million people. Someone invested in a computer for each of them, meaning they have a presence in the economy. In fact, they have average annual incomes of $3,000 each, most of it presumably disposable, creating a $37 billion market right there.

Jupiter Communications, meanwhile, has found that two-thirds of U.S. teenagers and one-third of U.S. children with Internet access had shopped or bought something online. At that rate, the U.S. youth market will be worth $1.3 billion in 2002, the firm concludes.

The figures foretell a future population of adults who are as comfortable online as offline and are likely to do their shopping in either domain.

➤ Young but Not Stupid . . .

Forrester Research has found that on-line youths fell into two categories:

1. *Netizens* who spend more than 10 hours weekly online and whose lives seemed to be dominated by the Web.

2. *Cliquers* who spend less time online and for whom the Web was just another daily activity. Both groups tended to multitask—eating, listening to music, or watching TV while online.

➤ . . . In Fact, Smarter than You Think

Forrester Research has also found that the hottest leading brands in the real world had no impact on their surfing, and they showed no interest in visiting the Web sites of those brands, a survey showed. Only usefulness and interesting interaction mattered—brand recognition had no pull at all.

Web-Grown Instincts

Young Netizens have developed specific attitudes and expectations that Web vendors must comply with at their peril, adds Forrester. The firm lists five Net rules:

1. Information is everything—extensive and accurate information should be available anywhere at any time.

This agrees with a Navidec poll that found that 70 percent of polled Internet consumers cited the quality of the information available on a product as a crucial factor in their decision to make an online purchase. (Of course—if they were satisfied to be passive recipients of canned propaganda, they would be watching TV. They expect your Web site to be an encyclopedia about your products.)

2. They know that personal information about themselves has value, which means marketers must offer something of value in exchange if they are going to poll Netizens about their preferences and behavior.

3. Choice is a basic right. Suppliers must offer a wealth of options and configurations. (Weren't computers invented to make such things easy?)

4. There is such a thing as a free lunch—your lunch, when they eat it. If you want to get consumers' attention, you have to be prepared to offer no-strings giveaways.

5. Spontaneous online trust is entirely possible. They don't need face-to-face trust-building interaction. (Apparently, they leave face-to-face interaction for non-commercial settings.)

➤ Delivery Issues

Order fulfillment typically means residential delivery. If you previously had thought in terms of shipping pallet loads of products to distributors or stores, you have to adjust to the idea of delivering individual items to the doorsteps of buyers. (And Forrester Research has found that 85 percent of Web merchants made no attempt to sell internationally because they could not handle the complications of cross-border shipping.)

➤ Pockets of Resistance

The two-thirds of Netizens who have not bought anything online express a number of reservations about the medium, according to The Intermarket Group, a research firm in San Diego, including the following areas of concern:

Product pricing	77%
Potential return problems	67%
Credit card security	65%
Privacy issues	58%
Confused by Web site	35%

(Of those who *were* buyers, a depressing 48 percent complained about confusing Web sites, meaning they made their purchase despite the site.)

Of course, that two-thirds have not taken part in e-commerce does not mean they never will, leaving room for considerable expansion.

■ WRAPPING IT UP

Where does this leave us? Basically, with a phenomenon—e-commerce—that will soon cease being a novelty and become a major part of the retailing scene. An ever-larger part of the public is online, is buying things there, and expects to see you there, too. If you are not there, a competitor will be and will siphon off more and more of your business.

Your move is obvious. As we'll show in the next chapter, it takes less time and money than you'd think.

EXPERTS SPEAK

Forget disintermediation, advises Harry Hoyle, vice president of the market research firm GartnerGroup Dataquest in Stamford, Connecticut (although he's in the London office.) (*Disintermediation* is the removal of intermediaries so that the public buys directly from the manufacturers.) Basically, unless they are buying commodities, the buying public needs intermediaries, he says.

"What has been successful in e-commerce so far has been CDs, books, flowers and gifts—low-cost commodity products that do not need an intermediary, because you know exactly what you want to buy when you go online," Hoyle notes. "But when you look at total consumer expenditure, there are huge areas, like health and beauty aids, apparel, and food and drink, that have barely been scratched."

In such areas, the purchase decision involves countless options and is based largely on personal taste, he continues. (And, he added, buyers may prefer "touch and feel" shopping.) All this creates what he called "friction."

"Our view is that there will be great success with these categories only with the help of intermediaries of some sort, who can come along and grease the wheel," he concludes.

DEFINE THIS!

E-commerce

You thought this was easy, huh? You thought this was what the book was about, so the definition must be obvious. Guess again. Try this:

While watching QVC, you see a Beanie Baby that steals your heart, so you dial the 800 number and buy it with a credit card. Is that e-commerce? After all, everything happened electronically. Or consider an electrical engineer who spends hours on the Web hunting down the specifications of components he is considering using in a design. When he finally makes his decision, he turns the part numbers over to the purchasing department, who negotiates a deal during a power lunch. The purchase may or may not take place online, but the shopping took place there. There are plenty of e-commerce Web sites that show you their wares in glorious detail, but when you click the "place order" button, you get a screen telling you to call an 800 number.

Basically, we take *e-commerce* to mean, "buying and selling things when the Internet is used to make the transaction." The two previous examples are *Internet-assisted commerce,* and that is the route to take in certain situations. (Some prices have to be negotiated—there is no way around it.) As for QVC, we're not sure what to call it.

Meanwhile, there are those who would reject this definition. E-commerce, they'd say, means that everything must be integrated. Data from Internet sales must be warehoused and then mined for insight, creating a loop-back mechanism that continually modifies your electronic-marketing efforts. Plus you need links to your inventory, accounting, and planning systems. They'll tell you to your face that if you are not spending a million dollars, then you are not with the program.

Go out and prove them wrong.

DEFINE THIS!

Business-to-Business E-commerce

You'll notice that the previously quoted predictions mentioned something called business-to-business e-commerce, foreseeing it to be about twice as big as consumer e-commerce. That is because it generally involves selling wholesale quantities in some segment of a supply chain. Electronics distributors, for instance, often have Web sites where a "qualified reseller" can log in, find what she needs at prices adjusted according to the discount level she has earned through previous orders, what the inventory level is and at which warehouse, and what the likely delivery schedules might be. Plus she can examine a wealth of technical data about the item. There may even be what's called a *configurator* to check if it will work with another specific item. There are PC vendors with Web pages for specific customers, where they can log in and order merchandise based on their contracted prices. But achieving such levels of sophistication takes a major effort, with deep, custom-programmed integration between the e-commerce function and the existing information systems of the entire enterprise. It is not something a small operator should be contemplating, initially or ever. (Meanwhile, business-to-business e-commerce is nothing new, having been done with EDI for about three decades now.)

DEFINE THIS!

Electronic Data Interchange (EDI)

EDI invoices the transmission of predefined, formatted messages from the computer of one business to the computer of a trading partner, covering about everything you'd expect: orders, acknowledgments, invoices, shipping notices, receipts, and even press releases. In fact, there are hundreds of possible EDI messages, many of them specific to an industry. Some corporations require their suppliers to use EDI, and if you need EDI, you have doubtless heard all about it by now. Otherwise, rest easy.

The previously consulted Boston Consulting Group estimates that the volume of EDI in the U.S. amounted to $579 billon in 1998, of which 86 percent took place over private networks.

DEFINE THIS!

Tulips

That's right, tulips. You'll eventually hear someone make reference to those bulbous herbs of the lily family in the course of any discussion of e-commerce and Internet companies. There was a financial bubble in Holland in 1634 caused by a speculation craze in tulip bulbs that makes today's Beanie Baby trade look stone-cold sane. It was the early days of large-scale capitalism, and people were just getting used to the idea that they could invest in something besides land. And here we are in the early days of the Internet, when people are just catching on to the idea of nonphysical commerce. The result: Although conventional firms are typically valued at 10 to 40 times their earnings, Internet firms have found they can get away with being valued at 10 to 40 times their gross revenue. That puts them in a stock-price range about 16 times higher than conventional firms. Let's just hope the bulbs sprout.

$$20 / 20$$

Prior to e-commerce hitting the scene, the splashiest gold rush was the one that took place in 1897 and 1898 in the Klondike region of the Yukon Territory. About one hundred thousand people set out, spending fortunes to equip themselves and get to Skagway, Alaska. From there, they struggled up a frozen mountain pass or took the well-named Dead Horse Trail, and then (when the ice broke) they rafted down the treacherous Yukon River to Dawson City. About thirty thousand showed up at that end, and maybe one-third of 1 percent got rich. (The man who made the biggest find blew it all and died penniless.) But about half of them just stood around on street corners until the summer thaw allowed steamboat service to resume, and then they trickled home.

The demands of the e-commerce gold rush, as we'll show, are dramatically less rigorous. With a little planning, you won't be left standing dazed on a street corner, happy to let the world pass you by. As for striking it rich, that's not the issue—the issue is staying in business. Having done that, well, maybe you can go on and be in that 0.33 percent.

$$20 / 20$$

"Anyone you talk to, nine out of ten will say they want to be self-employed," notes John Schulte. "And in the mail-order business there has always been the allure of a pot of gold."

Schulte warns, "There are people who say they will sell you their catalogue which you can put your name on and mail out, and be in business. But they just throw junk into it. Now they are doing the same with Web sites, saying 'Yes, honey, you can get rich on the Internet.' Just look at the ads in the business section of major newspapers."

20/20

J.D. Power and Associates, the automotive industry research firm (whose awards are often seen touted in car ads), estimates that as many as 40 percent of U.S. consumers who bought a car or truck in 1999 used the Web for shopping. That is up from 25 percent in 1998. But only 2.6 percent actually bought their vehicle over the Internet (although that amounted to 24,000 online purchases per month.) Among used car buyers, 26 percent went on the Internet to make a decision. (Other researchers found that 36 percent of car buyers used the Internet.)

EXPERTS SPEAK

The advantage of e-commerce (at least compared to mail-order business) is not that it lowers the cost of doing business but that it makes a business more agile. At least that's John Schulte's opinion.

"When a company has a dynamic Web site, they can make instant modifications or clear out merchandise that they ordinarily could not afford to put in their catalog," Schulte says. "If you have 500 blue size-10 skirts, that is not enough to put in the catalogue, and in the past you would only be able to close them out to a liquidator for a couple of cents on the dollar. Now you can put them on your Web site in the clearance section."

Chapter 2

Outsource It!

In the last chapter we highlighted how important it is to take e-commerce seriously. In this chapter we'll show how easy it is to get into e-commerce. That's because you can outsource nearly all the activity associated with it at a trivial cost.

Don't flinch. When we say outsource, we don't mean signing an expensive contract with a firm that will bring in a bunch of temps who'll treat your business like rental property. Consider the following scenarios.

You can set up a personal Web site by running a T1 line to your house; buying and setting up a server in the basement; and then loading, configuring, and managing a network operating system. But you don't have to do that, and (hopefully) very few people do. Instead, you can just call up a local Internet Service Provider (ISP) and give the folks there a credit card number. They'll set up your account and give you a password. Using your personal computer, with its modem and its browser software, you call into the ISP, and it connects you to the Web. The ISP may also provide server space for a Web site for you, which you can set up by creating the necessary files and uploading them or by using the ISP's site-creation tools. (Some firms provide only hosting, and to get to your site, you have to have an Internet access account with an ISP.)

So you've outsourced Internet access and Web hosting to your ISP. Wasn't too traumatic, was it? As this is written, the going rate for Internet access and space for a Web site in the United States is $20 a month. (Internet access accounts without space for Web sites go for about $10 per month.) By spreading the cost of ownership among multiple users, the ISP is able to cheaply offer you something that you'd spend thousands to undertake yourself.

Having done that, the ISP can then load something called *shopping-cart software* on one of its servers and offer you access to that, too, which brings the price up to, say, $40 a month. (It can be more. And though you'd think there would not be much room, it can be less.) The shopping-cart (or shopping-basket) software does what a physical shopping cart (and associated store personnel) does—captures what selections a site visitor makes as he or she browses through the store and then helps them check out. The checkout mechanism is an automated cash register, capturing necessary billing and shipping information, figuring totals with taxes and shipping, and so on. It can even take credit card orders, doing the processing online, or it may simply capture the card number, leaving it up to you to do the processing offline. (But to take credit card orders, you must separately have what is called a *merchant account,* as explained in the Glossary.) The order information is passed on to you, the merchant, so that you can ship the item because the host that provides the site and the shopping-cart software is not involved in warehousing, shipping, or other aspects of fulfillment.

Well, of course, there's more to it than that. Let's look at some actual offerings from some of the leading e-commerce ISPs (also known as ESPs), and you'll see what we mean.

> These examples are for illustration only, are in no particular order, do not constitute an endorsement, and are certainly not a comprehensive listing of ESPs and their services. Prices were current in late 1999 or early 2000. More ESPs are listed in Appendix B—and more can be expected to spring up all the time.

■ SOME REPRESENTATIVE ESPs

➤ EarthLink
www.earthlink.net
This ISP's e-commerce offerings (called TotalCommerce Entrepreneur Packages) begin with a 10-item "kiosk" for $20 a month and a $50 setup fee. There is, however, no online credit card

processing. EarthLink software guides you through the process of setting up the site, using a wizard and canned templates.

(This and the following EarthLink packages assume you already have a Web site and a domain name. Getting these from EarthLink costs $19.95 per month plus a $25 setup fee. So you need to add that cost to the others. For the money, you get a domain name with unlimited e-mail addresses, 10 megabytes of storage, and 500 megabytes of monthly traffic. Extra traffic is 10 cents per megabyte.)

A basic 50-item store with online credit card processing costs $40 plus a $175 setup fee. EarthLink will help you get your credit card merchant account set up. A "SuperStore" carrying 100 items costs $80 per month, plus a $225 setup fee; a SuperStore carrying an unlimited number of items costs $110 per month, plus a $225 setup fee. Additional features get fancier as the price goes up—you get more storage space, more management features, and even customized discussion groups that are part of the Web site.

SuperStore features can also be added to an existing Web site using one of the EarthLink TotalCommerce Developer Packages for $130 a month and a setup fee of $225.

➤ MindSpring

www.mindspring.com
This ISP offers a "Biz" package that starts at $79.90 per month for a complete e-commerce site with Web hosting for 50 items but without online credit card authorization. For 100 items with on-line credit card authorization, the cost is $109.90. For an unlimited number of items with online credit card authorization, the cost is $209.90. All three offer wizard-based site creation—and a $50 setup fee.

➤ iCat

www.icat.com
This division of Intel will get you going for as little as $9.95 a month (or $100 per year) for a store selling 10 items or fewer. The first 30 days are free. For up to 25 items, you pay $19.95 per month or $200 per year. For 1,000 items, the price reaches $249.95 per month or $2,500 per year. And your store is part of

the iCat Mall, so there is some built-in promotion. Site creation is done through a wizard and is said to take mere minutes.

However, certain things considered standard features elsewhere are not included—such as merchant account status and credit card processing. If you establish a merchant account through iCat, there is a one-time application fee of $195, a monthly statement fee of $15, a transaction fee of 35 cents, and a discount rate of 2.44 percent of monthly sales (or $25, whichever is greater). For online credit card processing through iCat, you pay $45 a month plus a $300 setup fee. The online processing includes address verification service (AVS), which you'll need to get the best merchant account rates for your bank.

You will not have your own domain name—you'll be at www.icatmall.com/yourname. However, you can get set up with your own name through an outside service. That costs $24.95 per year, plus a $25 setup fee, and InterNIC (see the Glossary) separately bills you for the $70 two-year standard registration fee. E-mail to the new address is forwarded to your original address.

To access the site, you'll want to have Web access through a third-party ISP.

iCat also has a service called iCat Commerce Cart, where you link an existing site to the iCat shopping-basket system by adding hypertext markup language (HTML) code to your pages. The price is the same as having an iCat site, starting at $9.95 per month for 10 or fewer items.

➤ Yahoo! Stores

store.yahoo.com
This branch of Yahoo!, the Web directory and search engine, charges a flat fee for stores: $100 a month for a site selling up to 50 items and $300 a month for a site selling up to 1,000 items. The Web address can be stores.yahoo.com/yourname, or you can register your own domain name. Yahoo! will handle online transactions if you have a merchant account, and there is no transaction fee—from Yahoo! However, the merchant account, which you can set up online through BankOne, costs $250 to set up and then $45 per month, with a transaction fee of about 30 cents.

As with the other services, site creation can be done through a wizard, using templates. The service submits your new site to search engines, but (oddly enough) you have to submit it to Yahoo! manually. The service supplies the usual managing and tracking tools, and you can link its shopping-cart system to an existing Web site.

➤ Verio

www.verio.com
Verio—the largest ISP on earth, thanks to various mergers—charges $199 per month for a store of 1 to 300 items, $299 for 301 to 2,000 items, and $399 for 2,001 to 5,000 items. (So-called bolt-on services to add e-commerce to an existing Web site cost exactly the same.) As usual, a site can be set up quickly using the service's templates—Verio says that a site with 100 items can be set up in less than an hour. Items listed in Verio stores are added to an e-commerce search engine called stuff.com.

Verio will help you apply for merchant status to get credit card transactions processed. The setup fee is $199, and the transaction fee is 35 cents each.

➤ Concentric Network

www.concentric.com
Concentric Network boasts four plans for the small merchant. The ConcentricHost E1 plan runs $44.95 per month, with a $50 setup fee, and includes space for 25 items in three departments, 40 megabytes of storage, and a monthly traffic allowance of three gigabytes but no online credit card processing. Similarly, plan E2 includes 100 items in 10 categories plus 60 megabytes of storage and a traffic allowance of 4 gigabytes for $79.95 and a $50 setup fee.

For online credit card processing and support for up to 10,000 items (with multiple product attributes) in 1,000 departments, you move up to plan E3, which costs $149.95 per month with a $195 setup fee. You also get 100 megabytes of storage and a 6-gigabyte traffic allowance.

The first three plans are based on site-builder templates. For full customization, you move up to plan E4, which will run you $265.95 per month with a setup fee of $295. Other than that, it looks like plan E3.

Credit card processing with E3 and E4 involves an application fee of $150, and approval takes about two weeks. Thereafter, the monthly statement fee is $10, the discount rate is 2.44 percent, and the transaction fee is 35 cents.

With any plan, you can get your own domain name through InterNIC, with Concentric Network handling the applications.

➤ SmartAge

www.smartage.com

Prices at SmartAge start at $99 per month for 1 to 50 catalog items, with free merchant account setup, and goes up to $389 for 5,000 items. A store-creation tool lets you build the site without knowing HTML, but you can compose your own HTML if you desire. Off-site shopping-cart support starts at $289 for 500 items. The merchant account that the service arranges for you normally has a $199 setup fee and a transaction fee of 35 cents each, subject to promotional discounts.

SmartAge stores are automatically part of an online mall called stuff.com.

➤ Sitematic

www.sitematic.com

Prices at this service start at $39.95 per month plus a $50 setup fee for 12 Web pages and 20 catalogue pages and go up to $79.99 for 25 Web pages and 100 catalogue pages. Online transaction processing through CyberCash costs $10 per month and a $50 setup fee, not including transaction costs. You can arrange for your own Web address or use its in the format www.yourname. offc.com. The Sitematic site-creation tool boasts of offering a hundred dramatic page designs.

A free service called ListManager lets you store 250 customer e-mail addresses and send 300 e-mail messages monthly. For $10 per month, it will store 10,000 addresses and let you send 250,000 e-mail messages monthly.

➤ Stores Online

www.storesonline.com

This service starts at $49.95 per month for up to 50 items, going to $299.95 for 1,000 items and 15 cents per item over 1,000.

Real-time credit card processing is available, as is off-site shopping-cart support.

For up to one hundred items, you can pay it to build the store, for $999.95 (be sure and tip them the extra nickel!) and 50 cents each for every item over 100. For that amount it will also scan 25 images, charging $2 per image over that number.

■ THINGS GET INTERESTING

During 1999, a new phenomenon arose: free e-commerce services. That's right: The monthly fees, such as the ones quoted for the previously described services, are dispensed with. Of course, we live on Planet Earth, where *free* does not always mean "without cost." You give up something; the question is whether that particular something is of value to you.

As before, the following list of services should be considered representative rather than exhaustive. Service details can also be expected to change, and some details were sketchy at this writing.

➤ eCongo.com

www.econgo.com
This service is free, and you get to build the site using a wizard and display an unlimited number of items. But the service provides no online credit card processing—you pay money for that to a third party. The Web address you get is www.yourname. econgo.com, but if you have your own domain name, you can use it. Credit card processing costs $39.95 per month and 30 cents per transaction. The service will submit your site to search engines. Reportedly, eCongo hopes to make money from the banks through merchant account referral fees and by licensing its services to third parties.

➤ Bigstep.com

www.bigstep.com
Bigstep offers a free e-commerce site with as many pages and catalog items as will fit in 12 megabytes of storage. You get a Web address that looks like www.yourbusiness.bigstep.com, but you are free to use your own domain if you have one or to use the Bigstep address initially and get your own later.

Not only can you create a page using a site-creation wizard, you *have* to: there are no Web files associated with your site. Your information is made part of a database program, which generates the file (according to your design specifications) when a user accesses the address. Likewise, you can't upload an inventory data file to ease the chore of creating the site. Bigstep does keep a database of customers who have used your site, and you can download that. The site has facilities that let you customize e-mail pieces and newsletters to send to those customers, and Bigstep will help you register your site with search engines.

But what you have at that point is a free on-line catalogue. Your site does not qualify for shopping-cart service until you get a merchant account from Bigstep's partner service; this involves a monthly fee of $14.95 plus a transaction fee of 15 cents, a 5 cent address verification charge, and a discount rate of 2.67 percent. If you already have a merchant account, you still have to use Bigstep's partner.

Bigstep does not get a commission fee from the bank. Apparently, it intends to make money from advertising and by charging for enhanced, optional services, such as accounting.

➤ Freemerchant

www.freemerchant.com
This service boasts that it does not have a billing department. But it apparently has an accounts receivable department, because it intends to make money from banner ads sold on its site.

Meanwhile, Freemerchant is not involved in payment—if you have a merchant account, you retrieve the customers' credit card numbers and do the processing offline. Or you can arrange for online processing through a third party—and the posted fees start at $65 per month and 35 cents per transaction.

The site address will be yourname.safeshopper.com, but you can also use an existing domain name.

■ FREE VERSUS PAID

So here we have a dilemma, one you're not likely to encounter often: Should you bother to pay for it? The cost of e-commerce is so low that there are people willing to give it away, hoping to sell you services or use you for advertising in the process.

But the choice is not obvious, because there are general differences between the paid services and the free ESPs: The paid ones offer more options and services. You can customize your pages more. You can track sales, page views, affiliate links, revenue trends, sales histories, and so on, with a few mouse clicks.

But if you just want to get your feet wet, you can't beat the price of the free sites. If your feet are already wet and there is a specific place you want to wade to, the paid services are more likely to have what you are looking for.

■ FEATURES TO LOOK FOR

Which brings us to the question of features—what can you expect, and what should you look for? There is (or should be) more to it than having an ISP with shopping-cart software running on one server. You will want to ask about a lot of extra features and services when approaching a service. As always, some may be deal breakers, and some you may not care about.

➤ Wizards and Templates

By using templates and wizards, you do not have to know HTML to put together a store—you just click on the page options you want. Typically, there are enough options to ensure that, combined with business logos and product photos, no two sites will end up looking the same. If you do know HTML, typically you can insert formatting tags into the text that you upload for the site, adding further customization. (Just don't get carried away—there is no end to futzing with appearances. If the thing looks good at first glance, it's probably good enough.)

Yes, using templates gives you less flexibility. And buying a house gives you less flexibility than having the requisite lumber, siding, shingles, sheet rock, plumbing fixtures, wiring, cabinets, and carpet delivered to a vacant lot. If you have the power tools and six months to kill, go for it.

➤ File Access

Even if you have no desire to write your own HTML files, there is still the issue of whether you can get at the HTML files if you want to. If you cannot, it may mean that no actual files exist on the server and that your site is embodied in various entries in the ESP's database, from which the pages are generated when a specific Web address is accessed. But if there are no files, then there is nothing for a Web search engine to locate, and you are cut off from a major avenue of Web access. If your site is intended for invited clients instead of the general public, you won't care.

➤ Merchant Banking Account Setup

Merchant status means that you have an account with a credit card company that lets you accept credit card payments. It has to be applied for just as for credit because that is what it is: You are paid the money before the credit card company/bank collects it from the buyer. Many ESPs have a favorite bank that will handle your application and subsequent processing. If you already have merchant status, using it online may not come automatically—you have to check. In online transactions, the card is not physically presented to the merchant, and criteria vary for evaluating the risks the situation involves. You may need a separate account for Card Not Present (CNP) or mail order/telephone order (MOTO) transactions. And a standard MOTO account may or may not allow Internet transactions.

➤ Online Credit Card Processing

Processing the cards online means that the event is handled automatically and that the money shows up in your account (in a few days.) You can also process them offline, downloading the buyers' credit card numbers from the service and processing them yourself. And you may prefer that option if you have offline business as well.

➤ Promotional Services

The ESP may help you post your site to various search engines. It may also have a shopping mall whose catalog and search engine will include your products.

➤ Security

Everyone claims to have adequate features. Ask what you would be able to say to any of your customers who express concerns over online security. The issue, after all, is the protection of their credit card numbers.

➤ Site Management Reporting Tools

The service should provide tools so that you can see new orders, track sales by various dimensions (category, time span, and so on), track site and individual page hits, record referrals from other sites, see what words the customers searched for using the site's search facility, and the like. A facility that lets you see from which Web address the users came is necessary to track the usefulness of any link exchange or Web banner programs.

➤ Items Carried

The cost of the site is usually based on the number of items to be sold there. The service may allow several versions per item, as in apparel color or size, or each version may count as a separate item. Be sure to ask. The service's templates may also have a way to divide the items into product categories.

➤ Storage Space

This is the amount of storage space that the ESP will allow for the files that make up your e-commerce site. The high end may be 20 to 50 megabytes. Although it is nice to know that the storage is available, remember: When it comes to using the space, less is more. Most of the storage space will be needed for graphics files. If you have a hundred items and a large (50k) graphic for each, you should not need much more than 5 megabytes. Your customers, however, will need the patience of saints as they wait for each image to come in.

➤ Domain Registration

To have a Web address that is your own domain name rather than a subdirectory attached to the address of your ISP (i.e., www.yourname.com rather than www.ispname.com/yourname) you need to register the name that you've picked with an InterNIC registrar. Your ISP should be able to help you do this (and determine if the name you want is available.) But it would not kill you to do it yourself. The InterNIC registration (generally) costs $70 for two years and is commonly billed separately.

➤ Accounting Functions

The system might as well also handle your accounting and inventory because you will then have a completely integrated system, with order entry triggering inventory adjustments and ledger functions. If available, this will be an extra-cost option. More commonly, the order-entry system will have file download options with formats designed for use with popular accounting software.

➤ Site-Creation Services

The service may offer to set up the site for you, based on your specifications. It may charge to do this or refer you to a third party that it considers qualified, and the third party will certainly charge for it. Or it may offer to do it for nothing. Be sure to check to see where it stands.

➤ Traffic Allowances

Some services attach a maximum monthly traffic allowance to a site, in terms of how many megabytes of data is sent out to the Internet. You will be charged a small fee per megabyte for traffic that exceeds the allowance. Many services mention no such fee. Because the traffic is triggered by visitors to your site, you have no control over it. But unless your site involves downloads of software or video files or you've gone berserk with product photos, the allowance is not likely to be an issue. And if you do end up paying overage, you have the consolation of knowing that your site has proven popular.

➤ Database Uploads

To ease the chore of creating a site with a large number of items for sale, you want to be able to upload the product information in one swoop, using a common file format. This is most commonly done using the comma-separated value or variable (CSV) format, which can be generated by most spreadsheets and database programs. (See the Glossary for details on the CSV format.)

➤ Friendly Contracts

Can you set up a site and take it down immediately, or is there a minimum commitment? If you are involved in an adult business, you may find that the service bans them, even if they are otherwise legal. If you plan to make a living off spam, you'll find every hand turned against you. Read the fine print and look for hidden costs.

➤ Shipping Extras

It is possible, through Internet links, to connect the shopping cart at your site to the site of a shipping service to calculate shipping options and costs in real time and add it to the total.

➤ Internet Extras

If you are a serious Internet hound, you may insist on doing your site's pages by hand in HTML. In that case, you will want file transfer protocol (FTP) access to the site to upload your files. And if you are selling software, you may want your site to include an FTP folder, because files sent via FTP do not run into the length restrictions used by many e-mail servers, causing them to choke on files longer than a megabyte or two or five. If the service lets you install common gateway interface (CGI) scripts, you can add custom, special-purpose features, such as adding password access to certain files.

➤ E-mail Tools

An interesting but rarely mentioned feature is an *autoresponder*—an e-mail address that, when it receives a message, automatically sends a reply containing canned material. You can send newsletters or other material to interested parties without manual intervention—they click the e-mail link and then, after the browser's e-mail window comes up, they click "send." The autoresponder sees the address on the incoming message and sends back the material.

Multiple e-mail addresses associated with the site are also nice—one for customer service, one for inquiries, and so on. And it is nice to have a last-resort mail address for all mail to yourname.com that otherwise did not match any existing mail address there so that you can get any mistyped messages.

➤ Customer Support

The customer, in this case, is you. Does the service have a help desk manned around the clock, every day? Or during business hours only? Or does it have an e-mail address that it promises to answer within 24 hours? Seventy-two hours? Are any promises at all made about customer support? Does the service even mention customer support?

➤ Infrastructure

The service should boast of periodic file backups and of uninterruptible power (i.e., battery backup and even a backup generator in case of a power failure). It should also boast of its Internet connection—T3, or multiple T1 lines, at least, with redundancy. Simply surfing around its site should give you an idea of how effective its servers are—if its response times seem as slow to you as the arrival of Christmas to a small child, your shoppers may be equally annoyed.

➤ Frills

Frills can include customized bulletin board–like discussion forums for your site, special sections of the site devoted to hot deals or discounted merchandise, customer feedback forms, customer order tracking, interfaces to accounting software (usually through file downloads in specific data formats), a full-text search engine, order notification options (maybe you'll want them faxed to you in the Bahamas), multiple shipping options, distinction between bill-to and ship-to addresses, and support for various so-called electronic wallets.

➤ Off-Site Shopping-Cart Support

Many services let you use their shopping-cart software from an existing Web site on another host. You insert HTML code at your existing site, linking it to the e-commerce site. Typically, the price for this support is the same for having an on-site store.

EXPERTS SPEAK

Web e-commerce is a realm of small businesses. Activ-Media found that just one e-commerce site in seven reported more than 100 transactions per month. Seventy-five percent reported fewer than 50 transactions, and 40 percent reported fewer than 10.

EXPERTS SPEAK

A survey conducted by Cyber Dialogue, a market research firm in New York City, found that among small businesses that were online in the first half of 1999, 56 percent regarded the Internet as essential to the success of their business. Among those conducting e-commerce, 71 percent said it was essential. (The others were using the Internet to buy supplies rather than to sell anything.) Among those engaged in e-commerce, 60 percent reported sales gains brought about by e-commerce. Internet sales averaged 23 percent of total sales. Half of the small businesses that were polled said they expected to save money by using the Internet.

EXPERTS SPEAK

In 1999, small- to medium-sized retailers had 50 percent of retail revenues but only a 9 percent share of Web sales, reported Forrester Research. The firm says that this figure will fall to 6 percent by 2003 as what it calls the "Wal-Marting of America" proceeds and larger national merchants grab more of the pie. *But this assumption is based on survey results showing that it costs an average of $1 million to set up a Web store.* If you are in the Fortune 1000 and want to integrate e-commerce with data mining, accounting, inventory, shipping, enterprise resource planning, and so on, that is undoubtedly true. Otherwise, as this book shows, setting up a Web site can cost less than a trip to Wal-Mart, especially if you avoid the toy aisles.

EXPERTS SPEAK

Paralysis is a problem when it comes to getting into e-commerce. Or so says Brian de Haaff, product marketing manager at Concentric Networks, a commerce service provider in Redwood City, California.

"The biggest point of paralysis is the personal pride they have in this business they have built," de Haaff says. "When they approach e-commerce, their desire to make it right the first time makes it a huge, complicated site that will do these different things. Big thinking leads to paralysis.

"Start with a simple plan," he urges. "Do a little research. It is actually very easy.

"The biggest problem is trying to do too much too early," he says. "Start small and get your feet wet. Park a domain and get a one-page site up. It can be as simple as a picture of a shirt and a phone number and—bang—you have e-commerce. But people often have grandiose plans, and you see a lot of pages that say 'under construction.' But if the page is not done, don't put it up. Keep the site simple."

The second cause of paralysis is simple fear—fear of wasting time and money, fear of hype and vaporware, and fear of being a guinea pig, although the industry is well past that stage, de Haaff notes.

"But once they get started, they are usually pretty pleased," he adds. "E-mail starts coming in and it starts to get exciting, as they realize this can do something for their business."

Lyerly Peniston, head of Little Moonjumper, Inc., in Chicago and its www.littlemoonjumper.com Web site, says she established merchant status through her bank after setting up her business to sell personalized baby blankets. When she set up her Web site (through iCat), she did not see the need for online real-time credit card processing and just let the iCat shopping cart collect the credit card information.

"After I get e-mail notifying me that I have an order, I log onto the site and collect the full order information, including the credit card number, and call it into the credit card service," she noted.

The HTML files were created by a relative after she did the layout using graphics software.

Carrie Hardy, at Scrappin' Happy and its scrappinhappy. safeshopper.com Web site in Aurora, Colorado, says she did not want online credit card processing because she also has mail-order and walk-in customers. Also, she wanted to figure in discounts before processing the orders so as to award discounts to customers with coupons or who responded to special offers.

"I chose Freemerchant because they were free. I had more than a thousand items in the store, and that would have been too expensive on Yahoo!" she notes.

Reasons You Can
Do This

In Chapter 2, we established that you could indeed get your business online reasonably cheaply and quickly. In this chapter, we will address a bigger question: Should you do it? As was said in the movie *Jurassic Park*, just because you can do something doesn't mean you should do it.

Below, we pose some questions that we think you should consider when addressing the issue. There is no correct answer. What matters is the process of answering them.

1. *How unique is your product or service?* If it is available only from you, that's good, for obvious reasons. If it is available only from you in your region, that's good, too, because you can stress the delivery or personal inspection angle. If it is available only from a limited number of suppliers, at least your competition is a known factor, and you can study them and see what you can offer over and above what they offer, or identify some niche that has yet to be served. If it is a widely available commodity, other factors will have to be put into play, such as price, delivery, service, detailed product information, and other marketing factors that you will have to create.

2. *Has what you are planning to sell been successfully sold on the Web by anyone else?* If no one else has done it, it may actually be because no one has thought of doing it or that everyone who thought of doing it immediately dismissed the idea—perhaps for good reason. But perhaps

your understanding of the situation indicates that everyone else's good reason for dismissing the idea was clearly wrong.

Perhaps someone is selling it on the Web but having little success, for reasons that seem clear to you—and you intend to do better. Or maybe someone is doing well, and the success this firm is enjoying validates the idea to the public and the supply chain—but you see a way to be different or better or bigger.

The answer can be any of these—but know which one applies to you.

3. *Does everybody and his brother appear to be already on the Web, selling what you want to sell?* If so, don't despair—you can still offer a Web site that is prettier; easier to use; and offers better prices, faster delivery, more options, or more detailed product information. Competition is a good thing if you are setting out to compete.

4. *Do you already have a Web site for your business?* That means you already have your product information displayed electronically. You can just put your 800 toll-free ordering number there, and you have e-commerce. Then you can move on to getting merchant status and accepting credit card orders. Don't feel bad about doing that—no one will look down on you for taking a gradual approach. Some big names have done that. Meanwhile, most ESPs can link to an existing Web site, even if it is located on another ISP. You just add some HTML code to your own site, linking it to the ESP's shopping cart server across the Internet.

5. *Do you have merchant status (i.e., are you set up to take credit card orders)?* If so, that's great. You can start taking orders as soon as your site is set up. If not, leading ESPs will help you get set up, which may take two days to two weeks. In the meantime, you can fall back to using a call-in number. (If you have merchant status, make sure its terms let you take Internet orders—you may have to upgrade or modify your account.)

6. *Are you familiar with the Web, browsers, and desktop computers?* We'll assume you are, to the limited degree

necessary. You don't have to configure domain name servers, but you will have to deal with file formats and sizes, understand that HTML files call up graphics files and all are formatted on your screen by the browser, and know the difference between uploading and down-loading.

7. *Are you familiar with HTML?* You don't have to be, because many providers have templates that will get you started. But as with driving a car, it can be good to understand what goes on under the hood so that you won't be helpless in the face of the smallest problem. (And HTML isn't rocket science—a computer-literate person can probably learn it in two hours.)

   But if you do the coding yourself or even if you hire someone else, always remain aware of the perils of "creeping featurism." Yes, you can keep adding things and playing with the appearance until you get it per-fect—or so you think. In reality, perfection is unobtain-able, and in the meantime you need to get the site running.

8. *Can you handle the additional business?* If no orders come in, that's disappointing—but you can go bowling. But what if 10,000 orders come in? Can you get the inventory? Can you ship it? If not, do you have some mechanism for alerting the customers?

9. *Can you handle the additional customer service demands?* If someone can buy your product 24 hours a day, they also expect—realistically or otherwise—to be able to reach you with a question 24 hours a day. If you can't do that, you need to say so on the site and state what your availability is, whether it's only at certain hours or all day and all night. And before you can do that, you have to determine what your resources are and how much of them you want to commit.

10. *Will your marketing plans include your Web site?* As explained in Chapter 11, if you build it, they won't come. Not only must your overall marketing efforts include your Web identity, your Web site additionally demands special promotional efforts. You must be willing to make

that additional effort to get the maximum benefit from e-commerce.

Meanwhile, *marketing* must also take on the additional meaning of "keeping customer files." You should begin keeping records of your online customers and prospects, including their e-mail addresses, for future marketing efforts.

11. *Your existing accounting practices—how will you integrate your Web business with them?* It may be done manually or through elaborate software, and the answer may be in constant flux, but you have to keep the question in mind.

12. *Are you willing to spend the money?* As this books shows, e-commerce can cost very little, but you cannot approach it thinking that it is genuinely cost free. Even if you use a free service, your time equals money, and you will have to spend some time learning how to do new things or how to do old things a new way.

    Beyond such software considerations, there can still be hard expenses. You may want to invest in getting product photos made. Or it may finally be time to get that faster modem you've been dreaming of. If you have never been involved in mail-order business before, you may at least need shipping boxes and labels.

13. *Are you approaching this as a business proposition, or as a get-rich-quick scheme?* Alas, this is a serious question. Scam artists and multilevel marketing schemes have discovered e-commerce, too. You never know who will be taken in. Just remember, in the real world of e-commerce the financial commitment is moderate, the personal commitment is great, and the risk is the same as it is anywhere, minus any need to commute. The scam artist will paint you a picture of a world where the financial commitment (paid, somehow, all to her) will be substantial, the personal commitment will be trivial, and vast profits are all but guaranteed. Yes, your main challenge will be adjusting to your new lifestyle at the country club while your Web site robotically churns out bushels of money. They even have a reference for you to talk to—called a *shill* or *singer* by those in the trade.

What's even sadder is that most of these come-ons are actually pyramid schemes in disguise. The product itself usually offers no hope of actual business profits or even ongoing operation unless you decide to start selling the scam to others. And so the scam propagates like a virus.

The Federal Trade Commission (FTC) of the U.S. government actually tracks these things, much as the health authorities track epidemics, and reports that popular scams include:

- *Medical billing services.* It sounds like a natural for an Internet-based home business. You just need to buy some oddly expensive accounting software from these smiling, friendly people. The only catch is that the field is already crowded with established, large, highly competitive firms.
- *TV access to the Web.* Sounds great—and this guy will sell you a distributorship, letting you get in on the ground floor. But Web/TV devices already exist and are sold through regular consumer electronics channels. Why would they feel any need to sell distributorships? And if they did, why sell them to random people outside the industry?
- *Internet access kiosks.* Put one in a hotel or airport terminal and you'll rake in big bucks. But the good spots are already taken. With great difficulty you might get your brother-in-law's cousin to put one of these expensive things in his bar.
- *Becoming an Internet consultant.* Yes, take a free seminar for that purpose. Unfortunately, you can't learn that skill in one seminar, and anyway the seminar turns out to be a high-pressure sales pitch to buy a bogus Internet-based "business opportunity."
- *Bulk e-mail.* Buy a distributorship for software that generates spam (unsolicited commercial e-mail)! Then spam millions of people with a pitch to buy the software, your spamming service, or a subdistributorship. As soon as you start using the software, your ISP will cancel your account for violating its anti-spam rules.

- *Stuffing envelopes.* Some viruses are too primitive to die. You pay for somebody to set you up as a work-at-home envelope stuffer. But in the end, the only envelopes you have to stuff are your own pitch letters offering to set up the recipients as envelope stuffers.
- *Cable TV descramblers.* They may have worked 20 years ago, but cable technology has changed. However, the law has not—such devices are still illegal.
- *"Wealth building."* Judging by the evidence, the best way to build wealth is to offer wealth-building seminars or books to the gullible public. The methods usually involve real estate, government grants or loans, or buying and reselling lottery winnings. Of course, if these folks had a method that worked, they'd be using it, not pitching it for a buck.
- *Chain letters.* These still show up in e-mail boxes, although they dance around the term or desperately claim to be legal. Just hit the DELETE key and go on. (But if you get a bunch of them, at least you have the consolation of knowing that you must be popular.)

14. *Are you already in business?* This is helpful, but not a requirement. If you are a veteran, e-commerce will demand that you relearn certain things. If you are a newcomer, you will have to learn business as well as e-commerce.

15. *Does what you sell traditionally require personal inspection by the buyer?* This can be a drawback or a challenge. Remember, there are people who choose spouses from what amount to (or actually are) mail-order catalogues. So if you are selling cherries and you find that people prefer to pick them out personally at their grocery store's produce department, perhaps you can overcome their reservations by offering live graphics or an interface to a personal shopper.

16. *Does your product involve a lot of customization?* If it does, good. Customization makes for unique products, and thanks to the use of hyperlinks, on the Web you can present lengthy option lists that would be tedious to deal with by phone and confusing on a printed page. But as-is products are not necessarily bad, especially if they repre-

sent the niche you serve. Meanwhile, it is possible to have too many options, to the point that (as in a fancy restaurant) dealing with a live person may be the only way to go.

17. *Do you depend on repeat business?* If so, that is good—your customers can bookmark your site on their browsers. But the opposite is not good. Having to depend on converting a steady stream of new site visitors into one-shot buyers means you are on a treadmill where you constantly have to generate new traffic.

18. *Your target buyers: Are they online? When online, do they buy things? (We'll assume they have credit cards.)* Hopefully, you already know that answer is yes to both. If you are not sure, check the resources in Appendix A to begin searching for an answer. If the answer is definitely no, then you have to ask yourself how you feel about being a pioneer. Someone always has to be first, but beware of those arrows.

19. *Is your niche dominated by small businesses?* If so, great. It is better to be a face in the crowd than a lone David facing a billion-dollar Goliath. (True, the original David prevailed. But note that the feat was considered so remarkable that it got written up in the Bible.)

20/20

You can have an e-commerce site for more reasons then just displaying wares and taking orders, notes Mary Jo Matsumoto, owner of the Mary Jo M site at www.maryjom. com. Although she does sell her designer purses online, her site exists mostly to display her designs to wholesale fashion buyers.

"It absolutely helps my business, but not in the sense that I get huge orders. A lot of reps can't represent you if they have already represent a conflicting handbag design," she explains. "Sending out color photocopies or color brochures is expensive and takes time to get there. But with the site they can click and tell me in 30 seconds if they are interested."

Then there is the topic of *channel conflict,* which she understands but which causes problems for some major companies. "I don't want to compete with my stores," she says. "I do take orders through the site, but my prices there are comparable to the retail prices in the stores, so that I don't undercut the stores."

On the other hand, getting set up as a Web merchant also meant that she became the only designer in her showroom who accepted three credit cards. This is helpful because she cannot always extend net-plus-30-days credit, but that is what a credit card transaction amounts to.

EXPERTS SPEAK

You should think of your Web site not in terms of how much it might cost you but in terms of how much it can save you, indicates John Schulte.

"Every time someone calls in asking us for an information package, it costs us about $1.25 to mail it out, so we may spend $10,000 yearly on postage," he notes. "Now we can ask them if they have Internet access. A good percentage of the time they do, so we ask them to get the material directly from the site (www.nmoa.org). Almost every time, they do it. So think of how much money you can save down the line by being able to refer them to your Web site," he says.

Chapter

First Things First

It is probably no surprise that you'll need to get certain things squared away before launching yourself online.

■ A PLAN

Business projects should be approached with something more than vague intentions. You should draw up a business plan. If nothing else, it should assure you that what you are about to do is worth the time and effort—and that assurance will make it much easier for you to muster the necessary time and attention. We will go over the details in Chapter 5.

■ A DESCRIPTOR

As explained in Chapter 11, most users will find you through search engines using keyword searches. And the search engines use the text that they find at your site, especially near the top of the opening page. So you must ask yourself, What words describe my business, my products, my niche, and my site? If someone were to look for me, what words would he or she search for? What words do I want associated with my site?

Remember, these can't be the puff words you intend to put in your advertisements: *new, convenient, centrally located, inexpensive, award winning,* and so on. No, they have to be words that a real person with a real need for your product would really use: *local, 120-volt, left-handed, counter-rotating, six-gear,* and *widgets with optional red racing stripes.*

Then you come up with your descriptor, which you will use, somewhere in the text on the first page (and not in marquee graphics, which the search engines can't read): "Your convenient source for the best-priced, late-model, 120-volt, left handed, counter-rotating, six-gear widgets in the South Megapolis area. Gold racing stripes available."

We'll discuss the use of descriptors in Chapter 7.

You also will probably need to settle on a domain name: www.yourdomain.com, where *yourdomain* is the name of your site. It should be something that speaks to the niche you are in but will not be so trendy or cute as to be embarrassing to talk about 20 years from now. Most ESPs let you get started without one. Many pundits, however, urge you to seize upon a compelling name first, register it, and then work on the Web site.

■ ORGANIZED PRODUCT INFORMATION

You can't be there to answer the questions of puzzled surfers as they stumble through your site—the site has to do that without your help. But you can't bog the reader down with endless technical information, either. Decide in advance what information is pertinent and get it organized. Don't assume it is all in your head; put in on paper and ask yourself if it is information that the buyer wants to see. As you do this, you will probably arrive at a conception of how the site should be laid out because the two are closely linked. We'll discuss how to lay out a site and use the information in Chapter 8.

■ ISP ACCOUNT

An ISP, as you know by now, is the service you use to get online and surf the Web. It need not be the same as your ESP (some of which are pure hosting firms and do not offer access services). We'll assume you know your way around the Web already—which means that you already have some kind of ISP account with somebody, somewhere.

■ ESP ACCOUNT

The ESP provides the e-commerce Web site, the site-creation system, links to the credit card payment system, and other features. It can be the same as your ISP but need not be; if you want maximum flexibility, it should not be. (If you keep them separate, you'll feel freer to switch e-commerce carriers, and if one service is having problems, you can check the situation by using the other one.) We'll talk more about this in Chapter 6.

■ PRODUCT PICTURES

Yes, you'll need pictures of the product. Even if what you're selling is software, you still need a box shot, and if there is no box, then have a screen shot. Things are virtual enough online; you want a picture to reassure the buyer that you and the product are both real.

You can scan existing photos, take a picture with a digital camera, or hire a studio photographer at $200 an hour to take slides that are then rendered as digital images. However you do it, get the photos. We'll talk about how to get them and what to do with them in Chapter 7.

■ MERCHANT ACCOUNT

You need a merchant account that lets you accept CNP or MOTO payments over the Internet. Remember, a particular merchant account may not permit CNP or MOTO payments, and one that does may or may not permit Internet commerce.

The ESP you sign up with may have a payment service it can recommend for getting a merchant account. We'll go into detail in Chapter 6.

■ FILE SYSTEM

Presumably, you are going to have some kind of bookkeeping system or software or already have one. You will need to keep in mind the need to incorporate e-commerce activity into it.

Because you are the one who knows your system, you don't need to be told how to do this.

Meanwhile, you need to think about how you are going to store customer information. The real potential in e-commerce lies in really knowing the customer, in terms of what he or she has bought or expressed interest in. Then, you can make better marketing plans and launch highly targeted direct-marketing campaigns using e-mail.

You can use elaborate database software or a stack of file cards. But you will be missing out if you do not make capturing such information part of your business process.

■ THE INFRASTRUCTURE

Of course, you need a PC with a modem and a browser. Even the cheapest PCs come with these things built-in these days, and there is no point trying to make a political statement by getting anything else. So we will assume you are equipped well enough to proceed and go on.

■ THIS BOOK

Section II will walk you through the process of setting up an online store, using example products and photos. The emphasis will be on time because that resource requires the tightest management by entrepreneurs. (This is especially the case with e-commerce, where low costs mean that money is not the paramount factor.)

We will go from day to day, with projects to undertake in the morning and evening, until by the end of the week you have an operating e-commerce site. We don't expect that you will actually mark these daily tasks down on your calendar, but we believe that you should take them as an indication of the attention to be given to certain tasks and in what order they should be done.

We will also supply checklists at each step, showing what information you need to have on-hand before starting.

Creating an E-commerce Site, One Day at a Time

Chapter

Sunday–Drawing Up the Blueprints

Today we will set about planning your e-commerce business in earnest. Note that this does not mean planning the site itself—that comes later in the week. Instead, we are going to look at the big picture, in terms of what you want to do (sell stuff) and why (to make money). But to arrive at useful answers, we have to address other questions, such as who is going to do the buying; where, why, and how; how much; and how often.

In the morning we will do some scouting. In the afternoon we will get into the nuts and bolts of what you plan to do by drawing up a business plan.

■ MORNING: RESEARCH

CHEAT SHEET
(one for each site examined)

- Apparent audience.
- Layout.
- Freshness.
- Overall artwork.
- Product mix.

- Prices.
- Delivery options.
- Product information.
- Company information.
- Opt ins.
- Customer service.
- Policies.
- Value adds.
- User community.
- Production value.
- Impediments.
- Sizzle or steak?
- Overall impression.

At this point, it's time to fire up the old browser and hit cyberspace with a mission: Find out what is going on out there in your field. Before you launch yourself into e-commerce, you might want to check out who else is doing it and how. And then ask yourself how you will stack up against them.

First, find them. Second, analyze them.

➤ Finding Them

The obvious move is to launch a search at Yahoo!, where human beings categorize the sites in terms of subject matter. If you want to sell cutlery online, you could go there, do a search of the word *cutlery,* and find a list of sites registered there that claim to sell cutlery—or said they sold knives but the Yahoo! staff knew enough to file them under cutlery.

That may be enough to get started on a session of analysis, as described later. But you should not stop there. Many sites do not apply for a Yahoo! listing, for whatever reason, or are listed under the main topic but the niche you are interested in is a minor sideline. So you need to also run a keyword search from a search engine such as Lycos.

When running the keyword search, include geographic descriptors to see who in your neighborhood is online. And make careful note of the keywords that lead to sites like the one you hope to create, because you will want to use them Tuesday, in Chapter 7.

➤ Analysis

Now that you have located some sites of interest, look over them, asking the questions about the following topics as you do so:

- *Apparent audience.* Who is the site aimed at? How is it made to appeal to that audience? Does the effort appear successful?
- *Layout.* Does it seem easy to find what you want? Or do you have to stumble past a bunch of mission statements and executive biographies?
- *Freshness.* Did the site seem fresh? If so, what gave you that impression? If it seemed stale and neglected, what gave you that impression?
- *Overall artwork.* Do they use a lot of it? Is there a theme? Does it seem appropriate? How does it make you feel that way? Do the product photos do the job of identifying and promoting the product? If so, how was it accomplished? If not, what was lacking?
- *Product mix.* Is it narrow or broad? If broad, how is it being promoted? If narrow, who is it targeted at? If configuring is appropriate, does the site let you do that? Is the configurator user friendly, and does it warn you against incompatibilities?
- *Prices.* Are they what you would expect? If they are not, why do you think that is?
- *Delivery options.* Can items be delivered overnight? If it is a local operation, can items be picked up at the counter? Or is there local, same-day delivery? Are shipping charges made clear?
- *Product information.* How much is offered? Does it seem like enough? Do you think the buyers would appreciate more?
- *Company information.* If you wanted the firm's address and phone number, can you find it here? Or are you left with the impression that this organization exists only in cyberspace, unconnected to the real world?
- *Opt ins.* Does the site do anything to entice you to at least leave your name and e-mail address?
- *Customer service.* What avenues are offered for customer service? Do the folks running the site promise to respond to questions within a set period? Do they, for that matter, mention customer service?

- *Policies.* Do you notice any statements concerning customer satisfaction or data privacy?
- *Value adds.* Did you find any information there—consumer, technical, financial, or whatever—that struck you as valuable? If so, what was it?
- *User community.* Is there a chat room or discussion board? Are they used?
- *Production value.* Did it seem well put together? If so, was there anything in particular that impressed you?
- *Impediments.* Was there anything that seemed jarring or out of place? Did anything make you wonder if the producers knew what they were doing?
- *Sizzle or steak?* Does their marketing appear to depend on glamour and hype or on illuminating the features and benefits of their product? Which appears appropriate?
- *Overall impression.* Was there anything about the site that seemed memorable? Anything that might make you feel like making another visit some time? If so, what?

By the time you analyze (not just look at) a dozen sites, you should have formed an impression in two different areas:

1. What the likely online competition is like and whether there is an evident niche that you can exploit, such as better prices, better service, better availability, or just a better-organized site.
2. In terms of site organization, what works, what does not work, and what just gets in the way.

Assuming that you have not been scared off by the thought of having to compete with legions of magnificent sites (an unlikely event, incidentally, from what we've seen out there), we'll move on into the afternoon and respond to the situation by drawing up a business plan.

(20)/(20)

"Before I started, I looked at as many sites as I could," says Carrie Hardy. "I looked at their site design and at what they were selling and how much they were selling it for, and how much I could sell it for less and still make money. I also looked at how much they were charging for shipping—most were, and it's expensive.

"If I could do it over again, differently, I could find out what the discount stores are selling and not sell that online. I have some inventory that is not moving, since the discount stores can sell it below my wholesale cost," she adds.

■ AFTERNOON: THE BUSINESS PLAN

CHEAT SHEET

- Spreadsheet.
- Cost projections.
- Income projections.
- Market projections.

The idea of a business plan is to force you to confront certain basic questions that you need to ask yourself before launching a business. Hopefully, you will arrive at answers you consider correct and thus convince yourself that your project will be time well spent. This will make it far more likely that you can and will muster the commitment necessary to accomplish your goal—any goal. (And if you arrive at answers that convince you that the project is a pipe dream, at least you got to that stage early.)

The secondary goal of the business plan is to give you data to pour into a handsome document that you can show bankers or potential backers. Such a document ought to be a fairly elaborate project, and creating it should take more than an afternoon, so we won't dwell deeply on the requirements. (And the entry costs of e-commerce are so low that we don't need to assume any need for backing.) But the basic material is the same—your conviction in yourself and your project.

We'll approach the plan by getting into the guts of a series of fundamental questions:

- What business are you in?
- Who are you?
- What is the competition like?
- What is your marketing plan?
- What is your projected income?
- Will you need to make a printed version of the plan?

Below, we'll examine those questions in greater detail and show an example of putting them to use.

➤ What Business Are You In?

In other words, describe the business as if to somebody from Mars. That will involve having a firm answer to these questions:

- What are you going to be selling?
- What are you absolutely *not* going to be selling?
- Why does the buyer need this product or service?
- What kind of demand do you expect?
- Where does the profit come from?
- Will you need any licenses or permits to operate?
- Will demand be steady?
- Will demand grow?
- How much time will this project demand from you?

If you had previously hung a label on your operation—"sells washing machine parts," for example—you might decide, after answering these questions, that the label does not do it justice. "Ends home appliance headaches," perhaps?

➤ Who Are You?

Forget the deep insights. You are your chief resource, so you must now analyze yourself and your situation. Try these questions:

- What experience do you have with this business?
- How much time will you have to devote to this project?
- What sources or information about the business are available?
- What professional organizations exist?
- Do you have partners? What is their place in this project?
- How much money do you need to live on?
- Will the project cover your living expenses? If not, where will the rest come from?
- What financial resources do you have that you are willing to put at risk in this project?
- What kind of accounting system will you be using? How familiar are you with it? Can it use order data downloaded from your e-commerce site?
- What kind of database system do you have? Can it be used to manage electronic mailing lists?
- What kind of inventory control system will you use?
- Will you need to hire anyone? How will you find them, and what will you pay them?

➤ What Is The Competition Like?

You already did some research into this in the morning. But competition includes more than other Web sites—it includes anyone selling something similar, be it from a store or a catalogue or the back of a pickup on the shoulder of a highway. And then there is indirect competition. Remember, a bowling alley does not just compete with other bowling alleys; as a form of entertainment, it competes with television, movies, paperback books, and hanging out at the mall. Try these questions:

- Who would be your direct competitors? Name several.
- Does their business seem to be good?
- What is their marketing like?
- What are their prices like?
- What are their strengths and weaknesses?
- How does your product or service differ from theirs?
- What is the indirect competition?
- How will you overcome it?

What Is Your Marketing Plan?

Marketing is a big topic, but you cannot expect to have a successful business without paying attention to it. It is not enough to offer a better mousetrap—you must reach the people with rodent infestations and convince them to call you rather than the friend of their brother-in-law who's an exterminator. Try these questions:

- Define the target market. In other words, who are the customers?
- Is that market growing or shrinking?
- How you do intend to reach that market?
- What kind of advertising do you intend to use?
- What is your pricing strategy? (Are you going to offer high quality at high cost, low quality at low cost, or some other combination?)
- How will your prices compare to that of the competition?
- Can you make money with these prices?
- Are you going to sell internationally, domestically, regionally, or locally?

➤ What Is Your Projected Income?

Here is the good part, where we plug in numbers and see if what you have is a viable proposition.

The idea is to make a spreadsheet—manual or computerized—with a column for each of the next 12 months and a thirteenth row for the annual total, summing the 12 columns in that row. Then you put in rows for each of these data items:

- Total net sales (revenue).
- Costs of sales.
- Gross profit.
- Gross profit margin.
- Variable expenses.
- Fixed expenses.
- Total expenses.
- Net profit (loss) before taxes.
- Taxes.
- Net profit (loss) after taxes.

Some of these entries are actually the totals of detailed breakdowns, as defined in the following sections. Hopefully, that last entry (the bottom line) will be a positive number—if not in the initial monthly columns, then at least in the annual column.

Total Net Sales (Revenues)

Figure how many items you expect to sell at the price you expect to use, minus expected returns, and any discounts you intend to give. Do not include anything not strictly related to this project. Start out with low sales in the initial monthly columns, ramping up to what you think sales should be in 12 months.

Cost of Sales

This should include inventory acquisition costs, shipping and direct labor, and the percent you pay the merchant bank for processing credit card payments.

Gross Profit

You get this figure by subtracting the total cost of sales from the total net sales.

Gross Profit Margin

You divide the gross profits by the total net sales (the revenue) to get this figure. This is of mostly theoretical interest. The average gross profit margins of businesses in various industries are available from reference sources, allowing you to compare yourself to the Fortune 1000.

Variable Expenses

Some optimists also call these *controllable expenses*. These can be almost anything needed to keep the business going but are not directly related to the acquisition of the product. In e-commerce, some items will be trivial, but include them for reassurance. Fees that occur only once should be put in the first monthly column. Variable expenses include:

- *Fees.* The service fee to set up your credit card merchant account is charged once, but the cost needs to show. The same goes for any license fees involved in your business.

- *Payroll/salary.* This includes paid vacations, sick leave, health insurance, unemployment insurance, and social security taxes paid by the employer.
- *Services.* These include any one-time services for special occasions, such as a photographer or a Web designer.
- *Supplies.* This includes the items bought for use in the business.
- *Repair/maintenance.* If you are using a car or truck for business, you'll need this entry.
- *Advertising.* Include desired sales volume and classified directory advertising expenses.
- *Travel.* This includes car expenses for buying trips as well as for meetings.
- *Office supplies.* You'll need them.
- *Dues/subscriptions.* There are probably organizations you should join and magazines you should get. Keep in mind that many of the best industrial magazines are free—but you have to fit the profile of the reader they want.
- *Utilities.* You'd think this would be a fixed expense, but you can control it by, for instance, turning the lights off. You need to include the telephone bill.
- *Miscellaneous.* Anything else that seems reasonable.

Fixed Expenses

Fixed expenses are the things that you cannot do much fine-tuning with—you either have them or you don't. But at least they can be assumed to be the same from month to month. These would include:

- *Web site.* The amount your ESP charges for your site is fixed.
- *Rent.* Include any rents for your office, trucks, or storage space.
- *Depreciation/amortization.* This is the cost of using something you already own.
- *Insurance.* This includes liability insurance and worker's compensation.
- *Loan payments.* If you borrowed money to start the business, paying it back is an expense.
- *Miscellaneous.* Did you forget anything? You will.

Total Expenses

Add your variable and fixed expenses to get this figure.

Net Profit (Loss) before Taxes

This is what they call the *bottom line* and is derived by subtracting total expenses from gross profits.

Taxes

Include all taxes that impact the business, such as inventory, sales, real estate, and excise taxes. Do not include income taxes on what you, as the business owner, will earn from the business—that is a separate matter. (Because sales taxes are paid by the buyer, for many ventures the taxes will not be a big consideration.)

Net Profit (Loss) after Taxes

Subtract the taxes from the previous figure.

EXAMPLE

You know from years of experience in the classic European car hobby that certain models have front-door winglet windows whose handles frequently break off, leaving no way to close the things from the inside. This produces annoying wind noises and drafts. Deep in the fine print of a 300-page parts catalogue you find a replacement clamp-on handle kit for $37.50, not including shipping and handling. You buy one, examine it, follow up on what you find, and determine that it comes from an importer of French car parts on the East Coast, who wholesales it for $19 and says they move about two thousand units a year, all to the catalogue house. They have a gross right now they can send you. Their distribution through the catalogue house is not exclusive.

You figure your friends will love these things and that with a little work you can capture most of this market by opening an e-commerce site called www.winglets-fixed.com. You commence answering the questions:

What Business Are You In?

You decide you are in the business of soothing annoyed European classic car owners whose winglet window handles have broken. You figure you can eventually get a good share of the current annual market for 2,000 units and perhaps even expand the total market through an awareness campaign. But whatever the true size of the market, it should remain steady as more winglet handles break. Because you can get them for $19 and you think that you can box and ship them for $3, it seems worthwhile to sell them for $35, shipping included, thus undercutting the competition.

Who Are You?

You have a full-time job but have a few hours a week to devote to this business as an outgrowth of your existing hobby. Foreseeable expenses can be paid out of pocket. You have simple accounting and database software that will do the job with one inventory item. Your garage is too crowded to store the inventory and do boxing, so you decide to get a storage bay at the local mini-storage facility for $50 per month.

What Is the Competition Like?

You assume that the business represented by the repair kits is beneath the noise level of the catalogue house. But it could be painful if they respond by lowering their price. You resolve to offer additional value by including in the box an illustrated flyer you created, detailing how to install the device. (The original product included only terse instructions in French.)

A search reveals no one else selling such items on the Web.

What Is Your Marketing Plan?

You already participate in the applicable classic car newsgroups, and they are open to appropriate announcements. There are newsletters and convention programs you can advertise in for nominal sums, averaging $50 an appearance. You can create the ads yourself with your laser printer.

What Is Your Projected Income?

Now comes the time to fill in a spreadsheet. Remember, we will figure for 12 months, with certain start-up costs shown only in the first month. (Representative costs are used—yours could be very different.)

Total Net Sales

We will assume that sales take off slowly, rising to 125 per month by the end of 12 months. (That would be three-fourths of the known market.) We are selling the winglet window handles for $35 each.

Cost of Sales

Each item costs $19, the cost of boxes and shipping averages $3 per item, and credit card transaction processing costs 30 cents per item.

Variable Costs

Credit card processing will cost $250 to set up. We'll plan on spending $50 per month for advertising for the first six months. There are no employees and no significant utilities or taxes.

Fixed Costs

We'll assume $100 a month for the Web site, $50 for the storage space, $45 per month for credit card processing, and no significant insurance.

The resulting spreadsheet, shown in Figure 5.1, indicates that you can expect to clear just over $7,200 on this venture over 12 months—if all your assumptions are correct. Assuming you put an average of an hour per workday into it, you would be making a little under $30 an hour.

Is that worth the effort? Maybe. Maybe not. But think about the second year. On the assumption that you can maintain the sales level achieved at the end of the first year through the second year, you'll clear almost $17,000 (not shown), and your hourly rate has more than doubled. You can then build on that success.

	M1	M2	M3	M4	M5
Items Sold	10	20	30	40	50
Revenue	$350.00	$700.00	$1,050.00	$1,400.00	$1,750.00
Cost of Sales	$223.00	$446.00	$669.00	$892.00	$1,115.00
Gross Profit	$127.00	$254.00	$381.00	$508.00	$635.00
Variable Expenses	$300.00	$50.00	$50.00	$50.00	$50.00
Fixed Expenses	$195.00	$195.00	$195.00	$195.00	$195.00
Total Expenses	$495.00	$245.00	$245.00	$245.00	$245.00
Net Before Taxes	($368.00)	$9.00	$136.00	$263.00	$390.00
Gross Profit Margin	36.29%	(See Chapter 15 for note on taxes.)			

Variables:		Fixed Expenses	
Sale Price	$35.00	Web Site	$100.00
Shipping	$3.00	Storage	$50.00
Purchase Price	$19.00	Processing	$45.00
			$195.00

Figure 5.1 Our spreadsheet shows initial losses followed by gains as sales grow. Not shown, of course, is the cost of your time to set up the site, do marketing, fill orders, and respond to customers.

Alternately:

- Sales might not take off until you find just the right marketing method—if that ever happens.
- Owing to limited computer use in your target audience, sales may never rise above a certain level.
- The competition might slash its prices, making your efforts futile.
- Sales could suddenly trail off, and you discover that all the classic cars have now been repaired—all along, most of those kits were being sold to golfers for use on golf carts.
- You target the golf cart owners and sales soar, forcing you to expand, hire help, and spend money on the assumption that this level of sales will continue, defeating your original purpose for launching a sideline.
- Either way, you might get sick of stuffing things in boxes and sending them to people.

You get the picture—the rewards are yours to keep, but the pains generated by the risks are all yours, too. Finding

M6	M7	M8	M9	M10	M11	M12	Y-Total
60	70	80	90	100	120	125	795
$2,100.00	$2,450.00	$2,800.00	$3,150.00	$3,500.00	$4,200.00	$4,375.00	$27,825.00
$1,338.00	$1,561.00	$1,784.00	$2,007.00	$2,230.00	$2,676.00	$2,787.50	$17,728.50
$762.00	$889.00	$1,016.00	$1,143.00	$1,270.00	$1,524.00	$1,587.50	$10,096.50
$50.00	$0.00	$0.00	$0.00	$0.00	$0.00	$0.00	$550.00
$195.00	$195.00	$195.00	$195.00	$195.00	$195.00	$195.00	$2,340.00
$245.00	$195.00	$195.00	$195.00	$195.00	$195.00	$195.00	$2,890.00
$517.00	$694.00	$821.00	$948.00	$1,075.00	$1,329.00	$1,392.50	$7,206.50

Variable Expenses		Cost of Sales @	
Setup	$250.00 initial	Inventory	$19.00
Ads	$50.00 six months	S/H	$3.00
		Processing	$0.30
			$22.30

Figure 5.1 (*Continued*)

backing may ease the pain in some cases, which brings us to the next section.

➤ Will You Need a Printed Version?

Previously, when approaching the business plan, we assumed you were talking to yourself, and in that mode doing the plan on the back of a napkin suffices if the result is sufficiently inspirational. (According to urban legend, that's how Compaq Computer Corporation got started.) But it does not suffice if you need to ask someone else for money, especially a total stranger in a steel-and-glass high-rise office building downtown. Then your business plan needs to be turned into a polished Business Plan.

Obviously, you need to fire up the word processor and produce a pretty document, with your projections rendered as tables and charts. But be assured that there is no set format or government-approved outline that you should follow. Every proposal is different. Just make sure that yours communicates your excitement for the idea and clearly explains the opportunity that you see. However, you might want to include the following elements:

Cover Page

Don't laugh. The proposal will get separated from the cover letter and so must include complete contact information. Reportedly, seeing to this detail is beneath the notice of many entrepreneurs, who then wonder why the phone never rings. Having a running head on each page with your name and number is a good idea, too.

Executive Summary

This is a page that contains a summary of your proposal, without resort to backup data. Don't delude yourself—this is the only part of the proposal that many will actually read, perhaps going on to have a flunky check the figures in the rest of it. Make the summary short and polished—and interesting. Cover the basic concept, the financial features and requirements of the project, and the current state of the business.

Industry Overview

The trends in your industry may be obvious to you but they may be a new world to your banker. Describe the industry and talk about the pertinent trends there, citing sources. Market research firms often issue projections; use these rather than your own conjectures. (The bare figures you need will often be included in press releases. Identify the research firms that cover your industry and then check their Web sites.)

The Balance Sheet

If you approach investors or a bank, they will want to see a *balance sheet* to see what resources you have committed to the business. Basically, you show assets and liabilities and the total net worth (which is assets minus liabilities.)

Assets include anything of value owned by the business or due it. Assets should be figured as net values: original acquisition cost minus depreciation and amortization. The breakdown might include:

- *Cash.* This includes petty cash, money on hand, and money in the bank.
- *Accounts receivable.* Money owed to the business by customers.
- *Inventory.* This includes both raw material, finished goods, and anything that has been purchased for resale.

- *Short-term investments.* Basically, stocks and bonds that you intend to sell within a year.
- *Prepaid expenses.* Including what you are using that you have already paid for, including office space, office supplies, and insurance.
- *Long-term investments.* Basically, stocks and bonds and savings accounts reserved for special purposes.
- *Fixed assets.* This includes equipment used in the business and not intended for resale, such as buildings, furniture, cars, and machinery. Land should be valued at the original acquisition cost.

Liabilities include all debts, obligations, and claims to be paid in the next 12 months. Typically, this includes:

- *Accounts payable.* Money owed to suppliers for goods and services used in the business.
- *Notes payable.* The payoff for any short-term debts and the amount due for any notes with terms longer than 12 months.
- *Interest payable.* The interest due on both short- and long-term notes.
- *Estimated taxes.* What you owe the government.
- *Accrued salaries and payroll.* What you owe the employees.
- *Long-term liabilities.* These are typically notes or mortgage payments with terms longer than 12 months. They are listed by outstanding balance less the current position due.

Finally, after gathering the finished report from the printer output tray, rush over to see an accountant or a business consultant of some sort or anyone but the person you intend to ask for money. You may only get one shot with that person, so make sure it is a good one by having a professional poke holes in the plan first.

EXPERTS SPEAK

The following pointers may keep you out of trouble when producing a printed business plan:

- Everyone wants to say that they are going to offer something of better quality but at a lower price than the competition. So if you bluntly come out and say it, you'll brand yourself as a rank amateur.
- Don't justify low prices purely with low cost estimates. Costs are often underestimated.
- When citing research, such as market sizes, always mention the source. It shows you did your homework.
- Stress how your business is going to be unique and how you are going to profit from that uniqueness. And have a second avenue of uniqueness in reserve, in case the competition matches your first one.
- If you have applicable business or management experience, don't hide the fact. Investors know that good management can make all the difference.
- When seeking backing, remember that asking for too little is more dangerous than asking for too much.
- Do not use the word *conservative* in the same sentence as *sales projection*. To a banker, it's a trite cliché. Present best-case, worst-case, and most-likely sales projections.
- Feel free to use industry jargon with everyone you know—except the banker.
- Never claim to have no competitors. Remember, bowling alleys compete with TV.

EXPERTS SPEAK

It is said that the most common mistakes of small businesses include:

- Hiring friends instead of qualified candidates.
- Underestimating costs.
- Underestimating sales cycles.
- Underestimating the competition.
- Trying to be all things to all customers.

EXPERTS SPEAK

Keep a file on each identified direct competitor. Collect their ads and catalogues or screen prints of their Web sites. Visit their stores or call their support lines. Get to know each one well.

Chapter

Monday–Signing Up

Today you will select an ESP and, on the assumption that you do not have one already, sign up for a merchant account.

■ MORNING: SIGNING UP WITH THE ESP

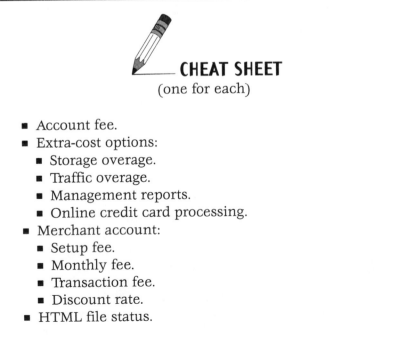

CHEAT SHEET
(one for each)

- Account fee.
- Extra-cost options:
  - Storage overage.
  - Traffic overage.
  - Management reports.
  - Online credit card processing.
- Merchant account:
  - Setup fee.
  - Monthly fee.
  - Transaction fee.
  - Discount rate.
- HTML file status.

- Infrastructure.
- Site-creation tools.
- Management tools.
- Contracts.
- Customer support.

Typically, you can sign up with an ESP online, giving your credit card number, just as you would order anything else online, and begin building a site immediately. We will deal with the chore of picking a service today and then look at preproduction considerations before actually building the site on Thursday. We want to register today so that we can then immediately apply for a merchant account. Approval may take several days, and because the merchant bank that handles the account is often partnered with the ESP, meaning that the account can be applied for through the ESP, we'll do both today.

First, though, you have to select an ESP. Don't feel limited to the ones used as examples in this book—the industry is growing rapidly, and by the time this book is printed and reaches you, there should be plenty to chose from. To get started, you can:

- Check Yahoo!
- Check ads in computer magazines.
- Check your ISP. (They may have begun offering e-commerce.)
- Listen to word-of-mouth from friends.

The last is always the most effective, especially in terms of negative reports. Having gotten a preliminary list, there are some issues we suggest that you discuss by calling up the ESP's customer service department, which is done primarily to see if it's responsive. But while you have them, ask about the following topics and mark up the Cheat Sheet accordingly. (Also, go over the list of possible ESP offerings for ones that seem particularly important to you.)

➤ Fees

Look for hidden surprises. For instance, if the monthly fee is based on the number of items for sale, how are they counted?

Are variations such as size and color counted as separate items? Are there additional charges for extra storage or data traffic over a particular monthly total? If there are, do they appear to be a problem? (You may never get close to the limit.) Do certain management reports involve an extra fee? Is online credit card processing (assuming you have a proper merchant account) part of the set fee, or is there an extra charge for that? If you have to upgrade to a bigger site, is there a fee for that? For that matter, is there anything at all that involves extra fees?

➤ HTML Files

You will probably be creating your site using an online site-creation tool. That's fine. But does the tool create Web (HTML) files? Or does it just keep your data and page specifications in a database and dynamically generate a page when someone invokes your site? If the latter is true, then there is nothing for a Web search engine to find, and you will be known only to those people whom you are able to reach with your marketing.

That may be a showstopper for a consumer site. For a special-purpose business-to-business site, where only existing customers will be served, you may not care.

Meanwhile, if you have existing HTML files, could you use them? And the HTML files that you are going to create and fuss over using the service's site-creation tools—could you reuse them if you switched to another ESP? This is not a big consideration for a one-shot hobby site. For a site that is being done as a sideline for a corporate division and that will be expanded if successful, it is a major consideration—you may end up moving it to the corporate server, for instance.

And if your site involves a substantial number of inventory items, is there any function that lets you upload the data and pictures in one file? Such a feature may be tricky to learn, but once you get it to work, you should be able to revamp the entire site with one upload.

➤ Infrastructure

Does the ESP have the usual high-speed connections, uninterruptible power supplies, and backup policies?

Meanwhile, there is the issue of hard goods (stuff you put in a box and ship to the buyers) and software goods (data that is transmitted to them.) If your business involves streaming video or audio, then the server will need facilities to pace the streaming. This is not a huge, expensive upgrade, but from looking into the situation, we got the impression that the ESPs offering it are in the distinct minority.

If your business involves downloadable software, you need to make sure in advance that the ESP's site-creation tools and shopping-cart support soft goods.

➤ Site-Creation Tools

They all have them. But ask what shortcuts each ESP has, such as database file uploads that would let you change the inventory with one action.

Also, what documentation does it have? Any? Our experience is that these systems can have a lot of power obscured by programmers who were basically talking to themselves.

➤ Management Tools

Is there a way for visitors to opt in and ask for a catalogue or to be put on your mailing list? As explained in Chapter 11, this feature is critical if you are to take advantage of the principal opportunity offered by e-commerce: cheap, targeted direct mailings. Remember, to simply send bulk e-mail ads into the blue is called *spamming* and will win you public scorn and the wrath of your ISP. But if you send e-mail to people who are on your database because they asked to be there, then the e-mail is no longer unsolicited, and you are no longer spamming.

In addition to this catalogue request feature, the service may have an online mailing list management feature, which may be useful chiefly in that it lets you download the names in formats that your database program can immediately use.

Meanwhile, is there a way to see what Web address your customers came from? (If you have link exchanges with other sites—see Chapter 11—you will not be able to judge their effect without this feature. Otherwise, you won't care.) It is also nice to see what pages have been visited the most (and least) and what search keys visitors to your site have used.

➤ Contracts

The question here is, Can you take your store down any time you want, or are you stuck with a lease? After all, some of the advantages of e-commerce are supposed to be flexibility and speed. If you can get a store mounted in a short time, you should be able to pull the plug on it with as little notice. If you are stuck with a long-term contract, you might as well go out and lease a storefront.

➤ Customer Support

If the ESP can address all the concerns we've just discussed, then it has a customer support function second to none, and you can sign up without hesitation. And you need to do this, because we have to get on with applying for the merchant account.

EXPERTS SPEAK

If you are going to have a unique domain name, you will probably get it through your ESP. Put some thought into the name, warns John Schulte.

"I have noticed a mistake that a lot of people make, in that they choose a name that has no connection with what they do," he says. "They go for cuteness. That may work if you are well financed. Write a bunch of words down based on the concept of your business. Then start searching to see if it is in use. If it is, you can often use other words. Then, even if you don't have any other money, pay the $70 to register it. You will have it for two years, and in the meantime you can start working on your business plan."

■ AFTERNOON: APPLYING FOR THE MERCHANT ACCOUNT

CHEAT SHEET
(one for each)

Have the following information on hand:

- Business general information.
- Business legal information.
- Sales and business data.
- Credit card processing information.
- Business owner information.
- Banking references.
- Funding information.
- Card type information.

As you have already learned, a merchant account is the arrangement that lets you accept credit card payments. (And also as mentioned earlier, online processing of the payments is another issue—you can have an account and do the processing offline, like a clerk in a restaurant.) Many services have online applications where you answer questions on your browser screen and then press the Submit button. However, applicants with declared credit card revenue over $150,000 per year would have to fax a signed application and supply additional data.

(If you are going to operate without credit cards—have the buyers pay in advance or bill them, ship COD, or use purchase orders in a business-to-business arrangement—then you do not need a merchant account and can skip this section. But if that is the case, you have to wonder if you need a shopping cart at all—just have an ordinary Web site that contains your catalogue, with an HTML form that customers can fill out to send you orders by e-mail. However, veteran Web buyers may be more comfortable seeing and using a shopping cart, and if you have a shopping cart, you can always add credit card processing later.)

If you already have a merchant account, you may still not be able to accept credit card orders over the Internet because an Internet account is not a standard account—it is a variation of the MOTO or CNP merchant account. Check with your merchant bank for details. If you do have an Internet merchant account, though, you can usually use it with a new ESP.

Filling out the online merchant account application provided by the ESP often involves opening your new store site and using the site management feature (such as picking payment method.) The forms can take 20 minutes to fill out, assuming you have the information at hand. The information is detailed in the Cheat Sheet, and we'll go over it below.

➤ Business General Information

This includes your legal name and your DBA (doing business as) name, if any; the business address; the name and title of the legal business signer; the business phone and fax numbers; and contact name. In cases where you are signing up through an ESP, you may have to give the store identifier, e-mail, and Web addresses.

➤ Business Legal Information

This includes the physical address, zoning, type of business, type of ownership, state you are incorporated in, federal tax ID number, the date the business was founded, the number of employees, and (finally) what you sell.

➤ Sales and Business Data

This includes your yearly cash sales and yearly credit card sales; the percent of credit card sales of your mail-order, telephone, and over-the-counter sales; sales tax percentage; and information on your credit card policies and methods of advertising and delivery.

➤ Business Owner Information

You'll need the names, address, titles, and Social Security numbers of your business's owners, partners, or officers.

➤ Banking References

This includes your bank's name, address, contact person, and phone number; the date you started doing business there; and your average daily balance, dollar total of accounts, and available credit.

➤ Funding Information

You'll need to give American Bankers Association (ABA) and direct deposit account (DDA) numbers from a business check.

➤ Card Type Information

Basically, you pick the cards that you want to offer.

Most services say you can expect to wait about three days for approval and that approval rates run to 98 percent. Most assume that you have a business checking account, but some will work with a personal checking account.

---

(20)/(20)

If you are in the consumer field, do not think that you can get by with not accepting credit cards, advises Carrie Hardy.

"Ninety percent of the customers use credit cards," she says. "Of those who put in an order and say they will pay by check, only half ever send in the money. There are sites that will not accept checks for that reason. If the check does not come in, I will send them a reminder, and sometimes that will cause them to get around to it. But for the others I just have to cancel the order," she says.

EXPERTS SPEAK

When the time comes to get a merchant account, apply with your bank first, advises John Schulte. You may be able to get it cheaper that way. In fact, he says, check with them about it when you first set up your business checking account. It's painful to set up an account and then later find that the bank can't or won't give you merchant status when you could have set it up with a bank that will, he notes.

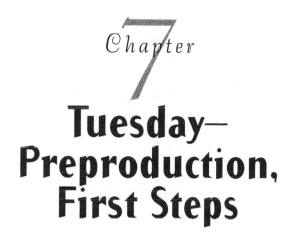

Chapter 7

Tuesday–
Preproduction,
First Steps

Today you will line up two pivotal ingredients for your Web site: the artwork and the descriptor text. We'll do the artwork in the morning and the descriptor in the afternoon.

■ MORNING: ARTWORK

CHEAT SHEET

- Graphics software supporting .gif format.
- (Each item): Product shots in .gif format. If not available, you'll need printed product shots and access to scanner OR a digital camera (and access to products) OR relation by marriage to studio photographer.
- Logo.
- Marquee banner.
- Color scheme?
- Edit out backgrounds of product shots (optional).
- Set transparent color in product shots (optional).
- Thumbnails (optional).
- Button artwork (very optional).
- Page background pattern (extremely optional).

You must have artwork. The customer must be able to see the product, dispelling tiny but ever-present doubts about whether you have it and whether you and he or she are really talking about the same thing. Even for something like software, having the blandest box shot is better than nothing at all.

Meanwhile, to achieve a truly attractive and distinctive Web site, you need at least a logo. Yes, you can probably get by without one, at least initially, but as you surf around, you will realize that your site looks painfully stark, even naked, without one.

Also, like a bride planning a wedding, you need to have a color scheme in mind. Do you use a distinctive color or color combination for your logo? If so, that should be carried over to the Web site, usually as contrasting background and text colors, or embodied in your artwork. Details are not important now— we'll show you how it's done as we go along—but you should be aware of your colors. (A decision to have no preference is fine, because they can be changed later.)

Meanwhile, you have probably seen Web pages that use a background pattern instead of a solid color. This is done using a small graphics file that, once downloaded to the browser, is tiled repeatedly until it fills up the page's background. It can be a nice touch, or it can make other graphics on the page look very messy. For simplicity, we will skip that feature in our examples.

Now, as we get into details, don't panic. The demands of Web artwork are far less rigorous than those of, say, magazine or book publishing, because the resolution and color depth are much lower. And if you did not understand the previous sentence, then we'll pause and go over the five things you must understand about Web graphics before proceeding.

1. *File formats.* You are probably aware that there are scads of file formats out there for graphic material. To ensure browser compatibility, graphics for the Web are limited to three of them: *.gif, .jpg,* and *.png* (pronounced ping.) Of these, .gif (sometimes called the CompuServe format) is the most widely used, and we will stick with it in our examples. Meanwhile, .jpg *(jay-peg)* is used for large color photos because it renders them into smaller

files than .gif does, whereas .png is a new format that does not seem to have caught on.

2. *Resolution.* Use the screen solution of 92 dots per inch (dpi.) This, you'll note, is dramatically less than the resolutions used in publishing, which typically start at 1,200 dpi.

3. *Color depth.* This term refers to the number of colors (or shades of gray) that can be rendered and the number of data bits needed. The standard is 256 colors, which requires 8 bits per pixel (We'll define that under the next heading). Yes, you can get photorealistic files using 16 or 24 bits, thus achieving millions of colors. But the result is huge files, and the browser won't show more than 256 colors anyway. (If you are handy with graphics software, you might experiment with your pictures to see if they will look as good in 16 colors, which takes 4 bits and makes the file even smaller. Line drawings should be rendered in two colors—black and white—that takes only 1 bit.)

4. *Image size.* The dimensions of the pictures are measured in *pixels*—individual dots on the screen. The standard Windows screen size is typically either 640 pixels wide and 480 high or 800 wide and 600 high. That does not give you a lot of on-screen real estate to play with. (Yes, users may be able to scroll across a graphic that is too large for the screen, but why force them to do that?) For product shots, therefore, shoot for 150 by 150 pixels. They can be bigger, because a larger image can be scaled to fit a smaller frame, and will look fine—you'll just have an unnecessarily large file. But if it's a small image scaled up to fit, the results may not look good.

5. *File size.* Because most people are still stuck with fairly slow modems, you want your files to be as small as possible. If the user has to spend five minutes downloading your exquisitely ornate page, she may decide to go to some place friendlier. But if you follow the suggestions in the previous four headings, you'll be okay.

➤ Product Artwork

Armed with the information given in the previous section, we can now approach the task of getting the product shots with confidence. Typically, you can get product shots from the manufacturer, which may have some in electronic format that they can send to you, or you can save artwork directly from its Web site. (Right-click [uni-click with a Macintosh] with the cursor on the image to save it as a file on your hard drive.) Perhaps they can supply glossy photos, or suitable pictures are included in their flysheets. Either way, you should ask for permission to use them, but that permission may be embodied in the fine print of your distribution agreement.

With physical pictures, the problem is that they are on paper and you need them in electronic format. These days, any large copy shop offers scanner services. Simply tell them the pictures are for Web use. If that does not mean anything to them, tell them the gist of the advice from the previous section: .gif file in 92 dpi, eight-bit color (two bits if it's a line drawing), and sized to about 150 pixels.

Meanwhile, office scanners are breeding like rabbits and are almost as cheap. If you have a multifunction fax/printer, it will include a scanner with sufficient resolution. The only question is whether it will have color capabilities.

Either way, make careful note of the file names.

Now, we run into problems if there are no existing pictures. You can take them with a digital camera and have the file immediately. Or you can take them with a conventional camera and have the photos scanned. However you do it, the technology takes a back seat to plain old artistry.

You want to achieve what's called a *hero shot* of the product, in which it stands out from the screen, uncluttered with distractions. You can start by thumbtacking a white bed sheet low on a wall so that it spills forward on the floor. Smooth it out. Put the product on the sheet, a little out from the wall. The camera angle should be from slightly above and to one side to give a three-dimensional effect. There should be sources of light from both sides, and one side should be brighter than the other. If you can, bounce the flash off the ceiling.

You can also pay a studio photographer about $200 an hour to do the same thing but hopefully with surer results. Be sure you explain exactly what you want. Don't be shy; he's heard it all.

➤ Advanced Topics

Once you have the product shots in electronic format, there are four more steps you might need to take: cropping, editing, adding a transparent color, and creating thumbnails.

Unfortunately, all four steps involve the use of graphics software. And that is a problem because you are probably using Windows, and the Windows Paint program can't help you because it does not support the three Web graphics formats (.gif, .jpg, or .png.) So if you are serious, you will probably have to acquire a graphics program such as Paint Shop Pro or Photoshop. Paint Shop Pro can be downloaded for immediate use from www.jasc.com. (You will need to pay for it at some point.)

Cropping means cutting back the edges of the picture so that only the product and a little of the background remains. There is no point in taking up transmission time for background pixels that add nothing to the meaning of the picture. With any graphics software the process of cutting will be fairly straightforward—just scan the Help index for "crop."

Editing is more involved and means removing unnecessary distractions from the image, especially the background. For instance, if you are selling an old car and the picture had to be taken in the driveway, there are probably bushes or parts of the garage appearing to poke out of the fenders. It is possible to edit those out and replace them with a plain white background. The simplest way is to draw a white line around the item and then "paint-fill" everything in the background with white. (The white line will keep the paint fill from spilling over onto the item.) Admittedly, you will have to spend a few minutes educating yourself about the software's tools, especially the freehand brush (for making the line), the fill command, and the color selection procedure (so that the line and the fill will be white.)

The emphasis on white backgrounds brings us to the concept of *transparent colors*. Using a white background in your photos will cause them to merge nicely with the background of your Web page—assuming the Web page is using a white background. But what if, after great soul searching, you decide to use a light blue background? Then your pictures will appear to be sitting in a little white window. Editing the pictures to change the background from white to light blue will not help much because the light blue used by your software is unlikely to exactly match the light blue filler rendered by your browser. Now your pictures will appear to be in a slightly off-color window. (Plain white, being the absence of color, can always be expected to match.)

The situation may not bother you. Or it may repel you. Fortunately, you don't have to worry about how your users will react, because with .gif files, you can set one of the colors to be transparent, which means that the background fill color (or pattern) used by the Web page will show through whatever part of the image is set that way. Assuming you made a solid background and you set the background color to be the transparent color, the product will now appear to be laying atop the background of the Web page—an arrangement that looks much neater and less distracting, as you can see in Figure 7.1.

The only drawback arises in cases where the background color also appears as part of the item. Perhaps some shiny spot on the front surface of the item reflected the camera flash and now sports a white splotch. Assuming you used white as the transparent background color, that splotch will suddenly take on the Web page's background color, with unexpected and probably weird results. The answer is to use the fill tool to replace the white background with some other color, one that does not appear elsewhere in the picture, and set that to be the transparent color. This will have no effect on any other pictures on the page because the color is set within each individual picture. (Your graphics software may have some proof facility that lets you view the image against some arbitrary background pattern to check what parts of the image have become transparent.)

Finally, *thumbnails* are miniature versions of the product photos, used for illustrative purposes in the product list. They are too small to allow for any inspection of the product but are large enough to show what you are talking about. Some systems will create them automatically from the product photo, so you don't have to create or upload a separate picture to serve as the thumbnail.

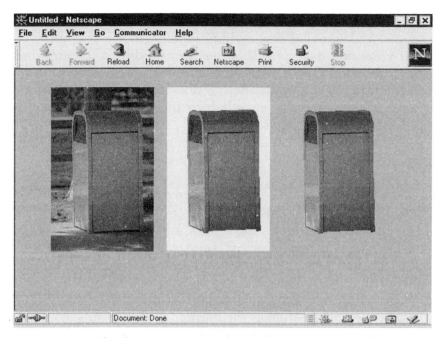

Figure 7.1 This browser screen shows three versions of the same picture. The first shows the picture as originally taken, without an edited background. In the second, the background has been edited out and replaced with solid white. In the third, the background has been set as a transparent color so that the page's background color shows through.

If you are called upon to create your own thumbnail pictures, simply load the product photo into your graphics software. (Again, it has to be a package that supports the Web formats: .jpg, .png, but preferably .gif.) Find a Resize command and set the height to about 40 pixels. Then save it under a new name.

➤ Logos, Etc.

It can be a modern, minimalist swoosh or an ornate relic left over from the nineteenth century, but it is good to have a *logo*—a graphic element associated with the identity of your business. If you have one, you should incorporate it into your Web site.

We can assume you already have one in paper form that can be scanned and edited as discussed previously in this section.

If you don't have one, this may be the time to create one. The time-tested way of arriving at a logo is to render your business's initials, using a distinctive but not overly ornate font. Once added to an image, each letter can be given its own color, size, outline, or special effect.

Again, this will require educating yourself about your graphics software—read up about its Text commands.

Having done that, the next step is to create a marquee banner, containing the business's name, to put on to the top of the page. The name will otherwise be in text, and no matter what font you use, it will look rather stark and bland. With graphics you have total control over its appearance, and you can add your logo and perhaps other special effects. Again, you will have to play with your software's Text command and then explore what special effects it has to offer. You might, for instance, be able to emboss the banner so that it appears to be engraved in parchment or add a border that makes it look like a large screen button.

It's up to you. Just keep in mind that any text contained in the marquee (being part of an image) cannot be read by search engines. And as explained in Chapter 11, getting good coverage by search engines is important, and the text that appears at the top of your opening page is critical to getting that coverage. We'll discuss what to put in that text in the afternoon section.

For the advanced user, it is possible to create images to go in the screen buttons of the Web site, perhaps with your logo. But also keep in mind that sometimes less is more.

Pixel

As you now know, each of the tiny dots on the screen is a *pixel*. Resolution, however, is usually spoken of in terms of dots per inch (dpi), for comparison with publishing, where the pixels are actually tiny dots of ink. You can get passable results with lower resolution on a computer screen than you can with a printed page, because each pixel on the screen can be a specific shade of color or gray. On the page, each dot has to be one of the three primary colors or black, and they must be clustered together to achieve the illusion of a shade of color or gray.

EXAMPLE

For the example site we are going to build in Chapter 9, we will create a logo and then a marquee banner incorporating that logo and the business name. We will also create artwork for each product, as shown in Figure 7.2.

The artwork was created using Paint Shop Pro. The logo was made using the Text tool and a heavy font. The logo was then pasted into both ends of the banner, which is

Figure 7.2 This browser screen shows the banner created for the example site and the three random items we will be selling. The product photos are shown 150 pixels tall, scaled to that size by HTML coding from somewhat larger photos. The backgrounds were edited out and replaced with a color that was then made the file's transparent color.

470 pixels wide and 55 pixels high. The name in the middle was done with the Text tool, this time with an ordinary font. The banner's three-dimensional effect was created with the software's Buttonize function. This can be done in a few minutes.

The time required and the degree of difficulty involved in the product photos depends on what sources are available and whether you feel the backgrounds need to be edited out.

David Green, president of Creative Design Group in Malden, Missouri, says that a scanner is fine for most artwork used on the Web because screen resolution is not that high.

"The advantage of a scanner is that many firms already have photos on file that are perfectly useable on the Net," he says. "Many have photos that were shot for catalogues, which we can use. And since we are aiming for quick downloads, we will give a little on clarity for nonvital photos."

But now and then there are vital photos, which, for instance, show the fine details of factory millwork. "Then we will set up our ministudio and use a portable camera to best advantage," he says. The resulting pictures will be turned into high-resolution images, typically in the .tif format, which surfers can download separately and view offline.

Carrie Hardy says that she created her site's artwork by scanning photos and saving them in .jpg format. But the process was a tedious one because she ended up redoing files that turned out to be too big.

"People would e-mail me, saying that a page took too long to load, so I would resize the picture to the screen size so that people would not have to scroll around it. That's one thing I look for when shopping on the Internet—that a site's graphics are reasonable. So if I had to do it all over again, I would use a digital camera," she says.

■ AFTERNOON: DESCRIPTORS

CHEAT SHEET

- Words describing your site.
- Five sites selling similar items.
- Words used on their opening pages.
- Your final descriptor list.

As explained in Chapter 11, shoppers are not just going to stumble over your site while hanging out online. The way they get to your site is by either:

1. Knowing the Web address and typing it in or, having been there before and bookmarked it, invoking that bookmark.
2. Following a link from another site to yours.
3. Finding you in a search engine.

The first is someone who already knows about you, and the second is someone who at least recognizes you. So although their mere existence may speak well of your existing marketing efforts, they are not new customers. To grow, you want new customers, especially ones who appear at your site spontaneously, free of cost to you, drawn not by an expensive marketing campaign but by the fact that you offer what they want. The way those people know that you offer what they want and get to your site is through search engines—they type in a word and get a list of sites that contain it. Typing in generalities, they get lengthy, useless lists. They soon learn to type in specific, precise descriptors and thereupon get short, useful lists. The trick, then, is to be on that list when they go looking for what you sell. And to do that your Web site—especially the opening text of the first page—must contain the words they will use when searching for what you offer.

These are not the words that you or your advertising copywriter would use if asked to describe your site—*new, exciting, original, great values, good deals,* and so on. Instead, they are the words that someone would use to describe your product and your site in the context of the Web: *wood train sets.* It may sound bland, but specifics are what will draw them in.

However, we've not been specific enough. Several questions that you should address will go through the mind of the Web surfer:

- *Market.* Wholesale or retail? Industrial or consumer?
- *Channel.* Over the counter or mail order?
- *Location.* Is the store around the corner or in Guam?
- *Intended users.* Are these collectibles, display items, toys, or elements of a rail service that transports forest products in the Pacific Northwest?

In this example, although children are not going to be buying the product, it is intended for their use, so you need to mention the word *children.* Because toys are often designed for a specific age range, you need to mention what it is. The city you are in is always of interest so that a Web user in South Africa can decide to look for a closer source. But because you don't have a store (we'll say), you don't want people showing up at the door, and so you need to say outright that yours is a mail-order business.

So you find yourself forced to say something like: *South Megapolis's mail-order source of wood toy train sets for children ages three to eight.*

We are not yet through, however. The next step is to go to the Web itself and find other sites that sell what you sell—find at least five—and see what keywords lead you to them as well as what keywords lead you completely astray, such as to the resume of someone named Wood in the railroad industry, leading you to decide to use *wooden* in the descriptor.

At each of the sites you find, examine the text on the opening page. Then look at the title—the top line in the browser screen, which can be set by the site's HTML code. Then do a View Source command to see if they have hidden away any lists of keywords that only the search engine will see, using meta tags. (See the Glossary for an explanation of meta tags.) If any are present, they will typically be found at the top of the screen. Make a note of them.

In our example you might discover that the other sites emphasized the brand names of the toys: *WhittleCraft, KidsRR, ChildFreight,* and *HoboBaby* and that they slip in the words *kids, toddlers, railroad, choo-choo, track, locomotive, accessories, bridges,* and *freight.*

Suddenly we have a list of words that can't be tied together into any kind of English sentence that rolls off the tongue. Don't worry about it. Using the words comes later. For now, just get them down on paper. We'll show you what to do with them in the next chapter.

---

(20)/(20)

"I ran into three sites just yesterday, brought to us by new clients to be managed, that did not contain any keywords or meta tags on the opening page," notes David Green.

EXAMPLE

For our on-going Wonder Widget example site, we settle on the words *widget, gadget, gizmo, wangdoodle, thingamajig, gimcrack, South Megapolis, retail, mail order,* and (we couldn't help ourselves) *affordable.*

Again, we'll show what we are going to do with these words in the next chapter.

Chapter

Wednesday—
Preproduction,
Final Steps

We are almost ready to produce the site itself. But before we dive into that chore, we should know exactly what we are going to do, rather than be floundering around while online. So today we will make all the decisions regarding the organization of the site, and then we'll write the text to go into it.

■ MORNING: SITE LAYOUT

CHEAT SHEET

- List of inventory items.
- Large sheet of paper.

There are certainly many e-commerce sites that consist of one long page of items for sale, each with a shopping-cart button beside it. That's okay for Army quartermasters working on replenishment tasks. But we feel that a consumer site should be more like the clerk at a jewelry counter, catering to the shopper's desire to inspect the object before making a buying decision, standing ready to answer any questions that may come up, and able to quickly offer alternate items if the first does not please.

So in this section we are going to design a site, not a page. Each page will be short and sweet, devoted to one particular purpose. The organization will be straightforward and easy for the visitor to follow, thus making this a serviceable site. If while reading this, you are struck by specific reasons that make our approach a bad idea in your case, that's fine—you're already catching on. The idea here is to lay foundation on which you can build. And the foundation, we think, consists of the following features:

➤ The Home Page

Also called the *index page,* this is the page that a visitor sees when first coming to the site. It should be attractive and uncluttered, but it needs to contain the descriptor words we nailed during the last section plus something about the wonders of your business and the superiority of your products. Then there should be links to the rest of the site.

The links will be inserted by your ESP's site-creation tool (relieving you of a significant programming chore) and will match the layout of the site, which we will address later.

➤ Product Family Pages

It is presumed that you have more than one product and that these products fall into logical categories: bicycle accessories, helmets, children's helmets. By going up the selection tree, the buyer can make her way to an intelligent, uncluttered selection.

➤ Item Pages

At the end of the tree, there's a page for each item, each with a shopping-cart button (placed there by the site-creation tool). Yes, you can have more than one item per page or a major item with accessories.

➤ Product Data Pages

One of the advantages of e-commerce is that your Web site can contain reams of data about a product such as you would not dare clutter a catalogue or advertisement with. Buyers do appreciate this effort on your part, and its inclusion can be a major differentiator between your site and your competitors' slick, glad-handing sites, which palm off the shopper with a few phrases of marketing hype.

The trouble is that you don't want to clutter up the item page with background data—nothing should distract that buyer from the Order button, especially an intimidating screen of data that he may or may not be interested in. So the trick is to have the background data on a separate page, linked to the item page. The shopper can click over to it and study it or print it out. Even if he does not make a purchase at that time, he may fondly remember you as a source of information.

➤ Information Page

This is separate from the product data page(s)—it is a page about your business, with background information that you think is appropriate in your setting. Items to include might be:

- Address; phone and fax numbers; and e-mail address.
- Background blurb or mission statement.
- Investor information if appropriate.
- Privacy statement saying how to opt out of the mailing list database and whether you sell your mailing list.
- Links to white papers.
- Copyright notice.

Do include your address and phone number. If you harbor some belief that doing so will somehow counteract the cachet of being an Internet business, snap out of it—everyone knows your business is composed of human beings, to whom other human beings might have occasion to speak. (We have discovered, through hard experience, that as many as a third of business or corporate Web sites do not include basic contact information beyond an e-mail address. We wish there was a rational explanation for this.)

➤ Opt-In Page

As explained in Chapter 11, it is vital to gather e-mail addresses from visitors to your site. You will, of course, get the addresses of

those who actually buy something, but you want more than that—
you want prospects who can be turned into customers. But it
seems a little brash to just say, "Click here to join our mailing list."
(Not that some sites don't do it.) Anyway, as noted in Chapter 1,
today's online citizens expect something from you in return for
their personal data and the 90 seconds it takes for them to enter it.

So instead, offer something that requires them to register,
all the while remaining open about the fact that all names will
become part of your mailing list. And you are also open about
the fact that they can get off the mailing list at any time by, for
instance, sending e-mail asking that it be done. Things you
might offer include:

- A chance to enter a giveaway drawing to be held at a given
  date. (Do hold the drawing and award the prize, announce
  it, and then start another drawing.)
- Money-off, limited-time electronic coupons, sent back to
  them as e-mail.
- A free catalogue.
- A subscription to your industry newsletter, sent electronically. (You *are* going to write one?)
- The option to receive periodic product updates.

That last item, of course, just means "put me on your mailing list" and may prove sufficient when the site is devoted to
industrial or high-tech products. There, the buyers' interest has
probably been triggered by genuine need rather than marketing
hype, and they may see your e-mail ads as news. In the consumer market it is not likely to get much of a response.

➤ Other Pages

The shopping cart and the pages it produces, including an
order-status page to show what has been put in the shopping
cart so far, are handled by the ESP's software, and you don't
have to worry about them.

The ESP's site-creation software can also be expected to
include a contents or index page and a generic help page. There
may also be a link to a search tool to search the contents of the site.

If you are exchanging links with other sites, then your site
will include a page of reciprocal links. You will need to generate

that page yourself, supplying the outside Web addresses. The site-creation tool will almost certainly have some way to add links to a page.

➤ **How to Proceed**

The trick, therefore, is to map out the site in terms of the product inventory, divided into sections that represent the product families, reachable by following a branching tree of links from the initial index page.

Also linked directly to the index page will be the subsidiary pages, such as the opt-in page and the information page.

For instance, going back to our bicycle accessories page, we might have three families of products: helmets, child carriers, and car racks. Under each we could have further families: children's and adult helmets; heavy-duty and light child carriers; two-, three-, and four-place car racks. Then, assuming no further subcategories were appropriate, we could have the items themselves. Linked to the item page, we could have a product data sheet.

So get out a big sheet of paper and draw a diagram: on the left, the index page, branching to the information page, the opt-in page, and the product family pages. From each product family page, draw branches to the subcategories or items. Label each with the item you will put there. If you have product data sheets, branch to them after the item pages.

If things get too crowded, you can branch to separate sheets of paper. But don't go looking for fancy organization chart software—things that can be done on butcher paper should be.

EXAMPLE

Our ongoing example is shown in Figure 8.1. Note the three product families—widgets, controllers, and support units—each of which has two items. (The Order button will be on item pages.) Below each item page, we have a product data sheet.

In the next section, we will compose the text for most of the pages, a process called copywriting. We already have the artwork we need, thanks to our previous efforts.

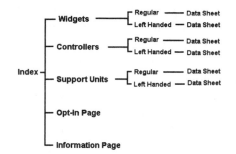

Figure 8.1 This diagram shows the layout of the example site we will be creating. It includes three product categories or families, each with two inventory items. Each inventory item has a product data sheet. Then there's the opt-in page and the information page.

"The main thing we have done to help the sites of some of our clients is to add a site map," says David Green. "A site map is a wonderful thing for whose who don't care about the animations and fireworks. Meanwhile, there are sites, whose operation we took over, where you could spend several minutes figuring out who to call. I can't see intentionally avoiding talking to a customer. And there have been sites where you could not even get to a convenient e-mail [button]—and I thought that would be the definition of having a Web site," he says.

EXPERTS SPEAK

Judging from the calls he gets, cost overruns in the site-creation phase are the biggest headache experienced by e-commerce entrepreneurs, says John Schulte.

The problem is that people use a site designer who is working by the hour. But they come in with only vague plans, he notes.

"You should have your Web site completely laid out on pieces of paper so you can say 'Here is the text, here are the buttons, they are oval, make sure they are linked.' If the programmer is making $100 an hour asking questions, you are burning up money right there. And you don't want programmers deciding strategy for your Web site since they are not salespeople," he cautions.

As for picking programmers, he has this advice: "Investigate what people say they have done. You can find a lot of people who say they know how to do something when they don't, and you can spend thousands of dollars starting over." Every new technical trend brings out people who not only want to learn the tools but want to bill you while they learn, he warns.

And what about picking software? "Use common tools," he advises.

■ AFTERNOON: COPYWRITING

CHEAT SHEET

- Descriptor composed in Chapter 7.
- Layout drawn in previous section.
- Word processor with a spell checker.

Now that we have the site laid out, we can commence to write the text that will go on each page. This should be done in advance of site creation for two very good reasons:

1. It makes site creation go faster.
2. More importantly, by doing it in advance, you can use a word processor with a spell checker.

If you have surfed any time at all, you have doubtless run across Web sites with misspelled and garbled text—and wondered what was going on with these people. Don't join their ranks.

Anyway, we will compose the text in a word processor and save that file. In the next section, when we create the site, we will cut and paste the text into the appropriate on-screen forms of the ESP's site-creation tool.

At this point we are not going to worry (much) about how the text appears on the page because we can do that in the site-creation phase much more handily. But text attributes that we absolutely know we want to use can be added to the text at this phase using HTML tags because most site-creation tools will let you insert them and will render the text accordingly. (See Appendix C for HTML tags that you might want to use.)

Instead, at this point we will be guided by a variant of the old KISS rejoinder—traditionally, "Keep It Simple, Stupid," but we will use "Keep It Short and Simple." Much as you may long for an outlet for your literary inclinations, an e-commerce site is not it. The text should do its job and then get out of the way. If the reader remembers the text, then the text is not doing its job, that of ushering her into and through the shopping process.

For a discussion, we will rely on the example site that we will be creating in the next section.

EXAMPLE: INDEX PAGE

In Chapter 7 we went to great lengths to nail down the descriptor words whose presence at the site should let interested Web surfers find us by using search engines. (As explained in Chapter 11, being found by search engines is of paramount importance, and including carefully selected words on the page is the best way to ensure being found.)

The words selected for our example: *widget, gadget, gizmo, wangdoodle, thingamajig, gimcrack, South Megapolis, retail, mail order,* and *affordable.* We have three avenues for using these words:

- The title text, which appears in the top line of the browser screen and is typically examined by search engines (and often used as the descriptor for the site when the search engine returns with its lists of findings).

- The body text of the opening page (i.e., the index page, also called the home page). Search engines find the initial text especially interesting.
- Meta tags, included as part of the HTML coding. (See the Glossary for an explanation.) Text in a page's meta tag will not be seen by the users but will be seen by many search engines.
- So we will compose the title text, using what descriptor words that we can:

```
Widget World, Retail Source of Mail Order
Widgets.
```

It gives the site name and can stand on its own in a listing of Web sites generated by a search engine. We will save it in a word processing file, put in a few blank lines, and go on to composing the body text. So we write a short sales spiel noting what can be found in the site—not forgetting the opt-in page—while including more of the descriptor words. The result:

```
If you need affordable widgets in the South
Megapolis area, then we are the answer. Yes, we
have:
Widgets
Controllers
Support Units
Register now and enter a drawing for a free
widget!
```

That would suffice, and we can run the spell checker on the text, save it, and go on.

However, we would like the bottom line to stand out. Making it red would serve that purpose. And the list of product categories should be distinctive. Centering them would do it. Also, we know from painful experience that HTML will run all the lines together into one paragraph unless you tell it not to.

So we will add HTML tags to add some desired formatting to the text: <br> for line breaks, <p> for full paragraph breaks, <center> to center a line or paragraph, <b> for boldfacing, and `<font color>` to set the color of the text. (These are all explained in Appendix C.) So what we end up with actually looks like this:

```
If you need affordable widgets in the South
Megapolis area, then we are the answer. Yes, we
have:<p>
<center>
<b>Widgets<br>
Controllers<br>
Support Units</b>
<br>
</center>
<font color = "red"><b>Register now and enter a
drawing for a free widget!</b>
```

The site-creation tool will supply the navigation buttons, and the banner was done in Chapter 7. So we can at this point declare victory and go on, happy that we ran the spell checker before adding the HTML tags, which would typically look like a bunch of misspellings.

We have forgotten one detail, however—we have some descriptor words left over:

```
Gadget, gizmo, wangdoodle, thingamajig,
gimcrack.
```

We will use these in the page's meta tag, saving them on a line of their own in the word processing file, and go on. (The site-creation tool typically has a way to insert user-supplied text into the meta tags. If you have to make your own, see the **Meta Tags** entry in the Glossary.)

EXAMPLE: PRODUCT FAMILY PAGE

As you recall from the layout we did in the last section, after the index page comes a page for each product family. Each product family page will link to the individual items that belong to that family.

The product family pages do not need to carry much except the link to the item pages, which the site-creation tool will insert along with links back to the home page, and so on. So we will just stick to a simple sentence:

```
As you can see, we have the finest widgets this
side of Tierra del Fuego. Select the model you
want below.
```

Because there is no material to set apart or highlight, we will not need to add any HTML tags. We will again add some blank lines to separate it from the other material and run the spell checker.

EXAMPLE: ITEM PAGE

Now we are down to an individual for-sale item, stock-keeping unit (SKU), product, or whatever you want to call it. The site-creation tool will add the picture of the item, the price, and the Order button plus the usual navigation buttons. You just need to write a blurb about the item such as you would see in any catalogue. Three sentences would be fine. Daring to include a compound sentence, we'll use two:

```
You can't lose with this baby. It comes with
all the options and accessories you've come to
expect from Widget World plus our famous
lifetime warranty.
```

Upbeat, yet (somewhat) informative. Again, put in a few blank lines to separate it from the other material, run the spell checker, and save it.

The page will need a link to the following product data page, but that can typically be done with your site-creation tool as we will show in the next section.

EXAMPLE: PRODUCT DATA PAGE

We could get by with being only marginally informative on the item page—relying on sizzle rather than steak, as is traditional in advertising—because we are going to put all the boring facts on a page by themselves. You might envision something like this:

```
Weight          8 lb
Color           silver
Size            16' x 12" x 8"
Composition     hardened steel
Rating          800 pounds
Rope Size       half-inch
Origin:         Sumatra
```

But if you just cut and paste the text, the material will probably not line up in a nice chart like this one. First, we would have to put in line break tags. Unfortunately, that will not be enough, because HTML does not have a tab function and multiple spaces are ignored. Unless you have a really smart site-creation tool, you are likely to end up with lines in which the material is jammed together rather than neatly separated.

There are two ways to ensure the material will be rendered reasonably close to the chart you intended:

1. Tell the browser to use the <pre> (preformatted) text tag. That will cause the text to be rendered as given, with entries on individual lines with the numbers lined up by the spaces. But it will use a fixed-width font.

2. Use HTML table tags to arrange the material, each phrase and number in a separate cell of a little display-only spreadsheet. This is not difficult to do—if you already know the HTML table tags. Otherwise, this is not the time to learn.

The second approach can give you more control over the final appearance of the material, but the first approach is by far the easiest, and is the one we will adopt. The only additional thing you might want to do is boldface the material to enhance legibility, by adding the <b> tag. (Trust us, this is always a good idea with fixed-width font material used on screen.) The text will look like this:

```
<b><pre>
Weight          8 lb
Color           silver
Size            16' x 12" x 8"
Composition     hardened steel
Rating          800 pounds
Rope Size       half-inch
Origin:         Sumatra
</pre></b>
```

Again, you don't need line-breaks tags because the text is preformatted.

The page will also need some kind of Up button to get the users back to the item page and its all-important Order button. You should be able to add one using the site-creation tool. If that does not prove possible, you can add text to prompt the shopper to use his browser's Back button to return to the item page. Either way, we can add some lines, save the material, and go on.

DEFINE THIS!

Fixed-Width Font

Text can be either *fixed* or *variable* (or *proportional*) width. *Fixed* means that each letter takes up the same amount of space in a line, be it an *M* or an *i*. The result looks as though it came from a typewriter. *Variable* (or *proportional*) means that each letter takes up space in the line in proportion to its width, and the results look like a page in a printed book. Using fixed text may produce a clunky, old-fashioned result, but when it comes to data, people will accept a utilitarian presentation.

EXAMPLE: ET CETERA

Now you can go back and do item pages for the rest of the products in that family, doing a catalogue blurb for the item page and a table of data for the product data page.

Having filled out the rest of the product family, you then go back and create another product family page for the second family and proceed with the item pages and product data pages, deciding what you want to say about each as you go along. Remember, keep it short, and if you are using more than one paragraph, include the line break tags.

EXAMPLE: INFORMATION PAGE

No, we have not forgotten the information page—although plenty of real-world Web sites manage to do so. We'll assume a basic, nonprepossessing information page, to include:

1. Company name and contact information.
2. Privacy statement.
3. Copyright notice. (In Microsoft Windows, you can get access to the necessary © symbol using the Character Map facility.)

We should end up with text that looks like this:

```
Widget World
123 4th Street
Townsville, South Megapolis 00001
Phone: 123-444-5678
Fax: 123-444-7890
E-mail: info@widgetworld.com
Privacy Statement: Our mailing list is for sale
at all times to the highest bidder. If you wish
to be removed, please send e-mail to
info@widgetworld.com with the word "remove" in
the subject line.
Site Contents Copyright © 2000 by Widget World.
All Rights Reserved.
```

Of course, by now you've come to expect more than just raw text. Due to the nature of the material, the text would look neater if it were centered. The company name ought to be in bigger letters, and *Privacy Statement* ought to stand out, so we will make that boldface. In keeping with societal norms, the copyright notice ought to be in fine print. And, of course, everything has to have line break tags. So we went up with this:

```
<center>
<font size=7>Widget World</font><br>
123 4th Street<br>
Townsville, South Megapolis 00001<br>
Phone: 123-444-5678<br>
Fax: 123-444-7890<br>
E-mail: info@widgetworld.com
<p>
<b>Privacy Statement:</b> Our mailing list is
for sale at all times to the highest bidder. If
you wish to be removed, please send e-mail to
info@widgetworld.com with the word "remove" in
the subject line.
<p>
<font size=1>Site Contents Copyright © 2000
Widget World. All Rights Reserved.</font>
</center>
```

Notice the use of the <p> (paragraph break) tag to separate the material into three blocks: contact, privacy statement, and copyright notice. As explained in Appendix C, the <font size> tag is based on text being in proportional sizes designated 1 through 7. So we've used the largest for the name and the smallest for the copyright notice.

EXAMPLE: EVERYTHING ELSE

The opt-in page will (we happen to know) actually be a form generated by the ESP's site-creation tool, which we can customize when the time comes. Therefore, no text needs to be written at this point.

The same is true for the order page, the order status page, the contents page, and the help page—all will be generated by the site-creation tool. If your ESP's software does not create them, don't panic—you can do without them initially, and possibly forever.

The thing you should consider adding at some point is a *site map*—a layout of the pages that your site contains, rather like the one we made in the previous section. But wait until you become familiar with how you add pages and links to your site.

Tomorrow, meanwhile, is the big day—we will pull everything together and actually build our example site.

EXPERTS SPEAK

A good Web page is largely in the eyes of the beholder. However, there is general agreement on what makes a bad Web page. As you set out, keep the following warnings in mind.

- People do not snuggle up to read a Web site. Instead, they scan the screen. If there is material below the bottom of the screen, there is no guarantee that they will scroll down to see it. They can be counted on to follow text below the bottom of the screen only if they have a serious interest in the subject matter. Catch them at the top of the page and don't assume they will stay caught.
- There is an HTML tag that will make the text blink. Don't use it. In fact, forget we told you about it.
- Continuously running animated graphics are fine in their place. We have yet to find that place.
- It is possible to change the color of links. Don't. The users have been trained to look for them in blue (unused) and red (used.) It's not nice to mess with their heads.
- Perhaps you have become fascinated with Web technology for its own sake and want to play with Java applets and running marquees, and the like. The users are not guinea pigs. Spare them.
- If a page takes more than 10 seconds to download, scrap it.

- Include some kind of common identifier on each page in the site so that the users can situate themselves if they happen to jump to it from the outside. (The site-creation tool we will be using pretty much takes care of that.)
- Likewise, use real words for page names, not code numbers. People do take note of the names.
- There are people who use yellow letters against a white background—or red against purple or silver against gray. Do we really have to explain why this is a bad idea? (Actually, this may be a promising new form of cryptography.)
- If you are in a position to use frames, do so sparingly.

Chapter
9

Thursday— Site Creation

Today we will create the basic site in the morning, uploading and configuring the material we created in the previous sections. In the afternoon we will finish the site and basically turn it on.

We will use Yahoo! Store for this example. This is not an endorsement of Yahoo! Store or an indication that the ESP you select will have a site-creation tool identical to that of Yahoo! Store. (Or even that, if you use Yahoo! Store, the process will end up going exactly as described—the system underwent changes while we were using it.) But to achieve the same ends, any system will end up having similar features. And the limitations of the environment mean that the interface will also involve form input through browser screens.

■ MORNING: BUILDING THE SITE

CHEAT SHEET

- Word processing file created in Chapter 8.
- Layout diagram created in Chapter 8.

- Artwork files created in Chapter 7.
- Access password for ESP site selected in Chapter 6.

For our example, we go to store.yahoo.com. Responding to the screen prompts, we get a password and then use it to log on. We are then given the Welcome page. Under the Getting Started section, we see the Create Store link. We click that and get the Create Your Own Yahoo! Store Account page, as shown in Figure 9.1.

The account ID will become part of the Web address. If you input (as we will) *widgetstore,* the address of the store will be store.yahoo.com/widgetstore. The second item is the name you give the site, to be used in the title bar of the browser screen and elsewhere where a name is needed (if you don't specify something else.) Predictably, we put down *Widget World* and click "Create."

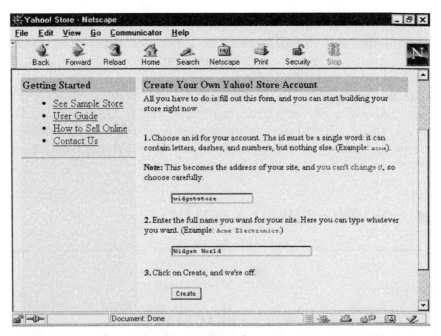

Figure 9.1 The Create Your Own Yahoo! Store Account page at store.yahoo.com, with the information filled in. You would have already registered for a user name and password. You can build a practice site free of cost, but you have to register to pay for it before you can start taking orders.

We then get an acceptance screen telling us how to log on in the future, and asking us to agree to their terms for the site. There's a link to read it (and the gist is, Don't be naughty). We click "I Accept" to go on.

There follows a guided tour concerning site creation. We will read along, but we won't bother to enter any text or upload any images so that we can start with a blank page. At the end, we can continue editing by scrolling down, where we will see the initial screen of our site, shown in Figure 9.2.

We have the main screen on the right and the navigation screen on the left. The main screen has the site name we gave earlier in large text, as a headline. Plus, the site name is in the title bar at the top of the browser screen. The site-creation tool has generated everything else that we see. So far, though, that consists mostly of the generic navigation buttons in the left column:

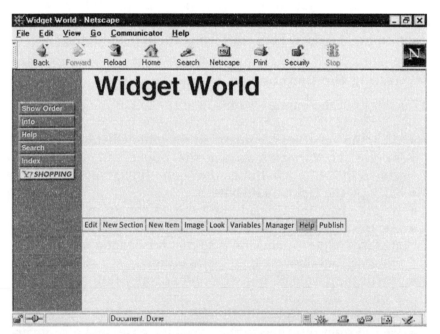

Figure 9.2 Initial screen of your new e-commerce Web site. So far there is only one page, which carries only the site name as a title. The horizontal (originally yellow) bar contains the site-creation tools. (You are assumed to have removed anything input during the initial tutorial session.)

- *Show Order.* This tells a user what has so far been added to his or her shopping cart.
- *Info.* This will link to the site information page, once we create it, using the text created in the previous section.
- *Help.* This links to a generic help screen.
- *Index.* This links to an index of the site's pages, listed alphabetically, generated by the site-creation tool (when we do have some pages.)
- *Y! Shopping.* Links to the Yahoo! Mall.

We are not stuck with these buttons—we can drop, add, and rename buttons, and we will go into that later. We can also put them at the top of the page, and we can upload artwork to go in them—but we won't go that far here either.

At the bottom is a yellow bar containing commands. These (as the guided tour demonstrated) are the tool buttons for the site-creation system. The first thing we do is click the Help command in the yellow bar. The screen will then refresh with a list of explanations below the command bar explaining what each command does. Let's start using them to build the site.

➤ **Adding the Banner**

First, let's put the banner we made at the top of the page.

- Click the Variables command in the yellow bar.
- We get the Variables screen, the upper half of which is shown in Figure 9.3. Notice the Name-Image section.
- Click on the Upload File button.
- We are given the Upload File page, as shown in Figure 9.4.
- Use the Browse button to select the banner graphics we created in Chapter 7, click on it so that it is loaded into the File window, and then click the Send button.
- It will then upload, but we don't see any fuel gauge–type progress indicator, just an hourglass cursor, which will go away when the upload is finished.
- We are then returned to the Variables page, and a tiny version of the banner now appears beside the Upload File button that we pressed a moment before.
- Press the Update button (at the top of the screen.)

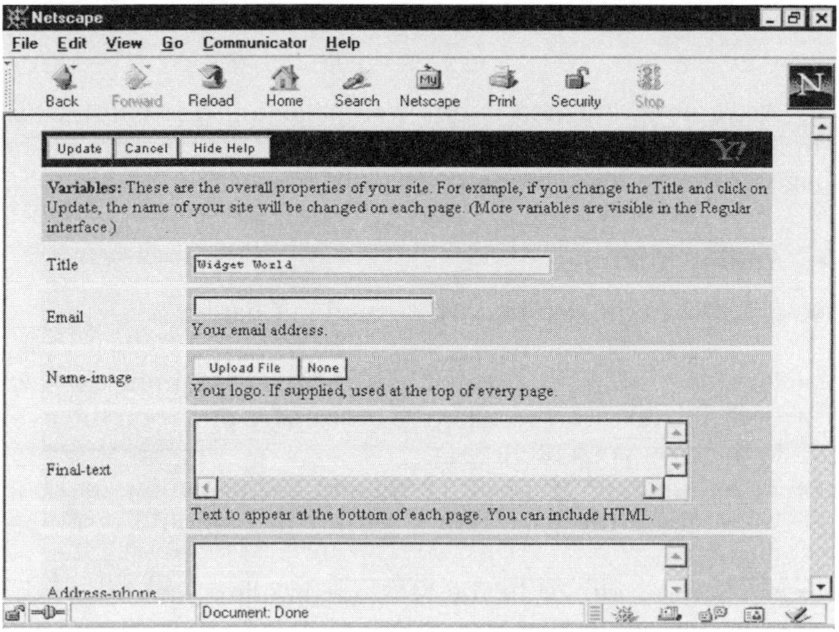

Figure 9.3   The top of the Variables page of the site-creation tool, where you can set various layout parameters used by your site.

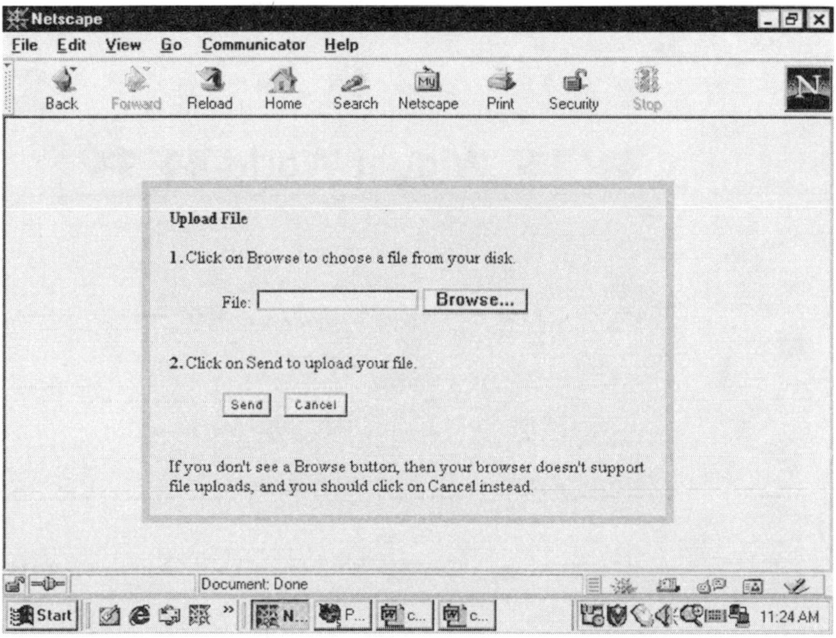

Figure 9.4   The Upload File page, which lets you upload pictures to be used as part of your e-commerce site. The Browse button calls up a file directory window that lets you look for a specific file on your computer.

We've now returned to our Web page, and the banner has replaced the name that had appeared as text at the top of the page, as shown in Figure 9.5.

➤ Adding Text

Now, we'll add the text that we created in Chapter 8.

- Run the word processor and load the file containing the text.
- Copy the text we wrote for the index page and then flip over to the browser screen.
- There, click on the Edit command in the yellow tool bar. We're given the Page Edit screen, which should resemble Figure 9.6.
- We put our cursor in the Message window and insert the word processor text (press SHIFT-INSERT.) It should appear inside the window.
- Then we press Update.

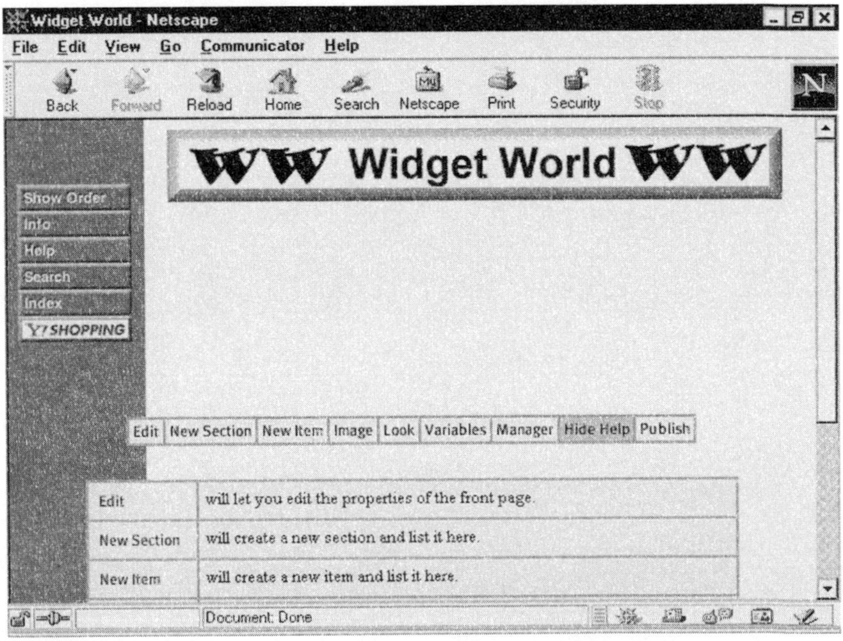

Figure 9.5 The e-commerce site with the banner file uploaded and added to the page. It automatically replaced the text title that had been displayed there previously.

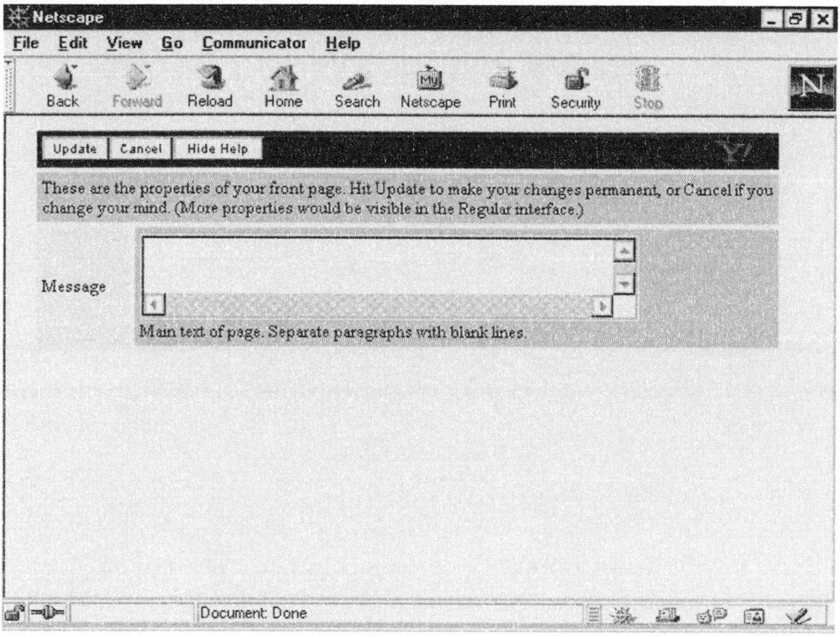

Figure 9.6 The Page Edit screen that lets you edit the properties of a specific page. Shown is the Edit screen of the Simple editor.

➤ Adjusting Text Size

Now we have a page that looks like Figure 9.7. And now that we see the text on the screen, it looks uncomfortably small. We can fix that.

- First, we click the Manager button in the yellow tool bar.
- We're then given the Store Management page, as shown in Figure 9.8. This contains a number of tools we will be using later, but right now the idea is to note the Edit column on the left and click the Regular option there.
- This returns us to the Web site using the Regular editor. (We had been using the Simple editor up to now—no offense.) Everything looks about the same, except the yellow tool bar has more options.
- Click on the Variables option again.
- This time we get a much longer list of options, scrolling far off the bottom of the screen.

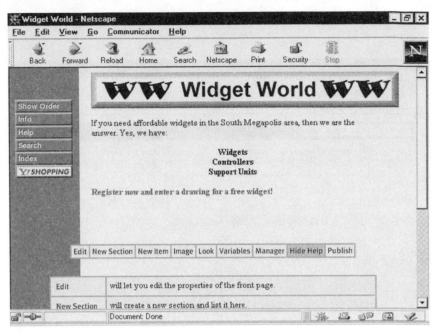

Figure 9.7 The opening page of the e-commerce site after adding the text. The text is shown using the default font size, which looks rather small on this page.

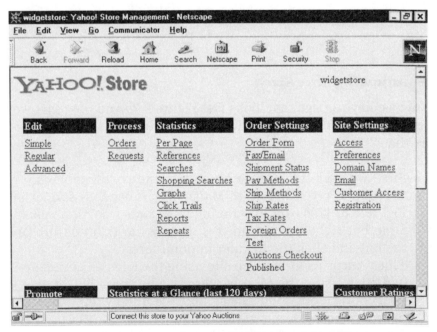

Figure 9.8 The Store Manager screen, reached through the site-creation tool bar, showing the editor options on the left and other site settings and control functions to the right.

- Scroll down until the Text Size option appears, and set it to 4 using the Options list.
- Click the Update button (at the top left of the screen.)

And the Web site returns—and the text looks much nicer, as shown in Figure 9.9. Why, the thing is beginning to look like an e-commerce site except that we have only the opening page. But that's a good start. For now, click thc Publish option in the yellow tool bar to save what you have done so far. Then log off and take a quick decompression nap. You've earned it.

➤ Adding a Section Page

We have the opening page, home page, index page, or whatever you want to call it. Now that we're rested, we'll go on and add a section page. Let's return to store.yahoo.com, register with our password, and go to the Welcome screen. On the bottom left of the page, there's a corner called Your Stores. (Yes, you can have more than one.)

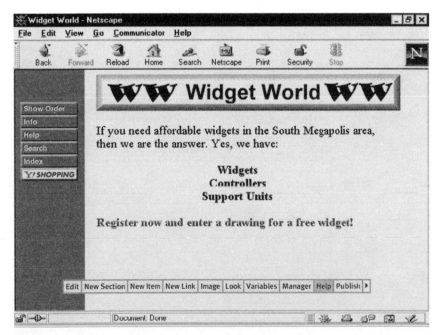

Figure 9.9 Our e-commerce site opening page, showing the text after the size was adjusted.

- Click on the one we're working on.
- We are placed in the Store Manager page, such as we saw in Figure 9.8. As we did last time, click on the Regular entry in the Edit column.
- Again, we end up back at our under-construction Web site, using the Regular editor.
- Again, call up the word processing file we created in the last chapter. Then flip back to the browser.
- There, back at our Web site, click on the New Section item in the yellow tool bar.
- We then see the New Section screen, as shown in Figure 9.10.
- In the Name entry window, we are asked for the name of the product family to whose items this page will branch. We put in *Widgets*.
- Flip over to the word processor and copy the text for the widgets product family page.
- Flip back to the browser screen and paste it into the Caption window. (For now, ignore the other text input windows on the form.)

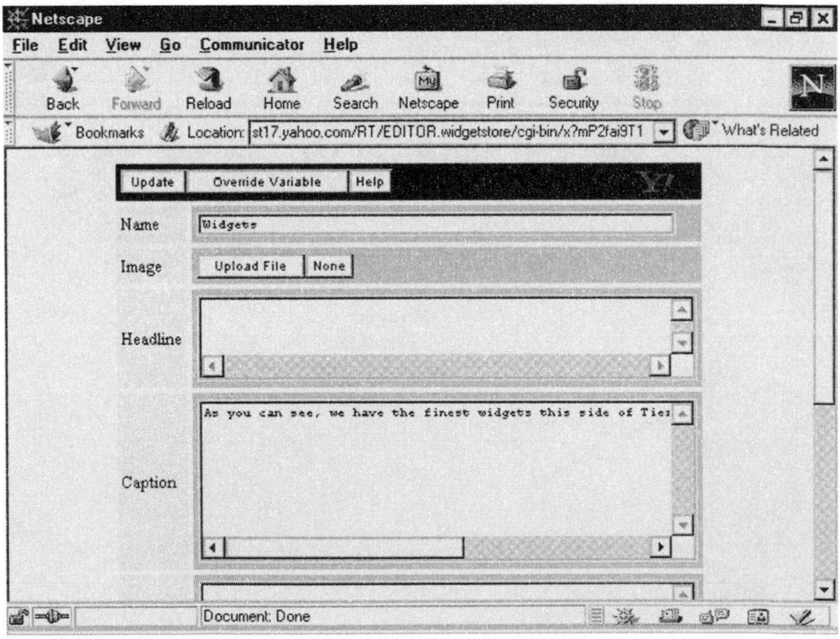

Figure 9.10 The New Section editing page of the site-creation tool, showing inputs. The text does not wrap by itself.

- As we have done before, we click the Update button in the top left corner of the page.

The results appear in Figure 9.11. The text-size variable we set earlier is still in effect. The product family name has been added as a subhead. And note the navigation buttons on the left—there is now one for Widgets. Clicking that will bring you to the screen we're at now. And there is a button for Home, which will take us back to the index page.

But the text refers to items that can be bought "below," and there is nothing there. To fix that, we must go on and add an item page, which will contain an actually inventory item, its price tag, and the Order button, which will trigger the purchase process.

➤ Adding an Item Page

To add an item page, we begin at the Section page that we just created. (This will make our embryonic site consistent with the

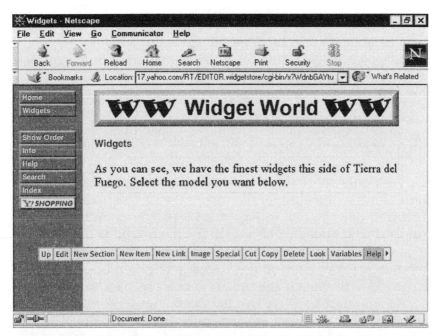

Figure 9.11 The Widgets section page created by the previous steps, before any items have been added.

layout we created in Chapter 8, but in theory we could add an Item page anywhere.)

- Click the New Item command in the yellow tool bar.
- We then get the New Item screen, and there are a number of things we need to do before we press Update. (Although after the page is added, you can always go back to it and use the Edit command.) We'll take them as they appear on the screen, skipping options that we will not use:

  Name. We'll put in the product name, which we'll call *Widget—Regular.*

  Image. As we did earlier, we will click the Upload Image button, browse for the file we want, and upload it. But this time we will be uploading the product photo of Widget—Regular that we created in Chapter 7.

  Code. Here we input the SKU number we use in our inventory system, or we invent something reasonable: *W-R1.*

  Price. Put in the price. We don't need the dollar sign.

  Orderable. If this is set to *yes,* the page will contain a shopping-cart order button.

  Caption. Flip over to the word processor and copy the text we created for this page. Flip back to the browser screen and insert it in the Caption text-input window.

  Shipping Weight. Input the number in pounds or kilograms—you can set the standard later.

- Skip the other fields. Figure 9.12 shows what the upper part of the page will now look like, with a tiny version of the product artwork displayed in the Image field.
- With everything done, click Update.

Suddenly we have a product page with a shopping-cart order button, a picture of the product, and other catalogue-like features, like the one in Figure 9.13. (Clicking on the product image, incidentally, will bring up the picture in its original size. The shopping-cart software scales it down to fit the page.)

But now let's click on the Widget navigation button that has been added to the left column. That takes us back to the Widget section (product family) page, and as you can see in Figure 9.14, a thumbnail of our widget product has been added to the page with a link to the item page. The other items that we add to the widget family will also be reflected here with a link and a thumbnail.

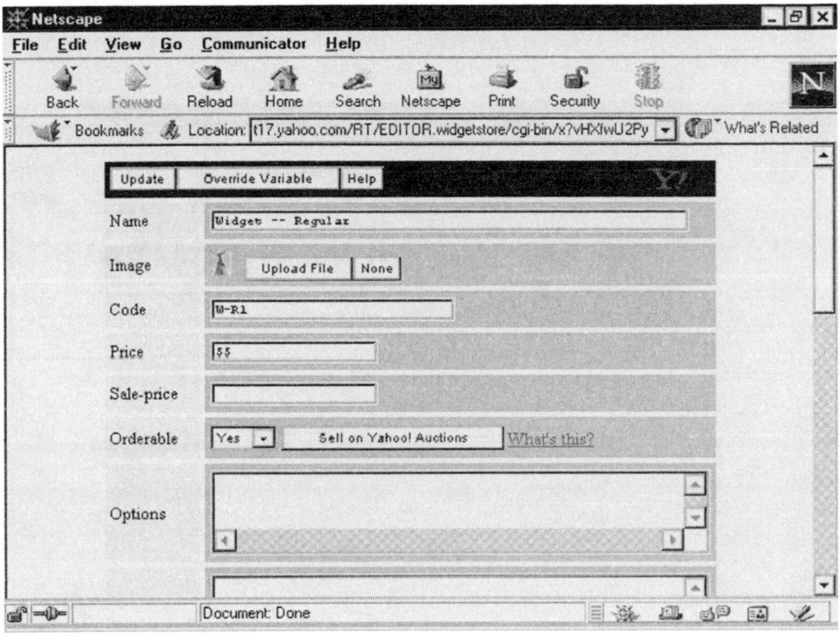

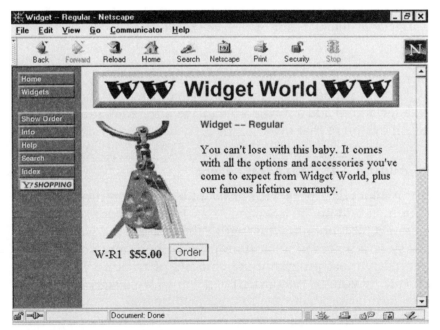

Figure 9.12 The initial items in the Item page-creation screen, with some items filled in. The product photo has already been uploaded, and its thumbnail version is shown on the Image line.

Figure 9.13 The Item page after creation, with the product photo, catalogue blurb, price and code, and the Order button inserted by the site-creation tool.

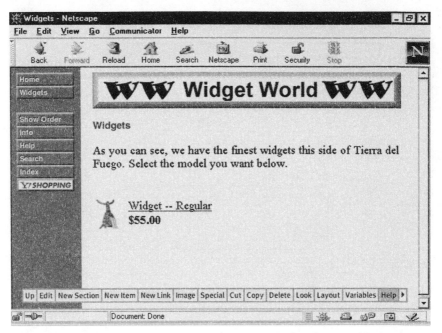

Figure 9.14 The Section page after an item has been added, with a thumbnail of the item's product photo and a link to the item's page, placed there automatically by the site-creation tool.

So far, so good. But in the layout we created in Chapter 8, we had decided to add a product data page after each item page. So let's move on to that task.

➤ Adding a Product Data Page

Our product data page will consist of text and a return (i.e., Up) button—it will not be a Section or an Item page per se. There is no direct tool for doing this (with Yahoo! Store) but we will trick the system by creating an Item page without an Order button. (Actually, most programming consists of tricking the system into giving you the results that you want.) We'll start at the Widget—Regular product page that we just created.

- On the yellow tool bar, press the red arrow at the right end.
- The screen will refresh, and we'll see that there are now two yellow tool bars—this is the Advanced editor.

- The new tool bar includes an Item function, which allows us to add an item to the page, just as the Regular editor could add items to a Section (product family) page.
- Click on the New Item entry.
- We get a creation screen, such as we saw when creating the page for the Widget—Regular item. (Because this is the Advanced editor, there will be more options.) We will make slightly different use of the options this time:
  Name. Remembering the product code we used, we'll put in *W-R1 Product Data.*
  Orderable. Set this to *no,* so there will be no shopping-cart order button.
  Caption. Flip over to the word processor and copy the text we created for this page. Then flip back to the browser screen and insert it in the Caption text-input window.
  Others. We'll skip Image, Code, Price, Shipping Weight, and the things we skipped last time.
- Click Update.

We end up with a nice product data page, as seen in Figure 9.15. Again, the text size we set earlier is still in effect. But something is lacking—there is no button to get out of here. Having reached this page, the buyer might want to go back to the Item page and its all-important Order button. So we add an Up navigation button to this page and to this page alone. Make sure you are using the Advanced editor and follow along with us:

- While on the product data page, click the Edit tool button.
- You will get the page editor screen, similar to the one we just used to create the page. The buttons on the top include one that says Override Variable. Click that.
- You will get a screen with a multiple-choice list of options.
- Scroll down and select the Nav-Buttons (short for *Navigation Buttons*) option.
- Click Update.
- You will be given the page editor screen again, but this time the bottom includes a new entry: Nav-Buttons.
- Click the Change button in that section.
- You will be given a list of possible navigation buttons that the site-creation tool can put in the left column. The ones in

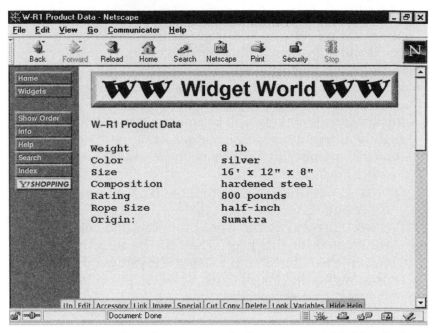

Figure 9.15 Product data page, with the contents added, but before the addition of the Up button.

use are listed in the order form at the top of the column, as you can see in Figure 9.16.

- Glancing over the list, you see that the highest number in use is 9, so you assign 10 to the Up button box, putting it at the bottom of the column. (You could, of course, take the opportunity to reorder the entire set of navigation buttons.)
- Click Update.
- You're now back at the page editor screen.
- Click Update.

We are now back to the product data page, and we see that an Up entry has been added to the navigation buttons on the left, as shown in Figure 9.17. Clicking it will bring you back to the Widget—Regular product item page.

(Of course, we could also just add a line to the button saying, "Click your browser's Back button to return to the item page." Alternately, you could go on and add Up and/or Down

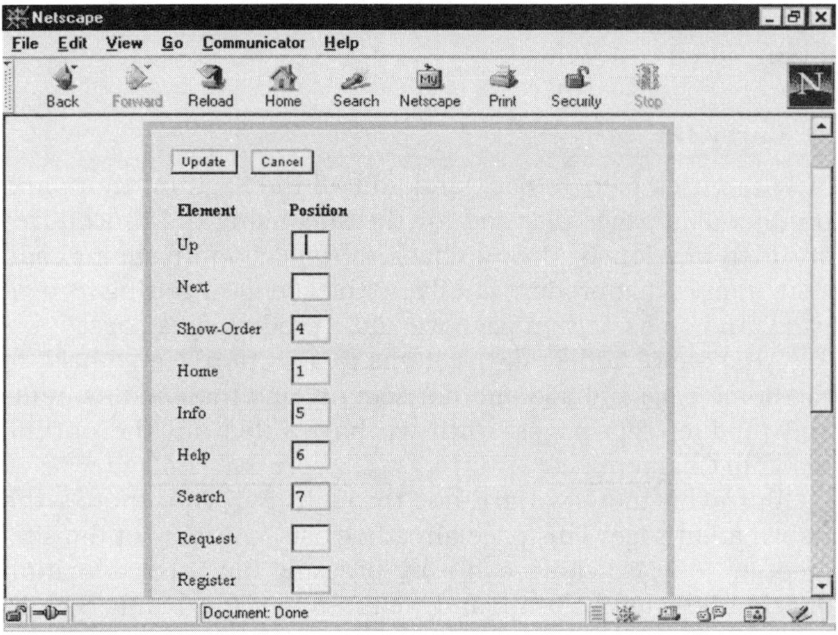

Figure 9.16 Top of the site-creation page listing possible navigation buttons that can be placed on a page.

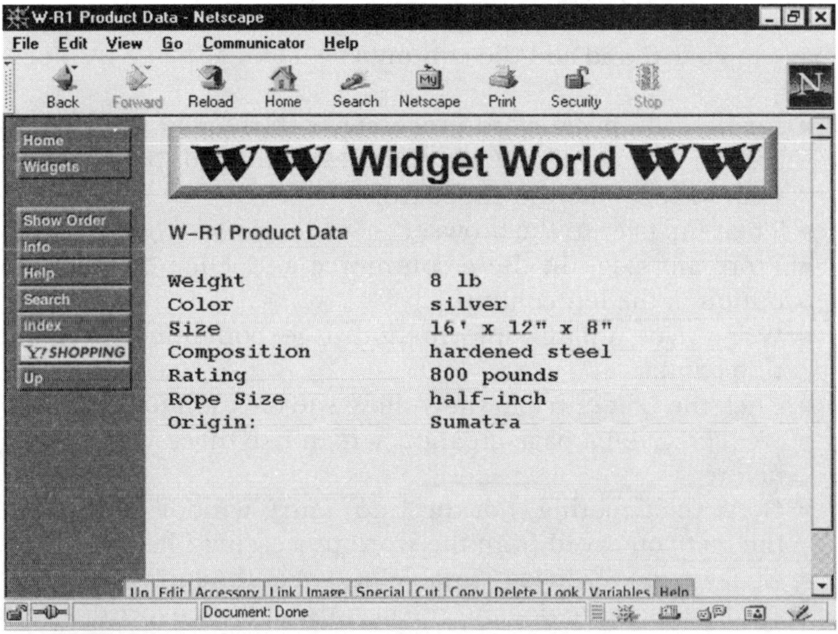

Figure 9.17 Product data page after the Up button has been added.

buttons to every page. There's always something you can do on a rainy day.)

➤ Carry On

Now the trick is to go back and add all the Section, Item, and product data pages planned for the site, using the procedures outlined previously. Just go back to the section page and add each item in that product family, with each item getting its own page. And on each item page we add a product data page.

After we've added all the items to a section, we go back to the home page and add another section, and then add its items and product data pages, until we have filled out the outline made in Chapter 8.

But even then, we are not through. For one, there's the information page. This page already exists, courtesy of the site-creation tool. We can reach it by pressing the Info navigation button in the left column, and we'll see that it is blank. So let's fill it in, using the text we prepared for it back in Chapter 8.

➤ Adding an Information Page

In the Yahoo! Store system, this page already exists. We just have to go to it and add the contents.

- Again, call up the word processor with the text file we created in Chapter 8 and copy the text intended for the information page into the clipboard.
- Then flip over to the browser.
- From any page in the e-commerce site, click on the Info button in the left column.
- We're given a blank information page, containing only the title banner.
- Click the Edit entry in the yellow site-creation tool bar.
- We'll be given a page-creation screen like those you've seen before.
- Go to the Greeting (not the Info) entry window and insert the text you saved from the word processing file.
- Click on the Override Variable button at the top of the page.
- As described previously, select a variable to override—this time, select the Name-Image variable.

- Again click on the Override Variable button and select the Title variable.
- At the bottom of the Edit page, we see two new sections, for Name-Image and Title.
- Set the Name-Image to *none*, meaning that the banner will not appear on this page.
- Erase the entry in the Title line, meaning that the site name will not be inserted as text where the banner used to be.
- Click the Update button in the top left corner of the page.
- You now see the information page as you wrote it, as shown in Figure 9.18, with no additional elements put there by the site-creation tool (except for some blank space at the top.)
- Now click the Home entry in the site-creation tool bar. There, the toolbar includes the Publish entry.
- Click it.

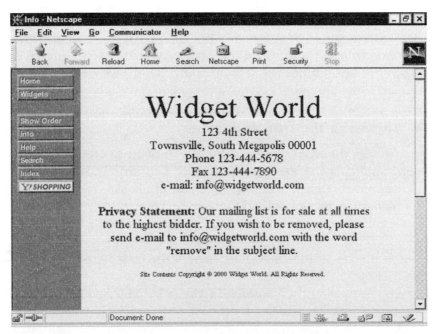

Figure 9.18 The information page after creation, using the Edit facility to remove the banner and title that would otherwise be placed there automatically.

Congratulations—you have created an e-commerce site. You can show it to your admiring friends, but it is not quite ready for prime time yet—we still have to do the opt-in page and set some parameters for the shopping cart. That's what the afternoon is for.

■ AFTERNOON: FINISHING THE SITE

CHEAT SHEET

- Descriptor text created in Chapter 8.
- Table of shipping charges.
- Merchant account ID, as applied for in chapter 6 (if granted).

Okay, we created the pages—but not the opt-in page. Meanwhile, we need to add the title and descriptor words that we wrote in Chapter 8 but did not use this morning. Then, we need to go on and set some shopping-cart parameters, and we'll be in business.

➤ Adjusting the Opt-In Page

As explained earlier, we need an opt-in page to create an electronic mailing list and realize one of the chief advantages of e-commerce: direct marketing by e-mail. As it turns out, the site-creation tool will add an opt-in page automatically, tied to a database system, if we just add one button to the home page.

- From the home page, click the Edit entry in the yellow tool bar.
- On the list of menu items in the Edit page, you'll see buttons. Click the Change button.
- You'll see a list of possible buttons, with an order-ranking window, as we saw in Figure 9.16.
- Find the one that says Request and put an order number in the box for it. In this case, we'll put it at the bottom of the

column, making it number 10. (Do not use the Register button, as it involves adding password registration to the site—unless that's what you want to do, of course.)

- Click the Update button.

We are now back at the home page, and there is a new button in the left column bearing the words *Request Catalog.* But this is not what we want it to say. So:

- Click the Variables entry in the yellow tool bar.
- We get the Variables page, with a list of options.
- Find the request-text line, which controls the caption in the Request button, and change it to *Enter Drawing* or whatever, as you wish.
- Scroll farther down until you see the request-options line.
- In the text-entry window, type *Enter contest and mailing list.*
- Go down a line and then type *Take me off the mailing list.*
- Click the Update button.

The home page will now have the Enter Drawing button on it, as shown in Figure 9.19. Click the Publish entry in the yellow tool bar to save what you have done.

Anyone visiting the store site and clicking on the Enter Drawing button will see the Request screen generated by the store system. As you can see in Figure 9.20, it has data-input fields and the two choices we typed in, to opt in and opt out. Tomorrow we'll cover how to handle the data.

➤ Adding Descriptors

As explained earlier, adding descriptor words is important to ensure that the site is adequately covered by search engines. We have already used some of the words we chose in Chapter 8, incorporating them into the leading text on the home page. That leaves the title and the meta tags. Both can be added using the Variable function of the site-creation tool bar—but make sure you are using the Regular or Advanced editor.

- Load the word processing file we created in Chapter 8, containing (among other things) the descriptor words we saved.
- Flip over to the browser screen.

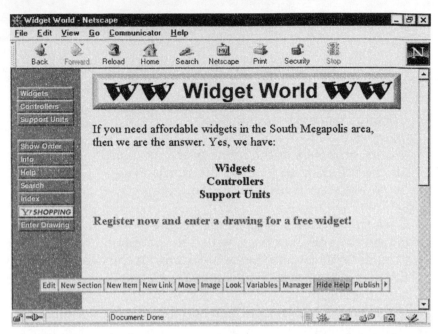

Figure 9.19 The home page with the Enter Drawing (opt-in) button added.

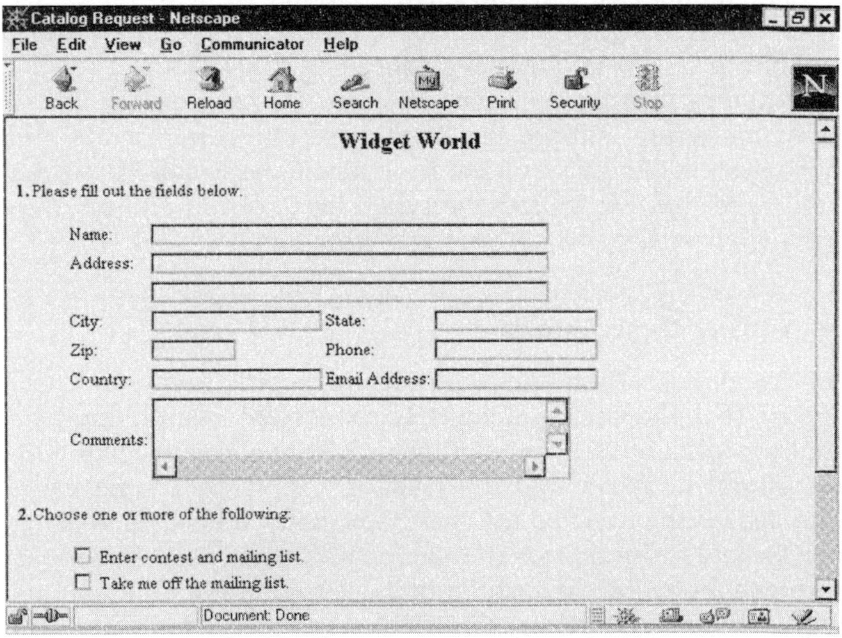

Figure 9.20 The page that comes up when a user presses the Enter Drawing button. It has fields for data input, as well as the opt-in and out-out settings.

- When at the home page, click on the Variables entry in the yellow tool bar.
- When the Variables screen comes up, we'll see that the first line is the Title field. Flip over to the word processor, copy the title *(Widget World, Retail Source of Mail-Order Widgets)* that was composed earlier, flip back to the browser screen, and insert the text into the field.
- Farther down the page, we'll see a field called Keywords (in the Page Properties section.) Flip over to the word processor and copy the leftover keywords: *gadget, gizmo, wangdoodle, thingamajig, gimcrack.*
- Flip back to the browser screen and insert them into the Keywords data-entry field. (The words entered here are used to generate the page's meta tag.)
- Click the Update button.
- We'll get the home page of the e-commerce site with the site-creation tool bar.
- Click its Publish entry.

We've done it—except there is no visible evidence that we've done it. To find some, we can visit the published site by clicking Manager and then, at the bottom of the Manager page, Published Site.

When we get there, the new title should appear in the title bar at the very top of the browser screen. Meanwhile, we can view the meta tag by invoking your browser's View Page Source command. When it comes up, the tag will be at the very top of the screen, as shown in Figure 9.21.

However, we are not quite through. We still need to set some operational variables and consider some other topics.

➤ Setting Operational Factors

The operation of your shopping cart—in fact, the whole site— involves a number of options, settable by you. In our case, the main ones can be set from the Manager page. Topics include:

- *Order page.* You can customize it using the Order Form entry under the Order Settings column of the Manager page. You can add the options of gift-wrapping and gift messages, customer comments and rankings, order and shipping information blurbs, a message from you on how to check order

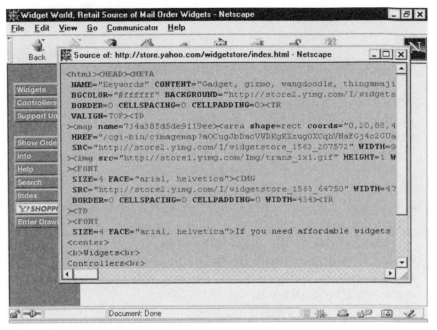

Figure 9.21 The Page Source window on top of the page it generates. In the source screen you can see the meta tag, with the descriptor words appearing in the second line. Users do not see this text, but search engines do. Note that the underlying page now carries the full title, selected earlier, in the title bar at the top of the screen.

status, and the all-important thank-you message. You can also tell it whether to add tax and shipping charges.

- *Opt-in page customization.* You can make some changes to that page using the previous facility so that it won't say *Request Catalog* when we want it to say *Enter the Drawing.*

- *Order processing options.* New orders can be sent to you by e-mail or fax, or you can check them online. The same is true for requests to the opt-in page. (Fax notification is not encouraged—those things run out of paper.)

- *Shipping status.* The system can automatically send e-mail to the customer when the status of his or her order is updated using the Shipping Status entry under the Order Settings column on the Manager page.

- *Payment processing.* If you are getting a merchant account, you can set up online order processing and select which credit cards you will accept using the Pay Methods entry in the Order Settings column of the Manager page.

- *Shipping.* You can select the shipping charges that the shopping cart will add to each order, using the Ship Rates entry under the Order Settings column on the Manager page. The charges can be calculated on the basis of the weight of the item(s) ordered, using the weight value that you entered during item page creation. You will need your table of shipping charges, as mentioned in the Cheat Sheet. (Or you can elect to not charge for shipping—but be sure to publicize this fact to the lucky customers.) Meanwhile, you can select shipping methods using the Shipping Methods entry under the Order Settings column on the Manager page. (You arrange shipping yourself—this entry lets the customer select the method that he or she wants used.) You can also list what countries you will ship to or state that you ship domestically only.
- *Taxes.* You can add them to the shopping-cart total or not collect any or tell the buyer that they may be added later. (Yahoo! Store can selectively add a state sales tax.)

➤ The Links Page

One way to promote your store, as explained in Chapter 11, is to trade links. That means that some other site has a page of links, which includes a link to your site; meanwhile, your site includes a page of links, including a link back to the other site. You then track how many customers come from the outside links and how much they sell, and possibly you give the other site a royalty on the revenue it generates.

With our site, you could set up a links page by going to the index page (while in the Regular or Advanced editor) and clicking the New Section entry from the yellow tool bar. Then:

- In the New Section window, type *Links* for the Title entry.
- In the Headline entry, type something like *You May Like These Sites as Well.*
- Click Update.
- You'll be given the new Links page, with only the headline on the page. The navigation bars in the left column will now include a new Links button.

- From the yellow tool bar of the site-creation system, click the New Link entry.
- You'll be given the New Link page. Enter its name and its full URL (including the http:// prefix). The other items on the page are not needed.
- Click Update.
- The Section page returns with the name of the link, highlighted so that the user knows it is a link to another Web site. Clicking it will call up the site you gave for its URL.

(If your site-creation tool does not have a facility for setting up external links, Appendix C shows how to do it manually.)

To track the volume of traffic from a partnering site, most ESPs will at least have a tool that lets you see what sites your visitors came from. Yahoo! Store has a special link-exchange facility that lets you register a linked site, and the system will track the number of visitors from it and how much they buy. On the Manager page, see the Create Links entry under the Promote column.

➤ Other Details

No, we are not through. There are still further details you might want to consider—although, having considered them, you may see no reason to act on them, especially during your start-up phase. These include:

- *Cross selling.* Someone interested in paint might be interested in paint brushes, so why not have links to them from the paint page? (Click the Variables entry in the yellow tool bar, and you will see a space for entering Cross-Sell Text.)
- *Specials.* Items being promoted on a given day can appear on the home page with thumbnail artwork. (*Special* is an item in the yellow tool bar that can be used to accomplish this automatically.)
- *Site map.* This involves a diagram, letting the user see at a glance whether the thing he is interested in is even there, and if it is, he can go there with one click. (You would have to make your own by putting text on a new Section page.)
- *Table of contents.* The Yahoo! Store system automatically creates one, called the Index in our example, with the pages listed alphabetically according to the title given to each. You

may think it is fine, or you may think it is useless. You can get rid of it by dropping its navigation button.

- *Registration.* Especially in cases of business-to-business e-commerce, (where you want only your customers to see the prices you are offering), you may want to give the site password protection. (In our case, the tools are in the Site Settings column of the Manager page.)
- *Help screen* The system provides a generic one, but there is no reason you can't drop it and then create your own with material specific to your site. In our case, you could drop the Help button with the Variables page and then create a new one as a Section page, with *Help* as the title.
- *Artwork.* You can add artwork to every screen button—in fact, you can have separate banners on every page. If a family member insists on contributing the work, go with it.

➤ Advanced Topics

It's now time to come clean: With Yahoo! Store and many other systems, you don't have to do most of the things that we have talked about in this chapter. You could compose all the material as one file and upload it, and the site-creation system would flip through it and create all the pages for you in one fell swoop. All you have to do is play with the appearance variables.

But you might want to forget using the bulk-load method because it has been likened to building a site with a chain saw. With the manual method, at least you can't wreck everything with one keystroke. But on the other hand, if you have 500 inventory items, using the manual method is not inviting. And with the upload method, sweeping inventory or price changes can be made at one sitting.

As for the dangers involved, there is typically some facility to check the contents of an uploaded file to make sure it will work before adding it to the site and a way to revert to the old site if you see something wrong.

Basically, you create a data file in the CSV format (explained in the Glossary) and then upload it as we did with the image files. (With Yahoo! Store, you use the Advanced editor to perform the upload.)

The CSV data file can be can be composed with just about any spreadsheet program. The trick is to study the documentation carefully, noting what field names to use, and to start with small practice files. The first line of the spreadsheet should contain the names of the fields being used. Subsequent lines contain the contents of those fields for individual pages.

With Yahoo! Store you can also upload the image files in one session, if you zip them together (compressed in the zip format) and name them in such a way that the system can match their names to the page names.

Truly large sites will run into the fact that browsers have a limit to the size of the files they will upload. But typically you can use the CSV method to add material to a site as well as to create a whole one so that you can break the creation task down into multiple smaller uploads.

➤ **Etc.**

The problem with Web publishing (and desktop publishing as well) is that you no longer face the constraints that existed in the good of days of publishing, when your whims had to be wrestled into reality by a staff of technicians in a small industrial facility. Today, thanks to an astonishingly powerful computer that probably costs less than the desk it sits on, your whims are a mere keystroke from realization. Want to see what your resume would look like in medieval lettering? You no longer have to face down a resentful typesetter to experience this mild thrill; you just pick the right font from the hundreds you have doubtlessly accumulated. Want to try a three-column layout? Two-color headlines? A page border with cherubic devices? A background with your face as a faux watermark? Etc., etc., etc.

This unrestrained process is called *futzing*, and there are those who wonder if it doesn't impact industrial productivity at the national level. At our level, the Yahoo! Store site-creation tool has Layout and Look entries in the tool bar that let you change the layout and color scheme of the site. Do try them— and then stop at some point.

Something attractive and distinctive that does not attract undue attention to itself is usually best. And a plain-vanilla, generic appearance at least won't repel anyone.

Chapter 10

Friday—Test Drive

Yesterday, you did it—you set up an e-commerce site. At least, we think it was an e-commerce site. Today, we'll reassure ourselves of that by walking through the site, testing it, and thinking about what to do next.

■ MORNING: TESTING THE SITE

CHEAT SHEET

- Password for your e-commerce site.
- Web address of your e-commerce site.

There are three things you want to do, now that it's time to take your site for a test spin:

1. Check the pages and links.
2. Try out the shopping cart and the opt-in page.
3. Try out the order and database retrieval facility.

We'll take it in that order. On your own site, when you get to this point, don't drop everything if you see something you want to change. Make note of it (and the next thing and the thing after that), until you have a list. Then plan your changes, make them at one sitting, and start drawing up a new list. As we'll explain in the afternoon section, the process never ends.

► Checking the Pages and Links

The trick is to make sure that a user can get to all the pages and that navigation is obvious. Simply go to the Web address—the URL—of the site. There, at the home or index page, just browse through the site as if you were looking at it for the first time. If possible, have someone with you who is indeed seeing it for the first time. Make sure all the pages are there as planned, that they are linked as planned, and that their contents are as you intended.

You'd be surprised what mistakes can happen.

Those noted, let's press on and explore the operation of the shopping cart and opt-in pages.

► Shopping Cart and Opt-In Pages

To see how the shopping cart works, go to an item page and press the Order button. You can see the button in Figure 10.1, placed there, as we explained yesterday, by the shopping-cart software. (It does not have to say *Order,* it can say *Buy Me* or *I'll Take It* or whatever—the setting is on the Variables page.)

Clicking it brings up the order-entry screen, shown in Figure 10.2. Here the buyer can change the number of items being purchased (the sum should be figured automatically), go back to shopping with the items on the screen remaining in the shopping cart, or proceed to checkout.

If the buyer opts to click the Keep Shopping button, she will be returned to the item page where she clicked the Order button and can go on shopping through the rest of the site. If at this point the buyer clicks the Show Order navigation button, the system will again generate the order-entry screen, as seen in Figure 10.2. Again, the buyer can change quantities, keep shopping, or proceed to checkout.

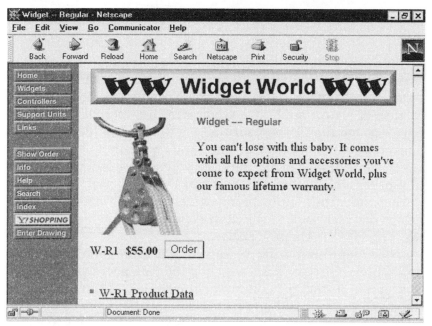

Figure 10.1   Completed item page with shopping-cart Order button.

Figure 10.2   Shopping-cart order-entry screen, which appears after clicking the Order button on the item page. Notice that the site's banner is carried over to this page. If you press the Keep Shopping button, you will be returned to the item page where you pressed the Order button. If you then click the Show Order navigation button, you will be presented with this same screen again.

At the checkout screen, shown in Figure 10.3, the system gets on with the serious work of taking the buyer's billing, shipping, and (if you are using that option) credit card information. In case of errors, such as a credit card number that does not have enough digits, the user will get an error screen that lets her return to the order-entry page and try again.

If everything is okay, the user will see an order confirmation page, such as the one shown in Figure 10.4, which can be printed out from the screen. Clicking the Continue button brings the user back to the item page where the last selection was added to the shopping cart.

Now that we are back at the site, it is time to check out the opt-in button. In our case, we click the Enter Drawing navigation button in the left column of the screen, which generates the screen shown in Figure 10.5. In our case it has the same address fields used by the shopping cart's order-entry system, and if an order screen has already been filled in, the opt-in

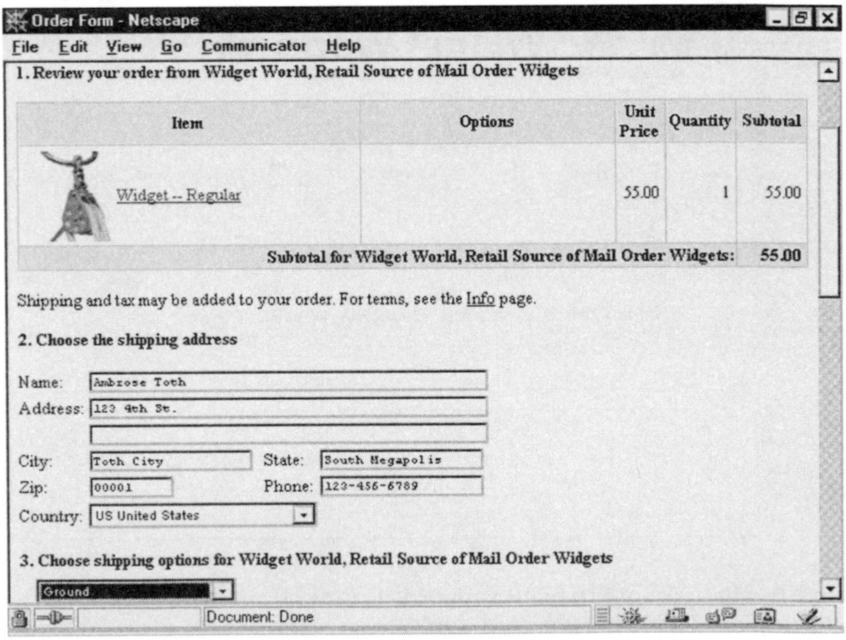

Figure 10.3 The checkout page, which appears after clicking the Check Out button on the previous shopping-cart order-entry screen. The page continues off-screen, with fields for the billing address, order information, and the credit card number.

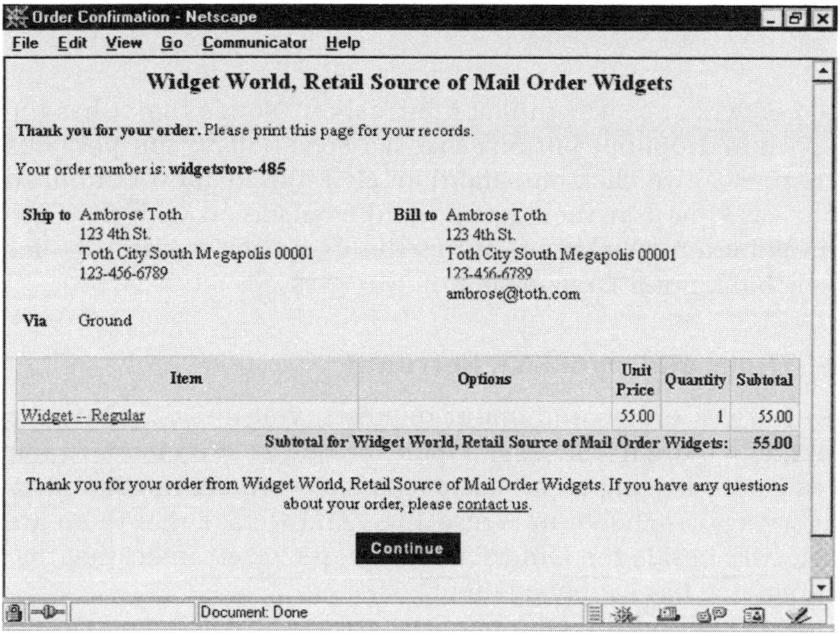

Figure 10.4 The order confirmation page, generated after filling out the order checkout page. Pressing the Continue button puts you back at the item page where you made the last order.

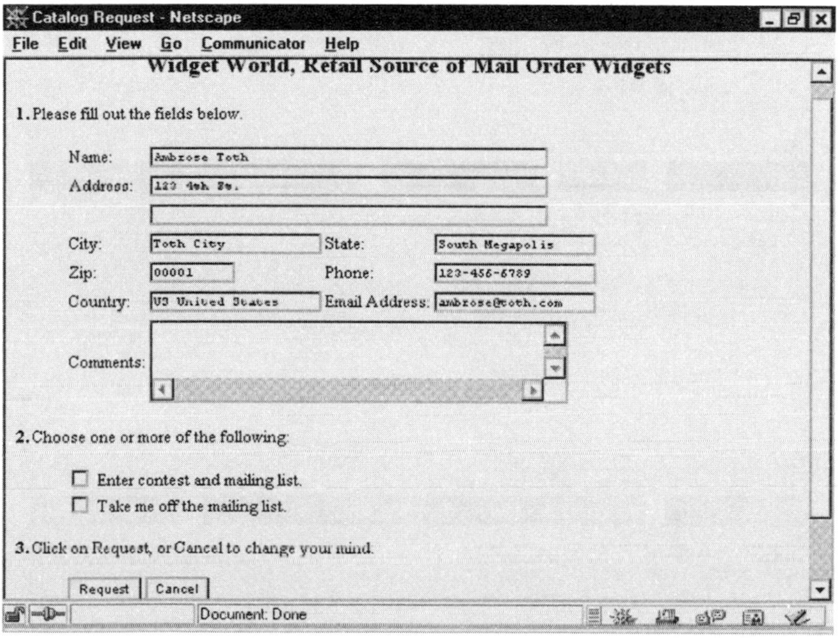

Figure 10.5 The opt-in page generated by the shopping-cart software. If an order has already been filled in, the data will be carried over to the same fields on this screen.

screen will appear with that information. Notice that it has the opt-in and opt-out buttons that we specified in the previous chapter. So we click one and then click the Request button. In our case the user then gets a thank-you screen with the Continue button. Clicking it brings the user back to the page for which the Enter Drawing button was pressed.

► Order and Database Retrieval

To retrieve orders and opt-in requests, you must log into the site, as we did in the last chapter to use the site editor. In our case, after logging on at yahoo.store.com, we get the Site Manager page, as shown in Figure 10.6. And we see that there are asterisks beside the Orders and Requests items, indicating that something has happened there.

Clicking on the Orders entry, we get the Retrieve Orders page, shown in Figure 10.7. Here we see that there is one new order and one order total, number 485. We can call it up and

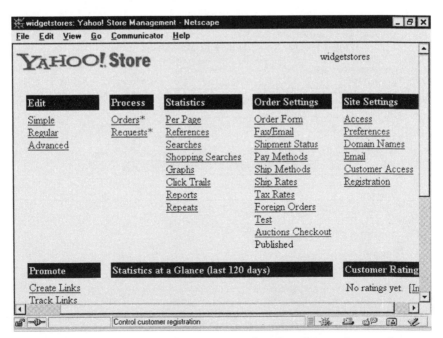

Figure 10.6 The Site Manager page, showing that orders and opt-in entry forms are available for downloading (indicated by the asterisk beside the Orders and Requests items in the Process column).

```
┌─────────────────────────────────────────────────────────────────────┐
│ ☼ widgetstores: Retrieve Orders - Netscape              _ ⊟ ☒        │
│ File  Edit  View  Go  Communicator  Help                              │
├─────────────────────────────────────────────────────────────────────┤
│  Y!    Retrieve Orders                              [widgetstores]    │
│                                                                       │
│  1 Total orders:              485-485                                 │
│  1 New orders:                485                                     │
│  [ View ]         a specific order:   [485     ]                      │
│  [ View ]         a range of orders:  [485 ]  through [485 ]          │
│  [ Summarize ]  a range of orders:  [485 ]  through [485 ]            │
│  [ Print ]        a range of orders:  [485 ]  through [485 ]  Format: [PDF      ▼] │
│  [ Export ]       a range of orders:  [485 ]  through [485 ]  Format: [MS Excel ▼] │
│                                                                       │
│  Note: for security reasons, credit card numbers are erased from orders more than 30 days old. │
│                                                                       │
│  Help   User Guide  |  Orders  |  Printing Orders  |  Exporting Orders │
│  Go     Feedback                                                      │
│                                                                       │
├─────────────────────────────────────────────────────────────────────┤
│  ⌑ ⊸         ‖Document: Done                     ≣ ⁂ 📇 🔒 🗐 ✎      │
└─────────────────────────────────────────────────────────────────────┘
```

Figure 10.7   The example site's Retrieve Orders page, with entries showing that one new order, number 485, is available.

look at it and perhaps set the shipping status. (When we change the status, it becomes one of the total orders and is no longer a new order.) Or we can download the information in a spreadsheet or database format and import it into whatever desktop accounting system that is in use.

You might want to do that now and establish the procedures you are going to use with your orders. It can be a $10,000 accounting system or it can be a box of file cards, but you need to have a system that you are comfortable with. So take time to:

- Download the various file formats offered by the system.
- Try importing them into whatever desktop software you are using. (If there is no format that your software uses directly, it may be able to use the CSV format.)
- Explore the data items they make available.

Clicking on the Requests item will bring up a screen similar to the Retrieve Orders page but with the information filled out by the users on the opt-in page. Likewise, you can download that in various formats, and you should explore what can be done with this data and how. The importance of gathering opted-in e-mail addresses and their appropriate use, is covered in Chapter 11.

■ AFTERNOON AND THEREAFTER: THE NEVER-ENDING QUEST

By now you've realized that the task never ends. You may have an operational e-commerce site on the Web, putting you on an equal footing (in some sense) with members of the Fortune 500. But having done it all in one day, you could change it all tomorrow and then again the day after that. Not that you should do it—but in the back of your mind, you might want to keep it as an option.

Remember: All worthwhile Web sites are perpetually under construction, and yours should be no different.

If you shop at a store for Christmas and come back at Easter and nothing has changed, what would you think? Over and above fiddling with aspects of the site that grate on you for whatever reason, periodically refreshing the site is a good idea for its own sake.

Other considerations:

- Determine what the signature elements of your site are (color scheme, logo, layout, etc.) and maintain them throughout future iterations of the site.
- Watch how the search engines list your site and adjust your descriptor text accordingly. But move slowly—it can take a month for all of them to react to a change.
- The currency of the Web is raw information. Product schematics, industrial data, historical trends, maps, formulas, free analytical software (usually in the format of spreadsheet templates), vendor directories—anything that might be of genuine value—will be appreciated by the users and thus likely to generate return visits to your site. While there, they may buy something. But if the material is posted for overt propaganda value, the users will perceive that you are

trying to influence them rather than help them, and the effort could backfire.

■ List pages, site maps, privacy seals, even chat forums are all nice ideas but will consume further time and effort. Make sure you can manage what you have before adding more.

In the meantime, remember two more things:

1. Have patience. If business is slow at first, that is no indication that it will remain slow.

2. Go celebrate. You built an e-commerce site—that's something. And remember, the thing can run itself. So let it for a while. Meanwhile, read the rest of the book.

Section Three

Open for E-business: How to Prosper as an Online Store Owner

Chapter

11

Finished.com—Now Comes the Marketing

Build it, and they will come. . . .

No way. Forget it. Put the whole idea out of your mind. That rubbish only holds true if you are building a cemetery, and not always then.

The truth is that marketing is always hard, and hoopla does not always equate to sales. (Consider one word: *Edsel.*) Certain things may be different on the Web, but that does not mean that they are easier.

Remember, there were (last time we checked) about sixty million Web sites out there. The Web is growing faster than any person could explore it, making its size, in practice, infinite. With all that cyberspace to go surfing in, why should anyone come to your site? If your store was on Main Street, any bypasser would see it, but there are no bypassers on the Web, only links that pass through no intervening space—that is, nothing. That being the case, how does anyone even come to know about your site?

The answer, of course, is marketing. In this chapter we will go over the various kinds of marketing and their applicability to e-commerce, plus several varieties specific to e-commerce.

But that's not the first step in the marketing process. The first step involves you internally processing the fact that you are now an e-commerce merchant, that e-commerce is a vital part of your operation, and that e-commerce is the key to carrying out your intention to stay in business for years to come. To remind the world and yourself of that fact, you need to start including your Web address in everything. Yes, that means:

- Your business cards.
- Your display window (right above the "Established in 1893" line).
- Your billboards.
- Your media advertising.
- Your vans and trucks.
- Your radio spots, with the announcer leaving out the http:// prefix. (Please!)
- Your Rotary Club speeches.
- Your license plate. (It's worth a try.)

E-commerce is now a vital part of your business. Make sure everyone knows it. (But do leave your URL off the uniforms of the Little League teams you sponsor. Enough is enough.) Make sure that your online and offline materials both share whatever visual elements, color schemes, catch phrases, swoosh-like logos or (shudder) mug shots that you decided, somewhere along the line, are going to constitute the visual signature of your business.

But, at the same time, if you have come to think of marketing as a weekly or monthly cycle of newspaper inserts combined with the merchandising of seasonal specials, then you will have to learn new patterns. With those old patterns, you knew what sold and when and you could form some suppositions as to why that was happening—but you ultimately did know not who your customers were or why they behaved as they did. With e-commerce, it is possible to identify each of them individually and even learn something about them.

How far that angle can and should be pursued is up to you; what's good for your business is what's good for your business. We cannot presume to tell you hard answers based on some overarching theory carefully formulated in some ivory tower (especially as none have been formulated because the field is so new). We can lay out some common approaches from which you might want to take cues. And we remind you of that old Texas saying: "A farm's best fertilizer is the footprints of the owner."

The common approaches include:

- Offline advertising.
- Online advertising.
- Getting posted in search engines.
- E-mail promotions.

- Newsletters.
- Online communities.
- Link exchanges.
- Customer reassurance.
- The final trick.

■ OFFLINE ADVERTISING

Yes, online entities advertise in the offline world—and the opposite is also true. Some general observations about traditional offline media:

- *Newspapers.* These are good for targeting a specific geographic region, and they increasingly have online versions where your ad can be linked back to your site. Small, local weeklies can also deliver local coverage.
- *Magazines.* Forget the national magazines unless you have already spent about $20 million creating brand awareness. But there are scads of trade, professional, and special-interest magazines serving almost as many niches as Usenet. Find one that serves your topic—you probably already know what it is.
- *National TV.* The same advice given regarding magazines applies to national TV, except that there are no trade, professional, or special-interest TV stations. There was once a small company that every year spent its entire advertising budget for one spot on the Superbowl. The fact that we can't remember which it was should tell you all that you need to know.
- *Radio.* Local radio stations are a much better deal, because they have targeted audiences, and many of the audience members listen not only on their way to work but also at work. And these days office workers often have Internet access.
- *Cable TV.* This medium has many of the advantages of radio in terms of price and local coverage, but the spots will cost more to produce.
- *Direct mail.* Done well, this can be very effective. Done poorly, it is a waste of time and money. Remember, you have the dual chores of producing the mailing piece and getting together the mailing list.

As for going about advertising, the trick is not to advertise before the store is ready and before you can afford ads. The theme of the ads, of course, is determined by what business you are in, and traditional advertising is a huge subject best left to professionals (or at least specialized books.) But whatever your message is, with the addition of e-commerce there are two things to add to it:

- There are advantages to shopping online. A customer can order at any time, in total convenience, from home, without dealing with overbearing, glad-handing salespeople (you don't have to put it that way, of course.) They can search the site for exactly what they want. The site can send them e-mail notification of new stock. Et cetera.
- Your store is a better choice than the other stores online in your niche thanks to its pricing, selection, brands, shipping, stylishness, snappy server-response time, or whatever.

EXPERTS SPEAK

A cheap way to promote a business through traditional means is through-post cards sent as bulk mail, says John Schulte.

"But you don't do it just once—you should have a marketing plan in place just to keep your name in front of the buyers," he explains. "You can mail every month for a year at a cost of $3.50 per year. You can gang-print the cards to make them cheaper and bulk-mail them for a few cents."

■ ONLINE ADVERTISING

Online advertising typically boils down to *banner ads*—those rectangular little billboard-like ads you see at the top of a lot of advertising-supported Web pages. Most are 468 by 60 pixels, and increasingly they contain animations or Java applets. Clicking it causes the users to jump to your site. Obviously, the idea is to put your banner ads in sites frequented by the kind of people you want to attract to your site. But where? Remember, there are 60 million sites out there. Therefore, creating banner ads and deciding where to place them should probably be left (like offline advertising) to an advertising agency.

One wrinkle you'll want to know about, however, is the fact that you can (in a way) buy search words at some search engines. When a user searches for that word, your banner ad is placed at the top of the subsequent results page. (One of the authors once approached Yahoo! for a client and found that all the desired words had been taken by Microsoft.)

Putting ads on small, special-interest hobby sites that cover the field you are in can be a cheap form of online advertising and will make the Webmaster of the hobby site in question eternally grateful. Unlike commercial sites, the general rule is that you do not pay money up front. Instead, you agree to pay a certain sum per 1,000 visitors—say, $50 to $200—for a month or two. You then examine your logs to see how many visitors you did get and if there was any apparent impact on sales. Based on your findings, you renegotiate.

■ SEARCH ENGINES

Search engines are the primary way that users approach the vastness of the Web. That makes search engines a constant fascination for e-commerce businesses. Basically, there are two considerations:

1. Getting noticed by search engines.
2. Getting a good position in the list of hits.

Getting noticed means registering your site with a search engine so that will send its *worm* or *spider* to catalogue its contents. (If your site is linked to from the outside, a particular search engine may find it anyway, as it follows the link from a site that it was already visiting.) With almost any search engine you can simply go to its site, click the Registration or Add Site icon, and register your site manually. There is no cost. You just fill out the on-screen form that the system will present. Unfortunately, there are hundreds of search engines, making the manual approach impractical unless you are satisfied with a very limited initial presence.

Because many people are not, registration services have appeared that will handle the chore for you, using automation. You fill out the master form that the registration service uses, and it feeds the contents to the registration forms of various search engines.

An automated submission service cannot tailor your data to the peculiarities of each search engine, so the results may be erratic. But as we will explain below, the results are very likely going to be erratic no matter what you do. At least with a submission service you won't be obsessing uselessly over the minutiae of manual registrations.

The most widely cited registration service appears to be SubmitIt, located at www.submitit.com. It charges $59 for registering two URLs. It lets you preview the forms before submission, verifies each submission, and produces a report. How long it will take for your site to show up varies greatly between search engines; it could take a month.

The reason you might want to customize your registration—indeed, your site—is that you want good ranking from each search engine. When a user triggers a search, the results may well be a list of hundreds of hits, which the search engine's software will happily stretch out over scores of screens. If your site is not ranked in the top 20 (and hence near the top of the list), the user is not very likely to ever get to you, and your inclusion by the search engine is meaningless.

So how do you get good ranking? If you are selling widgets and a search for the word gets 373 hits, how to make sure your site is in the top 20? Alas, that depends on how the search engine categorized your site. There are a lot of ways to do that, and the natural result is that each search engine does it differently. Basically, a page should make the list if it contains the word in the body text of its HTML file. As for how high up the list it is ranked, that depends on how much weight the search engine gives to various factors:

- *Title.* A Web page typically contains a title, designated by an HTML tag within the file, which is displayed in the title banner along the top of the browser screen. Many search engines weigh the title text heavily when ranking results, and some use the title as the site descriptor when listing the results.

- *Depth of search.* Some search engines dig through every page on the site, whereas others don't go beyond the first page so that only the contents of that page count.
- *Meta tags.* A *tag* is data in an HTML file (i.e., the kind of file used on the Web) that is used as a formatting directive to the browser. A *meta tag* is similar but does not contain information of use to the browser, which ignores it. The search engine, however, sees it when it sifts through the site. In a meta tag, you can insert the keywords you want the search engine to associate with your site and the description to use when it lists your site on a search results page. (Otherwise, it typically lists the initial text in the file.) Further information on meta tags is contained in the Glossary.
- *Word repetition.* There was a time when some Webmasters thought that the magic answer to ensuring good rankings was to repeat the keywords they were targeting as many times as seemed sane within the opening file of the site. They might do this in tiny type along the bottom, where few would notice, or assign the text a color that made it invisible. Sorry—search engines have since wised up and actually penalize ridiculous word repetition as well as ignore invisible or tiny text.
- *Word placement.* After the title, many search engines give the greatest weight to the initial text of the page, meaning that the keywords that you have targeted better show up early. Some ignore meta tags and use only the initial text, and some use initial text as the page descriptor in the results listing.
- *External links.* Some search engines use the number of links from other sites to yours to determine your site's popularity and then use popularity as part of the ranking process, ranking heavily connected sites higher than islands.
- *Overcooked layouts.* Some engines cannot follow links from image maps. Others have a hard time following links from frames. (Both are described in the Glossary.) Meanwhile, keep in mind that the search engines can only read text— any information embodied in marquee graphics will be lost on them.

Obviously, the best thing you can do to achieve decent ranking is pay attention to keywords. Figure out what keywords people are likely to use when looking for your site and make sure they are included in the title or text of the first page. But there is no magic bullet, as you can see from glancing at this list of major search engines:

- *Yahoo!* This site is not a search engine per se because the sites that it lists are categorized by human beings. Before submitting your site, examine the category tree it uses and decide what subcategory you'd like to be in.
- *AltaVista.* This search engine uses meta tags and will follow all links within a site.
- *HotBot.* This search engine will find your site if it is linked from any other. It uses meta tags and gives weight to the title text and then to the text, with repetition adding some weight.
- *Excite.* This search engine uses artificial intelligence to determine your site's dominant theme. Including clear descriptive phrases in the initial text of the first page will help. It does not use meta tags.
- *InfoSeek.* This site, like Yahoo!, depends on the judgment of human beings, who give weight to editorial value, traffic, and the number of external links to your site.
- *Lycos.* This search engine will sift your entire site. It uses meta tags, and gives weight to the title, initial text, text in HTML "heading" tags, and external links. Word repetition is penalized.
- *WebCrawler.* This engine sifts the first megabyte of text in your site, giving extra weight to the title.

Finally, we said there was no magic bullet, no universal weighting to ensure a good ranking. But what about money? you wonder. It always carries weight. Will not a search engine, for a consideration, ensure that my listing always shows up near the top of the list?

The simple answer is no. The major search engines do not do that, and moves in that direction have drawn a lot of heat. But, as mentioned, they sell ad space so that your clickable banner ad will appear whenever the keyword (or combination of keywords) is searched. But that will not affect your placement (or even your presence) on the list below the ad.

■ E-MAIL PROMOTIONS

The cheapest marketing you can do is to send out e-mail ads— there is no postage or printing involved. Meanwhile, those mass mailings that have been showing up in your mailbox all your life have a response rate of about 0.3 percent. But targeted, per- sonalized mailings, using names culled by data mining at the data warehouse, have a response rate of several percentage points. And with e-mail ads, the factor of 10 improvement is all gravy, because there is no incremental cost in sending out more ads.

The only problem is that by approaching the idea of using e-mail, you are flirting with the concept of spam, and if you do more than flirt, you'll find forces gathering to squash you like a bug. Many ISPs have zero tolerance for *spam,* defined as sending unsolicited e-mail or making off-topic postings in newsgroups. If they catch you doing it, they will cancel your account. They may also have a maximum number of e-mail messages that you can send in a day.

The way you get around this is by getting people to solicit e-mail from you by including some kind of opt-in feature at your site. There should be a button to push at your site to ask for a limited-time special discount coupon or a subscription to a newsletter (as we did in the last section) or an electronic white paper about current trends in your industry. Or the button could just state that they agree to receive e-mail. You gather their e-mail addresses, and then you have a list of genuine prospects to whom you can send e-mail without it being spam. Combined with the e-mail addresses of actual customers (whose buying habits are better known because they have bought something), you have a community.

Gathering entries for your mailing list must be an ongoing part of your overall business process. Your data warehouse can be the simplest electronic card file, and your data mining can be a simple sort procedure. But you must have something, some tool that lets your site reach out to people, or your Web site becomes an electronic tombstone.

Once you have your list, there are e-mail services that will handle the transmission of your mailing list (check Yahoo!), but you get can started by yourself using your personal browser or e-mail software. Look for two things:

1. Find the List facility that lets you list addresses under one name. When it comes time to address a message, you simply enter the name of one of your lists. The message is then sent to everyone on that list.

2. Look for a Bcc (blind carbon copy) facility among your e-mail program's addressing options. This lets you send e-mail to multiple recipients without each of them seeing the list of all the other recipients. (You have probably gotten e-mail where the message was lost below a long list of recipients. Whoever generated that message should have used Bcc—but such messages can be a great source of e-mail addresses.) Of course, make sure the Bcc option works with the list option. The Bcc option may require that there is at least one address in the To: line of the address field. You can use your own e-mail address there.

Meanwhile, you have to write the e-mail ad. No simple advice can suffice there, but do remember your audience—they are computer users like you who probably think they get enough e-mail come-ons. Make sure that your ad stands out from the background noise. A good way to ensure this is to make it short, sweet, and informative. Try to build rapport with the reader; a good way to do that is to demonstrate respect for the reader's time and attention. Approach the writing as if you know too well that you will have to stay up all night carving every word into a granite slab with a dull chisel. Make the words so clear that the reader will not notice them, because their meaning leaps directly into the mind. Then include a link back to your site.

It is possible to send e-mail in HTML format so that it can incorporate all the formatting and graphical adornment possible with a Web page. But this can be overdone. First, not everyone has e-mail software that can render the HTML code. Those without it will be left reading the raw HTML code, which may look like gibberish. Second, adding HTML graphics will inflate the size of the message. Anyway, you should be relying on short, simple messages, not flashy graphics.

Meanwhile, hang around long enough and you will start getting spam e-mail ads selling lists of millions of e-mail addresses on CD-ROMs. Don't brand yourself as an amateur by buying them.

---

(20)/(20)

Depending on search engines is a double-edged sword because they can lead to contacts from people you really may not be interested in doing business with, cautions David Green.

"If they have found us, then they have found a dozen others like us, and the bid request that I am reading is being read by a dozen other people around the country," he notes. "Because of considerations like the need to visit them, the problems getting artwork and dealing with text that is not in electronic format, and the desire to make money off the jobs we do want, we try to avoid business outside our geographic region. We will bid a little higher on jobs outside the region. We get ten or twelve a week arriving by fax and e-mail, and we don't get many of them.

"Now that Y2K is passed, many people are waking up and saying they need a Web site, but do not know why or what for," he adds.

But what if an organization does depend on search engine referrals? "If you don't have someone in-house specializing in search engine placement, things will not go as well as they should," he notes.

■ NEWSLETTERS

The very best online marketing results, according to those who have tried it, comes from publishing a free electronic newsletter about the topic you're doing business in. They establish not only brand awareness but also a presumption of trust—you are doing all this talking, so you must know what you are talking about. You are also demonstrating that you are a nice person because of your manifest willingness to share what you know. Your newsletter can be offered as a premium for those who opt in for your mailing list, as explained earlier.

But before committing yourself to producing a newsletter, there are drawbacks that you need to consider:

- It will have to come out at regular intervals if it is to have any impact and the readers are to take it seriously.
- It must contain information of genuine value to the readers.
- It must not read like one huge advertisement, even if you are convinced that it can still be one huge ad and meet the previous condition.
- It must be well written.
- It must be laid out nicely and printed nicely—these days, there is no excuse for a crude appearance. (For an electronic newsletter, that translates to using HTML coding. Most e-mail software will format it on the screen like a Web page. Subscribers can be asked if their software can handle HTML e-mail. For those that do not, you can have a plain text version.)
- If you get to the point of selling ads in it, you must not go overboard.

All things considered, putting out a worthwhile newsletter may demand more effort and attention than you are willing to put into it. If you have to do it all yourself, it may involve a dangerous diversion from your core business. If you hire a professional, it can run you a dollar a word. (Stick to 1,000 words: 400 for the main item, 350 for a second item, and the rest for short items and news.)

But either way, make sure that the writing style is not the same as the style used in your direct-mail or advertising pieces. A newsletter exists to win the trust, confidence, respect, and even friendship of the reader. Ads exist to get the reader's attention. (For this reason it has been argued that newsletters should always be printed and mailed rather than sent electronically. In print, they can be read at leisure. Online, they will be hurriedly scanned before the reader clicks on to the next thing.)

■ ONLINE COMMUNITIES

By *online communities,* we normally mean Usenet newsgroups, but the net result is the same for bulletin boards, echo networks, chat rooms, and mail lists. They all involve an electronic gathering place where participants place written comments . . .

and responses to comments . . . and comments on responses . . . until the sum total is a discussion (be it deep, fluffy, or acrimonious) conducted in text between people who may never see each other face-to-face.

The main difference between Usenet newsgroups and similar services hosted by commercial services or special-interest Web sites is than the latter are more likely to have a *moderator*— an editor who reviews each posting before adding it. Moderators can cut down on the heat and steer wandering discussions back to the avowed topic of the site.

Usenet newsgroups can be read using the news reader facilities that are built into most browsers. They will let you follow (or ignore) particular discussion *threads* (replies to a particular posting.) All you have to do is supply the address of the news server of your ISP, and you can start surfing Usenet.

The reason that you might want to do so is that there are about fifty thousand newsgroups out there (counting all languages), making it highly likely that there is one devoted to the niche your business serves. Aficionados of a particular car, software tool, politician, historical era, or sex act all have a place to go and talk about it. There are newsgroups where people trade car parts, recipes, insults, and jokes and even try to talk each other out of suicide (no kidding.)

Because there are so many newsgroups out there, a good way to approach Usenet is through a specialized, advertising-supported Web site called Deja.com (formerly called Deja News) at (predictably) www.deja.com. It has a carefully organized map of Usenet topics (especially product- or service-oriented ones beloved of advertisers.) You can drill down to specific newsgroups and read the threads or do a keyword search and see what newsgroups show up in it. You can then take note of what newsgroups follow your topic and read along either on Deja.com or through your ISP's news reader. Keep in mind that Deja.com has special filters that remove spam, which its management calculated in 1998 amounted to two-thirds of newsgroup traffic. The newsgroup feed from your ISP won't have this feature, and you'll see Usenet in all its savage untamed glory, rife with moronic come-ons from half-baked multilevel marketing schemes, get-rich-quick scams, cloying chain letters, and links to porno sites.

Many Web sites have discussion forums built into them, and there might be one out there devoted to your topic of interest that you should be following. They differ from newsgroups in that they exist only at that site and are under the total control of the Webmaster. A list of more than three hundred thousand Web forums is maintained by Forum One Communications Corp., searchable at www.forumone.com.

Similar to newsgroups are mailing lists, which operate via e-mail—postings are sent to an e-mail address and from there are remailed to every member of the group. There may be a moderator who combines selected postings into a sort of periodic newsletter, or a robot may do the remailings instantly and automatically. Either way, the effect is much the same as a newsgroup. A service called Liszt maintains a list of public mailing lists searchable at www.liszt.com; at last count there were about a hundred thousand. Having located one, the typical way to join is to send a blank e-mail message to the address of the mail list server with the word *subscribe* in the topic line. If you get tired of belonging, you can send a similar *unsubscribe* message.

The Internet also has its own real-time chat room facility called IRC (Internet Relay Chat.) A list of IRC channels (individual chat rooms) can be found at www.liszt.com, searchable by channel topic. The last time we checked, there were almost forty thousand channels spread over 27 subnetworks.

There are basically four things you can do by following a newsgroup, Web forum, chat room, mailing list, or whatever:

1. Find out what real people in the real world are really talking about. That they have been moved to talk about it online says loads. Of course, some people simply have a compulsion to talk; the fact that they are talking means nothing, and the subject is accidental. You'll be able to spot those cases.

2. Get acquainted with potential customers. *Do not send them unsolicited e-mail*—that would be spamming. Just watch for their names to show up at your Web site, and then you'll know that your marketing is having some impact.

3. Respond to questions from other participants with simple answers, which happen to include a link to your site. Say no more and do not start a new thread.

4. Participate personally in the ongoing discussion, offering the other participants the benefit of your vast wisdom and experience while shaping and molding their viewpoints until a decision to select your product is inevitable.

Number 4 requires a further word of warning. In fact, keeping just one word in mind may suffice: *carpetbagger.* Go look it up. (Okay, it means "meddlesome outsider seeking to manipulate the situation for profit.") The participants in the newsgroup were doing just fine until you came along and had collectively created this verbal space unto themselves for reasons that seemed good and sufficient to them. Then you showed up and sought to exploit its existence for profit. They are very likely to resent you. Your efforts could blow up in your face, with your every posting sparking a firestorm of vituperative responses. If you respond in kind, things can really get out of hand. Weary of reading verbal tantrums, the other participants will start to add your e-mail address to their junk-mail filters so that your postings will be automatically ignored, and every time they see your name or face, they will think the word *spam.*

Remember, this is a text-only world, without any of the facial, tonal, or body-language clues that modify meaning face-to-face, so that anyone inclined to find negative connotations in your words can always do so. Feuds can spring up from nowhere and rage out of control indefinitely, the participants apparently unaware of the dynamics of the process in which they are immersed.

It's a sad situation. You can arm yourself against it by reading the newsgroup extensively to get the general tone before deciding to participate. Do people contribute or shout each other down? Do other merchants participate openly, and how are they received? There may be a FAQ (frequently asked questions) file that is posted at regular intervals or archived somewhere. That file may lay out rules for participants (although more often it will be limited to questions about the group's topic.) Meanwhile, by reading the newsgroup you will see what questions that group has already considered at length and dismissed so that you can avoid looking clumsy by raising them again.

But there are always going to be some newsgroups that turn out to be feud-dominated places where people look for excuses to jump on each other. In such places you should keep a low profile, only responding to requests for hard information and not calling attention to your status. Or you might leave that to a boilerplate signature that you put on the bottom of each posting, touting your business, while the body of your messages never hint at your true identity. But it might be even safer to simply *lurk* (read without ever posting anything.)

Final note: In chat rooms on Web sites belonging to another vendor in your field, you might check with the owner before participating to make sure your presence will not be resented.

■ LINK EXCHANGES

On many sites you'll see a links page, which is a list of other sites that would logically be of interest to visitors to the first site: scuba-training schools on a site that sells scuba gear, for instance. The list is not there because the Webmaster was so moved on seeing those sites that he or she had to share the experience with others. (At least, that's not usually the reason.) The reason is to build traffic because those other sites also have links pages, which include links back to the first site.

Typically, no money is involved—you just add a link to another site, and the folks there add a link to your site. (In fact, be wary of demands for money—this is not advertising.) You don't use a banner ad, you just list their page much the same way that a search engine would. And the benefits are similar to having your site listed by a search engine—the end result is that people who are interested in your topic are more likely to come across your site.

There are three steps involved:

1. Identifying suitable sites.
2. Identifying the Webmaster.
3. Approaching that person with the idea.

Identifying suitable sites is the main chore and may end up being part of your ongoing marketing efforts. It should be a worthwhile site that would be logically of interest to the same people you want visiting your site. And the site should already have a links page, showing a preexisting acceptance of the idea. But it should not be an actual competitor.

Figuring out whom to contact can be sticky because a shocking number of sites list no contact information. Some sites provide an e-mail link to the Webmaster for comments, and that is a good place to start. If all else fails, many places have a default e-mail address of *info* in front of the @ symbol. If you want to link to www.wonderwidgets.com, try sending e-mail to info@wonderwidgets.com.

One way to find out who is behind a site is to track down to whom the site is registered, assuming it is a unique domain name. You can do this using InterNIC. (See the Glossary entry for background.) Go to the InterNIC site at www.internic.net and use the Whois function to find with which registrar the site was registered. Then go to the site of that registrar (through links at the InterNIC site) and use its Whois function. It will return the name(s) and phone number(s) of an administrative, technical, and billing contact for that site. (They might all be the same person.) Although, that person might not be the right one to contact for a list exchange, he or she will probably know who is.

Having found someone to contact, send a friendly letter stating your purpose. If he responds in a manner that leads you to suspect that he sees himself as too big to be bothered, reply to the effect that a link to your site will not draw any visitors from his site and that in fact the link from your site may bring in some extra traffic. If he still can't be bothered (or simply doesn't have and won't consider having a links page), consider adding a unilateral link to his page anyway. As a courtesy, seek permission.

But whatever you do, do not format your site so that links seem to be part of your site.

Meanwhile, a link exchange is different from an *affiliate relationship,* where you sell items at your site for another site. The deal is completed at the other site through a link from your site, and you get a commission.

20/20

Carrie Hardy says that she had tried a number of online advertising methods and found that the best response has resulted from joining message boards at sites that specialize in her topic (i.e., where people talk about their hobby of keeping scrapbooks.)

"I'm able to help them without spamming them, and there are a ton of scrapbook message boards out there," she says. "I join the message board basically as a fellow scrapper. Other users contact me because they see my link (on the link exchange page of the site's message board.) If they ask if I carry an item, I say that I do and that this is my link, but I don't send them e-mail or start a message thread, since that would be spamming. But if someone brings it up, I am more than happy to say that I have it." Yes, even this low-key approach still brings in business.

"I've done free classified ads, and those were a waste of time. I was involved in a banner ad exchange with another site and of about four thousand hits, it was clicked through six times. My ad was just littering someone's site and I had to show their ads on my page."

And what about link exchanges? "About 20 percent of the people I contacted would let me do it. The rest did not say no—they just never answered," she marvels.

Her site also includes an opt-in button, and hundreds of people have added themselves to her mailing list by using it. She says she sends the newsletter out promptly at the first of the month, with news of the latest product announcements and a special offer good only for newsletter subscribers. "If they don't get it, I hear about it," she notes.

Search engines also bring people to the site, but she is not sure if they buy anything.

"The secret," she says, "is targeting your audience."

■ CUSTOMER REASSURANCE

The problem with the online buying public is that it is not dominated by gullible rubes perfectly willing to send their money to anyone who asks politely for it. On the contrary, they are painfully aware that you could be an electronic façade with nothing to back up your intentions, however honorable they may be. At least in a three-dimensional store they can assume that what is on display is in stock, that you will be there later so they can bring back their purchase if it proves defective, and that you look honest—or, at least, are present, conscious, well-groomed, appropriately dressed, and at times lucid.

Online, there is the added issue of privacy. Because you typically cannot make an online purchase without disclosing personal information, people would like to know that you are not going to sell their name to a mailing-list broker or e-mail spammer. As mentioned in Chapter 1, 58 percent of Internet users who had not bought anything online expressed reservations about the issue of privacy (as determined by The Intermarket Group, a research firm in San Diego.) Adding a privacy statement will not automatically reassure them because, again, the users have no way of knowing if your words are more than words.

The answer to both the fraud and privacy dilemma is privacy seals. Like the Good Housekeeping seal of approval, they indicate that a responsible third party has examined your operation and found nothing wrong (or at least found that you are doing what you say you are doing.) The seal is displayed on your Web site, and clicking it will jump the user to the Web site of the issuing organization. There, she can check a list and make sure that you are displaying the seal legitimately. There are three main privacy seal organizations:

➤ CPA WebTrust Program

www.cpawebtrust.org

This program is sponsored by the American Institute of Certified Public Accountants (AICPA) in New York City and is the most rigorous and expensive of the three. Basically, a certified public accountant (CPA) who has been certified by the AICPA WebTrust program must audit your firm every three months to assure that you are doing what your Web site says you are doing, not only in terms of privacy but also in terms of credit card processing, fulfillment schedules, information protection, complaint resolution, and so on. Because the seals are granted by individual CPAs on the basis of audits, there is no set fee for getting the seal.

➤ BBBonline

www.bbbonline.com

You've probably know of the consumer protection and complaint resolution programs of the Better Business Bureau (BBB)—although only at second hand, we trust. The BBB started a reliability seal program for the Web in 1997 that required BBB membership. The privacy seal program, begun in March 1999, does not require membership. Instead, you pay a registration fee of $75 and then get a self-reporting questionnaire that asks for about one hundred seventy items of information. A compliance analyst then goes over the questionnaire with you and issues the seal once all requirements are met. Don't be alarmed if you don't get it after the first conference with the analyst—no one does, reportedly. After the seal is granted, there is an annual fee ranging from $150 to $3,000, depending on revenue.

➤ TRUSTe
www.truste.org
TRUSTe is the oldest and best subscribed of the privacy seal programs, having been started way back in 1997. Applicants fill out self-assessments concerning what they do with consumer data, and TRUSTe periodically reviews the site to see make sure the practices as described have not changed—or if they have, that the change has been reflected in the site's privacy statement. Participation costs between $299 to $4,999, depending on revenue. Of the complaints TRUSTe gets, most concern fears that the complainant's name has been sold to a spammer. Second is the complaint that using the opt-out feature to remove one's name from the site's database did not produce immediate results.

■ THE FINAL TRICK

It's called patience. Trickles can turn into floods. Acorns turn into towering oaks. You just have to give it time. Only you can know just how much time to give it, but with any luck, after giving it some effort and some time, you should start seeing results.

20/20

Christopher Swainhart, president of Resource Marketing, Inc., in Fort Thomas, Kentucky, signed up for the CPA WebTrust program. It cost him about $5,000 for the audit, and it took about 160 working hours to bring his firm's shopping cart into compliance.

The result? "In three months there was at least a 50 percent increase in sales and a 90 percent decrease in terms of people asking us questions, so the cost of sales went down," he recalls.

Because his firm sells banner ads, the buyers have little way of knowing if the service was provided as contracted, so the seal is reassuring to customers, he notes.

"The $5,000 has easily paid for itself," he says. "People no longer ask if we really deliver the product. They just purchase it or they don't, and the hand holding we were doing is being taken care of by the WebTrust seal."

20/20

David Green chose the BBBonline seal. "We have seen it quiet [prospects'] anxiety," he says. "We have found while making presentations on Web site designs it is a factor in some cases, minimizing the fears some people have of doing business on the Internet. Many of our clients come through our Web site, and when they see the BBB seal, it lends credibility."

When the certification started, his site was already largely in compliance, Green recalls. "They suggested some changes, and everything we heard was good ideas. It was easy to do, and they walked us in the right direction. As the Internet becomes more intersite marketed, it is important that customers know we offer services only and will not make money selling their names as well."

Chapter 12

Won't You Stay for a While?

Let's talk about a very important term: *customer acquisition cost.* It refers to the amount you spend on marketing divided by the number of buyers (not surfers) it brings to your site.

Mercer Management Consulting, of New York City, figures that the average retail site has an average customer acquisition cost of $34. That does not sound like much. Gosh, you could spend $3,400 and get 100 buyers. But if your gross product margin is 10 percent, that means that each of those customers would have to spend $340 before you made a profit just on the marketing costs. Maybe your niche allows a greater margin. If it's 25 percent, each customer has to buy only $136 worth. If it's 40 percent, they have to buy only $85. If it's 50 percent, a mere $68 will cover it. And then you can go on and cover your other costs with whatever else they spend and maybe then make a profit.

And maybe you will—but it will be much easier to do if each customer that you get for your $34 keeps coming back so that the next $34 brings in a new customer.

Admittedly, how well that works depends on what business you are in. If you are selling large pieces of equipment that last 20 years, then repeat sales are not an issue, and you need a business model that lets you make enough from each sale to keep going. Most people, however, sell related products or services to a defined niche of customers who have an ongoing need for them. Profit becomes not a one-shot deal but a process that unfolds over time, as the customer comes back, buys more, and generates more revenue. Each customer, once acquired, does not have to be reacquired and takes on a value to your business.

Which brings us to another important concept: *customer value*. How much is it? That again depends on the business, but there are ways to estimate it. For instance, the average retail business has a customer turnover of 20 percent per year, if only because the average American moves every five years. If each customer buys $150 worth of items yearly, each customer will have an average value to you of $750. And that makes the $34 acquisition cost looks like a much better deal—if indeed she keeps coming back and does spend that $750.

This is one of the reasons for the excitement over e-commerce among the big players. Combined with the higher margins possible with online sales (because you don't have to fill a store), revenue growth and profitability look inevitable—if you can hang on to the online customers you acquire. The potential, at any rate, looks more exciting than it does for offline vendors, who are chained to their stores, each of which represents a large fixed cost and can handle only so much business without an expensive expansion.

So that brings us to our third important term for the day: *customer retention*. In most businesses you have to have it. Typically, if each buyer never comes back, what you have is a recipe for financial disaster, an endless treadmill that requires you to spend money just to stay aboard. The search for new buyers never ends, and you never enjoy the advantages that e-commerce can offer.

But be aware that you are unlikely to get customer retention by simply offering the best price—if anyone else on the Web is offering a better price, bargain hunters will find it using search engines. Price cutting will simply put you on another treadmill. (And remember the Mercer study quoted in Chapter 1: 82 percent of users saw value in the Internet because of the information, 75 percent because of the convenience, and only 49 percent because they could save money.)

Realistically, there are two avenues that e-commerce gives you to compete for customer retention with the offline world:

- Customer service.
- Personalization.

Customer service is a big issue, and we have devoted a separate chapter (Chapter 13) to it. We'll look at personalization below.

■ PERSONALIZATION

When we use the term *personalization,* we mean tailoring our messages and offerings to the known situation of the recipient. When you walk into the little corner drugstore and ol' Mr. Whippel pulls out what he knows you need, filling you with a warm fuzzy feeling, that's personalization. However, you probably went to the mall instead, where you had to show a picture ID before they would take your check. This leads us to two truisms:

1. People say they want personalization.
2. They are not willing to pay for it.

And frankly, even if you won the lottery and were willing to shell out $50,000 for so-called customer relationship management software so that you could achieve the nirvana of computer-generated personalization, a small Web site with moderate traffic is not going to gather enough data about its customers to accomplish anything meaningful.

So let's drop our illusions—you are not going to be able to remind someone buying new spark plugs that his truck is due for an oil change. Instead, what you can set out to do is create the illusion of personalization for most of the people most of the time. Here are some approaches:

➤ Canned E-mail

Create a library of canned responses to common e-mail inquiries. When there is an e-mail to respond to, you can put in the salutation, string together the pertinent paragraphs, and send it off. This is what a lot of politicians do, and none have yet been run out of office for that alone.

➤ Customer Segmentation

Segment your customers in various groups, based on geography, age, purchase history, and so on, and send out sales letters personalized for that group.

At some point, you need to decide which customers are your best customers—not in terms of friendly interaction but in terms of how much revenue they generate. (A bank, for instance, may become very fond of problem customers who keep bouncing checks but also keep paying the resulting service fees.) Follow the 80–20 rule, which states that 80 percent of your profit comes from 20 percent of your business. Set aside the best 20 percent of your customers and tailor a sales promotion just for them. If you can keep them coming back, they are worth a few more discount points.

➤ Affinity Programs

Create a program that rewards points for frequent buyers—why let the airlines have all the fun? Again, analyze your customers' buying habits and identify the characteristics of the top 20 percent. Then come up with a system that rewards points to those who reach the top 20 percent. Put a page on your site that explains the point system and inform the customers by e-mail of their standings. Things they might get after accumulating enough points could include:

- Ten-percent-off coupons.
- Free gift wrapping.
- Free shipping.
- Access to a password-protected branch of the site with select merchandise.
- Access to a mailing list for special offers.
- A subscription to your newsletter, the same one that (if truth be told) you'd be happy to give away.
- Entry in a contest or drawing.
- A small gift.

But any personalization effort must be ongoing. You can't just get tired and drop it. Instead, you have to analyze the results and make whatever changes look promising.

For all this to work, you have to be keeping an ongoing customer database, one that tracks each sale to each buyer. But remember—it's all about relationships, not data. Study your best customers until you feel you know them. From that point, a relationship will come naturally.

$$\overline{20}/\overline{20}$$

Each customer gets a surprise gift with each order at the Scrappin' Happy scrapbook supplies site at scrappinhappy.safeshopper.com, says owner Carrie Hardy. "It is not something expensive, but it is something I know they will like." Repeat customers get a ten-percent-off coupon.

"I don't know what the rate of repeat business is, but it appears to be pretty high," she adds.

Chapter 13

Love Thy Customer: Customer Service Aspects

This is an actual e-mail sent by a large online retailer in response to a customer's e-mailed complaint:

> Your e-mail message has been received and is being reviewed. Customer comments are extremely important to us. Thank you for taking the time to share your thoughts and concerns with us.

Nothing more was heard from the retailer. This brings to mind a story so old that it concerns passenger trains and bedbugs. A passenger sent a letter to a railroad company complaining about having gotten bit by a bedbug while traveling in a sleeper car. He got back a long letter with paragraph after paragraph of fulsome prose about how aghast the railroad company was, how this had never happened before, and how every effort was being made to fix the problem. In the envelope he found his original letter. Pinned to it was a note that someone forgot to remove: *Send this [expletive deleted] the [expletive deleted] bedbug letter.*

And so we see how far we have come in the intervening seven or eight decades: The vendors have perceived that customers want shorter, terser prose. And they are providing it, rapidly and at little cost, thanks to computerization.

Perhaps even now a twinge of protest is rising in the back of your mind, slowly forming itself into words. Perhaps the words are: *That isn't customer service!*

So you say. But those missives served the purpose of the organization, momentarily satisfying the demands of an outsider while managing to remind one and all that although it is too big to be bothered, it is gracious enough to acknowledge her existence. If the outsider persists, it will move to another level of response and so on, until in a few cases they have to turn it over to the legal department. It's a perfectly rational, bureaucratic process for a corporate world of and by lawyers.

But that world is not the real world of struggling, small firms, desperately hoping to please their visitors enough that they will recommend the site to others. Positive word-of-mouth recommendations are always the best advertising, and you are going to get them only if you make a visit to your site a satisfying, pleasant experience.

However, cold, bureaucratic sites appear to set the tone. The astonishing truth is that if you make any reasonable attempt to keep the customer happy, you'll be ahead of the pack. Even the lip service just detailed would be, well, something, and the situation is getting worse, not better.

Jupiter Communications, the consumer e-commerce market research firm in New York, announced that it sent e-mail requesting simple service to 125 top retail sites during the 1999 Christmas shopping season. Forty-six percent got a failing grade, meaning that they took five or more days to respond, never responded, or did not even post an e-mail address so that someone could attempt to contact them. A year earlier, the number that failed had been "only" 38 percent.

Among shopping sites, the failure rate was 40 percent, although on the other hand, half of the sites responded within one day. In 1988, the failure rate had been 28 percent.

Among travel sites, the failure rate was 48 percent, up from 36 percent in 1998. On the other hand, in 1999, 40 percent did respond within two days.

E-commerce vendors' commitment to service, the firm sadly announced, was largely lip service, meaning they were missing a golden opportunity to differentiate themselves through computer-aided multichannel customer service. Jupiter urges just such an approach, including:

- E-mail.
- Toll-free phone numbers.

- Live chat rooms.
- Bulletin boards.
- Search functions.
- FAQ files.

But it found that only 37 percent of vendors used a multichannel approach, and even when they did, the implementation was often so uncoordinated as to be detrimental.

Meanwhile, according to Forrester Research, the market research firm in Cambridge, Massachusetts, fully 37 percent of all online shoppers have asked for customer support from a Web site. The customers evidently appreciate how easy it is to do so—after all, e-mail is built into the browser, whereas in a store they have to snag the right employee. They also appreciate being able to seek customer support from home. And 90 percent said they think customer service is a critical issue when selecting a Web merchant.

In fact, Forrester's findings also indicate that Web shoppers expect customer service at each step of the transaction. The three critical areas appear to be:

1. A well-staffed, responsive service organization.
2. A simple return process.
3. Easy order tracking.

And these are beautiful thoughts, but how is a tiny entrepreneurial start-up going to fulfill them? Don't panic—you can. We'll take it one step at a time.

■ SERVICE AT EACH STEP OF THE TRANSACTION

Service throughout the transaction means making the site pleasant and easy to use. It also means that help is never far away. When we built our site in the last section, there was an ever-present Help button. If you have one, make sure the text is actually helpful and add tips specific to your site. If your site does not have one, consider adding one. You don't need an elaborate set of context-sensitive help screens that tell the user what needs to be done in the next second. This is not rocket science—one well-organized Help screen ought to be able to explain how to do everything that needs to be done at a site.

Well-written FAQ files about your products, their features, and the rationale for those features will make a good impression.

➤ A Well-Staffed, Responsive Service Organization

Make service a priority. Check frequently for e-mail and respond immediately to customer queries. If you don't have an answer, say you are looking for one. Be honest and straightforward and do not use any stock phrases about how important customers are to you lest they think that you protest too much. Anyway, they don't want to hear that sort of mush—they want an answer.

People prefer to use e-mail, with the phone coming second, adds Forrester Research. We assume you followed our advice and included your phone number on the Web site. This will reassure customers that they can call you if e-mail is not fruitful.

If they are angry, do not answer in kind. If they do not seem reasonable, do not point it out directly, just remain reasonable yourself and trust that your example will prevail. If their emotions do not seem justified to you, remember that they apparently seem fully justified to the customers. Do, however, move things to a conclusion. This is business, not therapy.

We are also assuming that you are operating in an honest, open-handed manner and have nothing to be evasive about. Should that attitude fail in some eventuality, remember: Dwell on trivia.

➤ A Simple Return Process

You may have run into vendors that required you to get authorization from the right person, get the right authorization code, and send it back in the original packaging, by the original carrier, using the original level of service, with the code and/or authorization letter displayed just so. And you had the feeling that they were setting you up because somewhere in that rigmarole was a requirement that you would trip over and then they would not have to comply.

So right there you have a negative example. Do set a straightforward returns policy and include it in your Web site. Questions it should answer include:

- How soon do they have to send it back?
- Do they need to contact you in advance?
- Will you send a replacement item or attempt to repair the old one?
- Who pays shipping?
- How are refunds handled?

➤ Easy Order Tracking

You are probably not in a position where you can put a link between your Web site and your back-office system through which a customer can input an order number and find out where it is in the system.

But you can do the next best thing and send them e-mail to acknowledge the order and then another one to announce shipping (and yet others to announce any other milestones between those two events.) The shipping announcement can include the waybill number from the courier service so that the customer can track its progress.

EXPERTS SPEAK

Programs are available that let customers get a live keyboard connection through the Web site for one-to-one telex-like interaction. Doing so may sound spiffy, but from all accounts the results are likely to be disappointing. Typically, people can type at about one-tenth the speed they can talk. This applies to the customers, to the support staff, and to you, making keyboard conversations excruciatingly slow. Therefore, if you are going to have live support, using toll-free phone lines is likely to give much better results. You'll spend less time dealing with each caller, and the callers will not associate you with getting a headache.

EXPERTS SPEAK

Jupiter Communications, as cited earlier, urges a multi-channel approach to customer service, meaning people should be able to reach you more than one way. Sites should concentrate on offering phone service and live chat to qualified customers who intend to make a purchase. Content sites (offering news, entertainment, and links) should round out search and e-mail channels with well-maintained FAQ files, reserving chat functions for special circumstances, like live events, says Jupiter.

20 / 20

"E-mail is the key to customer service—answering questions and being fast about it," says Carrie Hardy. She checks her e-mail every 15 minutes and may get 20 messages an hour, although not all require a reply. (And the computer gets turned off when she goes to bed.) She also has a toll-free phone number.

"People know when your reply is canned, and I personalize every one—but as the volume goes up, I may have to do away with that," she says. She acknowledges that having a FAQ file on her site could eliminate a lot of query e-mails and has been working to create such a file.

Her return policy is simple—anyone can send a purchase back within 30 days for a refund. She does not know how well the policy works, because no one has yet sent anything back.

Chapter 14

Auxiliary E-commerce

Where there is business, there are business services. On the Web, there are services and associated Web sites that will let you expand your operation in several directions, including:

- *Auction sites,* for holding auctions with little effort on your part.
- *Shipping services,* to get items delivered in ways that can be tracked via the Web.
- *Affiliate programs* that basically let you add to your product line by linking to someone else's online products.
- *Online malls,* where you can add your store to an online mall and its search engine.
- *Net markets,* which replace phone tag with a Web site (sort of).

■ AUCTION SITES

You may have one-of-a-kind or handcrafted or surplus items or business equipment on which you are hesitant to place a price. Perhaps you have items you are willing to part with at almost any price, but you are not sure that there would be any demand at all for them.

If so, you should consider an online auction. You have probably heard of sites such as eBay (www.ebay.com) where anyone with a credit card can post an item for sale. The sellers pay a fee, usually consisting of an insertion fee plus a few percentage points of the winning bid (which is known to the system, of course.) At eBay, for instance, sellers are charged a sliding insertion fee from 25 cents (for items under $10) to $2 (for items over $50), depending on the minimum bid. After the sale, the percentage the site takes ranges from 5 percent of the winning bid (for items up to $25) to 1.25 percent for amounts over $1,000. (It is done incrementally, with the percentage for the various ranges within the total price stacked atop each other.) Vehicles require a straight $25 insertion fee and $25 sale fee, and real estate is $50 up-front, with no sale percentage.

Buyers typically pay nothing except to the sellers. The site typically is not involved in the transaction itself. Participants who draw complaints about nonperformance or nonpayment are barred from the system. But even participants who see every reason not to trust each other can nonetheless use escrow services (discussed later in this chapter) and still do business.

With the success of eBay, there has been a flood of auction sites penetrating previously little-known niches—surplus vats of chemicals, Hawaiian real estate, exercise machines, antique stock certificates, yarn, The Who records, business investments in Thailand, and so on. But although a lot of the things you see for sale have simply migrated out of the owner's attic, it's a mistake to equate auction sites with electronic garage sales—there is plenty of genuine commercial activity there, too.

Auction sites typically display the item for sale on its own page accompanied by a detailed description written by the seller, optionally with a picture, with the starting bid (set by the seller), the bids as of that moment, and the time left for bidding. (Most auctions go on for several days, with the time set by the seller.) You could probably rig something like that at your site with manual controls, using e-mail forms to send in bids, but there is no reason to go to the trouble. You can link your site to the auction site and let the auction site do the work for you. The reasons:

- You're likely to run into all sorts of trouble enforcing bid increments and deadlines, with sore losers blaming your system instead of themselves.
- The auction site is likely to have more traffic than you ever dreamed of having at your site.

- By posting items at the auction site, you are publicizing your site to the people who frequent that category at that site—people who have displayed a definite interest in your field.
- It's easy to do.

It can be done in three steps:

1. Register at the auction site and add your item. Copy the Web address of the resulting auction page.
2. Back at your Web site, unhook the shopping cart on that item page and add text stating that it is being auctioned off.
3. Add a link to that page to the auction page you just created at the auction site.

Then be sure and follow up. At the end of the auction, get rid of the item page on your site. Or if you feel good about the results, leave the item page but take out the link, replacing it with a note about the auction results.

(Your ESP's site-creation tool will probably have a facility for adding an external link to an item page. If you have to do it by hand, see Appendix C for the necessary HTML code.)

After the sale, the buyer and seller contact each other to confirm the price and terms (especially shipping). The seller usually supplies the buyer with a tracking number from the shipping service being used (an issue covered in depth a little later) so that they can confirm that it was sent.

But auctioning is a world unto itself, and before proceeding, you might want to familiarize yourself with the following terms and practices.

➤ Auction Type: Standard

The *standard auction* is the kind with which most people are familiar, involving a single item or batch to be sold to one buyer. Bidding starts at a minimum price, continuing higher and higher until no one proves willing to offer more within the time limit. In exchange for the privilege of bidding, the high bidder is obliged to buy that item at the final price—unless it did not match or exceed the seller's reserve price.

➤ Auction Type: Dutch

A *Dutch auction* is used when you have multiple buyers and multiple examples of the thing being sold. The result of the auction determines not only what price will be paid but also how the goods will be divided among the buyers.

Imagine a barge loaded with tulips passing under a bridge. On the bridge are tulip dealers. They buy flowers in bulk. As they look over the tulips, they individually decide how many they want, how badly they want them, and consequently how much they would be willing to pay apiece.

Thus, in a Dutch auction the bidders state how many they want and what per-item price they are willing to pay. The person who bids the highest price gets to buy the number of items he or she bid for—but at the price offered by the lowest winning bidder (whose bid exceeded the minimum price set by the seller.) In fact, all the buyers use the lowest winning bid, and their orders are filled according to the order of their bid—the second-highest bidder's order is filled second, and then the third-highest is filled third, and so on, until the stuff runs out. The bidders are required to accept, and pay for, whatever quantity they end up getting. In case of tie bids, the first bidders get priority. (Ties appear to be the norm in many electronic venues, where previous bids can be seen.)

➤ Auction Type: Private

If you are a celebrity gone broke and you are offering your house for sale to, presumably, other celebrities who are still rich, this method may appeal to you. The bidders (who are probably there by invitation) are not identified during the auction, and only the buyer and seller are notified of the results. (Private auctions are also used for adult material because the bidders' identities are not disclosed.) But by its nature, an auction is a nonprivate event—most sellers would want the widest possible participation—and so this method is rarely used.

➤ Auction Duration

Often you can select the duration of your auction, from a couple of days to a couple of weeks. A longer period will give the item more time to accumulate bids, and some niche items will need that. With other items, a short period will spur the bidders to action. Either way, the trick is to schedule things so that the auction ends at a time when you are available. You will want to contact the winning bidder immediately to arrange payment and shipping.

➤ Proxy Bidding

With *proxy bidding,* a bidder can tell the system to keep him or her in the top bidding position by incrementally topping any further incoming bids up to a maximum amount set by that bidder. Proxy bidding should protect against *snipers*—bidders who wait until the moment before deadline to place the high bid.

➤ Bid Increments

Of course, people could keep upping each other by a penny, holding down the price and dragging out the process forever. To prevent this, the auction sites typically impose a minimum bid increment, which is determined by the price range of the current bidding for that item. For instance, on eBay the increment ranges from 5 cents when bidding is under $1 to $100 when bidding exceeds $5,000.

➤ Shipping Costs

It helps when you calculate in advance what the likely shipping costs will be and figure that in with the price. That way the bidders won't be worrying about hidden costs.

Another reason to check this in advance is that online escrow services may have their own shipping requirements. But the buyer may insist on overnight shipping or be content with fourth-class mail or may live in Greenland, so this detail is usually not finalized until the last moment.

➤ The Title Line

As with the descriptor text for your Web site (discussed in Chapter 8), you need a catchy and informative title for your auction item page. (You'll probably have 80 characters for the line.) Potential bidders will search for keywords of interest and will get a list of item title lines. Obviously, there needs to be something in it to confirm the bidder's interest, make it stand out from other items in the list, and draw the bidder in. So you can't just say:

```
'67 Chevy. Gears stripped. OK otherwise.
```

No, you have to say something like:

```
'67 Chevy. Lovingly restored. Lacks functional
transmission.
```

The site probably does not let you use HTML tags inside the title line, lest listing a bunch of them on the screen after a search produce an unreadable typographic mishmash. So people have been known to resort to bizarre punctuation or capitalization to highlight individual words in the title or otherwise make the title stand out. The result is another kind of mishmash, and the Amazon.com site, for one, reserves the right to alter unsightly titles. So don't rely on gimmicks—just stick to the (appropriately embroidered) facts.

➤ Item Descriptor

The same advice goes for the item descriptor, except that you have much more room to play with. HTML tags may be allowed, but gimmicks will be seen for what they are. Check it carefully because the site will probably not let you change your description after bids have started coming in. This is the place to get away from puffery and stick to the facts, using as much detail as an intelligent reader should need. Show some respect for the bidder—especially for his or her ability to be misled. Even if you do so inadvertently, misleading the buyer can cause the whole thing to blow up in your face. Avoid jargon and strive for clarity. If there is a passage that can be misunderstood, it probably will be, so revise it. The text can, of course, embody a link back to your site. You'll have to input the HTML code manually, and Appendix C shows how.

➤ Illustrations

As with the site-creation tools of ESP sites, you can upload a picture of your item for inclusion on the page. However, the auction sites are typically less sophisticated, and your artwork will not be resized to fit the page. You will have to do it yourself with graphics software. The site will probably have size limits for pictures, both in terms of physical dimensions and file size.

➤ Categories

To augment keyword searching, the site will probably have a category breakdown, with possibly hundreds of categories you can select to list your item in. Obviously, you will need to browse the lists in advance to see where your item fits. You can typically choose all the categories that seem appropriate.

➤ Minimum Bid

The *minimum bid,* set by the seller, is the price at which bidding must begin. A bid below the minimum is not binding and might not even register. But a bid at the minimum will buy the item if no higher bids come in. Your agreement with the auction site binds you to honor that bid—unless you set a reserve price that was higher than the minimum bid.

➤ Reserve Price

The *reserve bid* is the lowest amount that you, the seller, will take for the item. If bidding falls below that, it is not sold. If you set a reserve price, use a reasonable sum, because you may otherwise alienate potential customers. People have been known to stir up interest with a nonbargain reserve price yoked to a very low minimum bid, especially at an auction site that tells the bidder that a reserve price has been set but does not say what that price is. In that situation, bidders may get the impression that the item might be gotten for a little above the minimum bid when in fact is it not for sale at that price level. Predictably, the bidders typically lose interest as the bidding approaches fair market value. Also keep in mind that the site will probably not let you fiddle with the reserve price after bids have started coming in.

➤ First-Bidder Discounts

If the site lets you offer a *first-bidder discount,* you should seriously consider doing so. The idea is that the first person to put in a bid will get a discount—say, 10 percent—on the final price if that person wins the auction in subsequent bidding. Because the first bidder knows that he or she will pay a discounted price, that bidder is motivated to keep bidding, perhaps pushing the price above the point where it would otherwise have stopped. If nothing else, offering the discount should spur the arrival of that ice-breaking first bid.

➤ Take-It Price

A *take-it price* is used when you honestly don't know what the item is worth but would be very happy to sell it at a certain price. The moment someone offers the take-it price, the auction ends, and that person gets it. If bidding does not reach the take-it price, there is no effect, and the auction continues normally. (If you set a reserve price, obviously the take-it price must be higher, or there is no auction.) Take-it prices cannot be used in Dutch auctions.

Obviously, with a take-it price you run the risk of selling for too little because you don't know if bidding would have gone higher than the take-it price. But it is a good way to speed up the auction because as bidding rises nearer and nearer to the take-it price, bidders will be increasingly tempted to simply pay the take-it price.

➤ "Going, Gone" Option

If the site automatically stops bidding at the end of the sale period and awards the item to the highest bidder at that moment, it may be cutting off a feeding frenzy. For all anyone knows, the price may have gone higher and higher. With the *"going, gone"* feature, if a bid is made in the last few minutes of an auction, the auction is extended a few more minutes and is not cut off until there have been a certain number of minutes without a new bid.

➤ Location Entry

When dealing with heavy items that require expensive shipping, the bidder would like to know at a glance how far away the seller is. This is often done with zip codes because privacy is maintained and there are many tools that let you determine the distance between two zip codes.

➤ Relisting Option

If your item does not sell, you may have the option of letting the site automatically relist it—starting the auction process over—until it does. Even if it does sell, you have still have the option of relisting it, on the assumption that you have more of the items. (With a Dutch auction, you should be able to relist with the sold quantity subtracted from the original quantity or to restart the auction with the original quantity.)

➤ Escrow Services

An *escrow service* is an independent third party that holds the buyer's payment in trust until the buyer receives the item and decides it's okay. Nor does the buyer have to send credit card information to an unknown party if that is an issue—an escrow service also buffers the seller against credit card fraud or bad checks. They arc uscd when buying through auction and classified-ad sites, where the parties have no previous relationship and are unlikely to have one again. The procedure is as follows:

- Both buyer and seller contact the escrow service, demonstrate an agreement on the terms of sale, and decide which one of them pays the escrow service.
- The buyer sends the payment for the item to the escrow service.
- The seller ships the item directly to the buyer while supplying the escrow service a traceable waybill number.
- The buyer receives and approves the merchandise.
- The escrow service passes the payment on to the seller.

If the buyer rejects the item, typically the buyer has to pay for return shipping and for the escrow service.

The escrow service used by eBay is I-Escrow, found at www.iescrow.com. Its charges start at 6 percent for credit transactions under $500, falling to $90 plus 1 percent of the transaction for cash transactions over $2,500. Other e-commerce escrow services include:

- D & M Internet Escrow Service (www.int-escrow-serv.com).
- Escrow.com (www.escrow.com).
- Internet Clearing Corporation (www.internetclearing.com).

- SecureTrades.com (securetrades.com—no www).

20/20

Carrie Hardy says she's had good luck getting customers through eBay, the auction site. She posts surplus items there and auctions them off, and she includes a link back to her site in the item description field. The awareness created by her presence at eBay, plus the link itself, generates a level of sales second only to participation in discussion boards, she says. (Third is word-of-mouth.)

■ SHIPPING SERVICES

Unless you are selling downloadable software or hard goods to be picked up at your place of business, e-commerce involves shipping things. Determining how best to make the shipments is, therefore, a big part of your cost structure. If standard shipping is included in the price, you have to understand shipping costs thoroughly before you can set your prices. If shipping is extra, you have to be able to quickly tell the buyer what it is. (Often it is both—standard shipping at no charge, with overnight shipping for an additional premium.)

Unless you are doing bulk business-to-business shipments (which would put you in another league), e-commerce typically means using *courier services*—delivery networks, at the end of which a truck pulls up and the driver takes the box out and hands it to someone or leaves it at their door. (The U.S. Postal Service also offers courier services, over and above putting letters in mailboxes.)

Aside from being able to offer overnight or two-day delivery, courier services also offer traceable shipments. Each address label—*waybill*—includes a unique serial number with a bar code. The code is scanned each time the box is handled, such as when it is put on a truck or a plane, passed through a sorting facility, or shunted to a customs warehouse in Hong Kong (as temporarily happened to one of the author's packages one time, for obscure reasons.) This data is sent to the service's central computer and can be accessed through its Web site simply by inputting the waybill number.

Therefore, it is possible to simply e-mail the waybill number to the buyer, who can go to the courier service's Web site, be immediately assured that it is a valid number, and then watch the progress of the package as it crosses the country. As mentioned previously, Internet escrow services typically require that the seller supply a traceable waybill number. (Of course, there is no assurance that the goods in question are actually inside that box.)

You can also calculate shipping costs through the Web site, figure out where to take the boxes for shipment, arrange pickup at your place of business (although that typically adds to the cost), and ask for more address labels and shipping containers. The main services and their Web sites are:

➤ U.S. Postal Service

- Calculate shipping costs:
  www.usps.com/business/calcs.htm
- Track packages:
  www.usps.com/cttgate/
- Drop-off locations:
  www.usps.com/ncsc/locators/find-po.html

➤ United Parcel Service

- Calculate shipping costs:
  www.ups.com/using/services/rave/rate.html
- Track packages:
  www.ups.com/tracking/tracking.html
- Drop-off locations:
  www.ups.com/using/services/locate/locate.html

➤ FedEx (Federal Express)

- Calculate shipping costs:
  www.fedex.com/us/rates/
- Track packages:
  www.fedex.com/
- Drop-off locations:

www.fedex.com/us/dropoff/

➤ Airborne Express

- Calculate shipping costs:
(Not posted—too dependent on volume and other variables).
- Track packages:
www.airborne.com/trace/
- Drop-off locations:
www2.airborne.com/DropBoxLocator/default.asp

➤ iShip.com

This site does not do any shipping but does have aggregated shipping-rate information from all the major carriers so that you can make meaningful comparisons between carriers and shipping terms. (Next-morning courier delivery can cost 12 times more than second-day standard postal delivery!) The site will also let you pay there and print out the shipping label, with tracking bar code, using your laser printer. (As of this writing, it offered only United Parcel Service (UPS) labels.)

EXPERTS SPEAK

Shipping gurus urge the following:

- Know the *shipping weight* of your items (actually, of the items plus the box and packaging) and not just the *net weight* (the item by itself).
- The ship-to address usually needs to be a street address rather than a P.O. box. Only the U.S. Postal Service can deliver to P.O. boxes, and large items won't fit anyway.
- Use corrugated cardboard boxes, sealed with packing tape—not string, masking tape, or cellophane tape.
- Note the weight capacity of the box and do not exceed it.
- Use bubble wrap or other packing material as needed. The output of a paper shredder will often suffice. Try to leave two inches of cushioning material on all sides.

- Spray foam peanuts or similar packing material with antistatic spray so that they will not stubbornly cling to the recipient.
- Free boxes can often be supplied by courier services.
- Put a duplicate address label inside the box in case the outside one gets torn off.
- Buy no more insurance than you think you really need.
- Many people would rather receive packages at the office, even personal ones, because otherwise the packages will be left unattended on their doorstep at home.
- With that in mind, do not put anything on the outside of the package calling attention to the value of the contents.

---

(20)/(20)

Carrie Hardy says that she uses priority shipping with the U.S. Postal Service and has found it to be cheap and fast enough for most buyers, and at her post office she never has to stand in line.

"Delivery usually takes two or three days, and the customers are ecstatic at getting it that quickly," she notes. "And you can get free boxes from them, and you can order them online. They just carry a little note saying it is a felony to use the boxes for any other purpose."

"But expensive shipping defeats the purpose of e-commerce," she says. On the other hand, offering free shipping makes most international orders too expensive to deal with, she adds.

■ AFFILIATE PROGRAMS

Affiliate programs, also called *associate programs* or *partner programs*, involve an elaborate expansion of the link exchange mentioned in Chapter 11. Basically, you put a link at your site to another site (usually a banner supplied by the other site), and every time a person clicks to that site and buys something, you earn a commission.

Indeed, there are so many affiliate programs out there now that you might think that it is possible, at least in theory, to have an e-commerce site with no product or service of your own. You just add a bunch of links, announce to the world that you are selling refrigerators, books, flowers, and so on, and wait for the checks to start arriving.

Although it is possible, and people are doing it, you may well have to wait a long time for those checks because engaging in this practice puts you in competition with the big price club and e-commerce portal sites. They practice drop shipping, where the order is passed to the manufacturer, who sends the item out under the Web site's name. With no value being added, the only reason the shopper goes to the site is out of conditioned response to advertising. This puts the site on an endless promotional treadmill, as it constantly seeks to drum up new users. If the main question you face in advertising is how many tens of millions of dollars you are going to spend this year, this may be your game.

Otherwise, affiliate programs work best where there is genuine affiliation. There appear to be two types of scenarios most suited to this arrangement:

1. You are involved in a club or association whose members could be motivated to help raise money for it by buying their refrigerators, books, flowers, and the like through affiliation links at the group's Web site.

2. You find an affiliate program whose products form a logical augmentation to the offerings of your site. If you are selling books on sailing, then links to sites offering sailboat equipment and boat rentals would seem natural. (There are Webmasters who claim success without any logical affiliation, but there is probably some second-order affiliation that they have not noticed.)

In any event, traffic is everything. Two percent of your visitors might click over to the other site, and 2 percent of those might thereupon buy something. If your name does not happen to be Lycos or Yahoo!, you should probably think of adding an affiliate link as a way of offering something extra to your visitors rather than as a way to afford that beachfront property you've been dreaming of. If money does come in, so much the better. (And it is more likely to come in if you make the effort to promote your affiliation when you promote your site.)

Some concepts to be aware of include:

➤ Banner Farms

Also called *flea markets* and probably a lot of other things, these sites have been oversold on the idea of affiliate programs and are loaded with banner ads, with no logical connection or theme.

➤ Commissions

These range from 5 percent to 50 percent. Services or sites that offer basically one product (such as a book written by the Webmaster) typically give a cash commission. Because you are going to be sending people away from your site, you should be rewarded. But a high commission offered by a blah site with a so-so product may not be worth your while. And if the other site is going to make your visitors unhappy, it is poison. Meanwhile, is the commission paid only for that sale or for every sale that referred buyer makes from then on? Do commissions increase with volume? And are they paid in cash or discount points? The former is more likely to get you a good table in a restaurant.

➤ Click-Through Programs

Some programs pay (usually a fraction of a penny) for each person who clicks over, whether they buy anything or not. Or the program may pay for each person who fills out a questionnaire. Another name for click-through is *pay-per-click*.

➤ Fine Print

In the program's written agreement (assuming it has one), does it demand to be the only link of that type from your site? Does it demand control over the nature, appearance, or wording of your link? If so, does this bother you?

➤ Minimum Earnings

Some programs may require that you earn a minimum before they will send a check during a payment period. If a program that you are interested in does that, make sure the balance carries over from one period to the next.

➤ Tracking

The nature of the tracking that the affiliate program uses is very important. Will it send periodic, detailed reports concerning what referrals it received from your site? Is there a Web site where you can check the status of your referrals? Or do checks mysteriously appear or not appear? With the former, you can intelligently fine-tune your approach to linking; with the latter, you can't do anything.

➤ Two-Tiered Programs

Two-tiered programs are affiliate programs that pay you a full commission when someone you refer to the site buys something or a split commission when someone you signed up to be an affiliate refers someone to the site who buys something. If this sounds like a multilevel marketing operation, it certainly involves the same drawback: If you sign up people rather than do the real work of selling, you will probably end up signing up people who, like you, are more interested in signing up other people than in doing the real work of selling. Nothing gets sold, and no money is made. If a program is selling distributorships and seems more interested in selling distributorships than products, alarm bells should go off. Otherwise, treat a two-tier system as if it were a one-tier system, and treat any split commissions as found money.

➤ Affiliate Operators

Recently a new kind of business has sprung up—matchmakers who marry Web sites to online vendors who offer affiliate programs. You go to a site, pick the vendors and products you want to be affiliated with, and get started. Getting affiliated is free. The main ones appear to be:

Affinia
www.affinia.com
This service boasts more than a million products from more than a thousand vendors. The shopping-cart pages are generated by Affinia and are not pages on your site, but you can customize those pages to a considerable extent. (You can also use Affinia as an ESP and offer your products through its affiliate program.)

Vstore
www.vstore.com
This service boasts a link back to your site so that you never lose the customer. It handles the credit card processing, and its selection of brand-name items makes it appear that you could turn your site into an online department store in a short time.

Nexchange
www.nexchange.com
Nexchange boasts total control over how the link is made and presented, with no loss of the customers to another site.

EXPERTS SPEAK

General advice on affiliate programs, gleaned from across the Internet, includes:

- Ask for references to sites that are in the affiliate program. Ask the person at that site if he is happy about the program, and if not, why. (If he is totally happy, that usually means he is not involved.)
- Many sites across the Web do not display contact information. If the affiliate program you are looking at has such a site, you should ask if the omission was inadvertent or if it prefers not to be reached. If it's the former, ask for the information; if it's the latter, go somewhere else.
- If the program has a written agreement, read it carefully. If it does not, put your understanding of the

agreement in a letter and send it to the program's contact person.

- Does it seem professional, and does it quickly reply to your questions? Or does it not want to be bothered? (You should contact the program with a question just to determine this.)
- Talk up the link. For instance, link to a page containing a review of the product. Realistic reviews, with pros and cons, actually carry more weight.
- Consider fine-tuned links, such as links from a book about a composer at your site to CDs of his music at another site, rather than just linking from a links page to a home page. (This is the equivalent of hand-selling and can increase volume fivefold.)
- Remember, you are handing traffic from your site over to another site. If the result is not a positive experience for both you and your site visitors, don't do it.

➤ Offering an Affiliate Program

Okay, you caught the bug, but you think that you ought to be the one offering the affiliate program, with scads of Web sites out there selling your product while you head out to the golf course. People do it, but you'll need to cover three bases:

1. *Decent commissions.* Is 5 percent enough to get your attention? If not, why do you think it would get someone else's attention? Be generous. And higher volumes—do they rate higher commissions? And does a referred customer generate a commission on all subsequent sales or just on that first sale?

2. *Promotional participation.* Just signing up sites may be a waste of time. They need to promote their participation, and you need to reward them for doing so. Are they going to mention you in their ads? If that's not worth a cash contribution, maybe it's worth a higher commission.

3. *Tracking.* This is the hard part. Read on.

Your ESP may have a tracking mechanism that lets you know how many hits came from a specific Web site plus how much those referred visitors bought. (Chapter 16 shows an example.) Lacking that, you could create separate item pages with shopping-cart buttons for each affiliate. Each would use SKUs with a different prefix, and in the end you could tell at a glance which sales resulted from which affiliates. But if you have a lot of affiliates, it could be an arduous task to create a separate set of pages for each. Predictably, vendors have come forth to help, with tracking software and services. The chief example appears to be Be Free Inc. (www.befree.com), with a service designed for affiliate networks.

An explanation of the tracking system needs to be included in the affiliate agreement because savvy Webmasters will pay as much attention to it as to the commission structure.

20/20

Although sites such as Amazon.com report that a third of their business comes through affiliates, success is not an assumption that you can make for affiliate programs. Carrie Hardy says that she joined an affiliate program for an office supplies vendor set up by Freemerchant, her e-commerce host. Visitors who clicked a smaller banner ad at her site would jump to the vendor's site and then she and Freemerchant would share a small commission. But nothing came of it.

"I never saw a dime from it," she recalls. She decided the banner ad was just littering her site and dropped out of the program.

A separate mall-like affiliate program that she joined did not produce a single hit, she also remembers.

■ ONLINE MALLS

There's strength in numbers—or at least a certain degree of comfort. But as people grow confident, they no longer feel the need to cling together, and so they disperse.

And that about wraps up the oscillating history of online malls. Back in the nearly forgotten dark ages of e-commerce (say, 1996), people thought that the development of Web commerce would parallel that of corporeal commerce, with big-name vendors making massive investments with developers who offered the right real estate. Or so the promoters of online malls hoped, because they saw themselves as the developers who were going to get rich. But it turned out that on the Web, one piece of real estate is about the same as another, and if the idea was to bring in customers through simplified navigation, the search engines did that for free. And even if they did not balk at the price, the big firms that were first on the scene discovered the e-commerce was not magic and saw no reason to tie their brand identity to that of a third-party mall. So the original malls dried up and blew away.

More recently, there has been a flood of smaller e-commerce vendors who see no reason to leave any marketing stone unturned—if it could be turned cheaply, with minimal hassle. The result has been malls whose business arrangements more closely resemble a combination of ESP and affiliate programs, with minimal up-front fees. Listed merchants become part of the mall, which chiefly means that their products can be searched for through the mall's search engine. The mall may also provide hosting, credit card processing, site creation, and other services.

And it may be that many of the vendors who join malls will branch out on their own after they get firmly established. In the meantime, there's enough interest to support scores of malls. The site www.malls.com, which lists and categorizes malls, counted about four hundred twenty in early 2000. Of these, about thirty were considered large, and the others fit into various categories, such as regional, ethnic, electronic villages (largely local ISPs hosting local small businesses), and theme, which includes gifts, Western, outdoor, Hawaiian, marine, and scads of other interests.

Yahoo! listed about seven hundred malls, with a similar breakdown, although price clubs and large discounters were included as if they were malls.

Three fairly random examples of this new wave of low-cost malls would include:

➤ ShopNow.com

www.shopnow.com
This site lists more than seventeen thousand stores, from arts to auctions to sports. (Some are themselves malls.) You can list

your store for as little as $19.95 per year. For reserved words in the shopnow.com search engines and better placement in the listings, you pay more—quickly rising to $3,999 per year for 100 search engine words and the right to use your logo with the listing. There is a search engine that lets you search all the listed sites for a specific item and compare prices.

➤ NetMall

www.netmall.com
This site resembles Yahoo!, but it is devoted to listing online stores. Store managers can register their stores here, selecting a category, listing keywords, and inputting a descriptor paragraph. Visitors can then search the database. Registration is free and the site is supported by advertising. At last count it listed more than two hundred thousand stores.

➤ Mallpark

www.mallpark.com
This site lists nearly three hundred thousand stores in 1,200 shopping centers within 50 malls (meaning subcategories and categories respectively.) A listing consists of descriptor text, keywords, and a link back to the site. You can be listed free, but to ensure a good place in the listing, you'll either pay $15 per month (to be in the top 10), $10 per month (to be in the top 30), or $2 per month (to be on the first page.) The free merchants (called *tent stores*) are listed on a second page that the visitor has to click on separately.

■ NET MARKETS

Net markets are also called *e-services, e-markets, e-marketplaces, netmarkets, I-markets, vertical hubs,* and anything else within reason. (Butterfly imagery is sometimes used, in apparent reference to the way such insects carry pollen between flowers.) They represent a fairly new concept and connect buyers and sellers through third-party Web sites that add something to the equation, such as project management and tracking software.

Let's pretend you're the head of the documentation department of a software company. The manual for the latest product is finished. It just needs to be printed. You discover that you are supposed to handle this chore. You could spend days calling printers, explaining your needs to them, waiting for bids to come back, analyzing those, going back to the ones you seemed to click with, explaining to them what you now realize you really needed, getting more bids, and so on until you nail down something, you let the contract, you make adjustments when you realize that several screen shots need to be updated, and you track the project until final delivery and then approve the invoice.

With an e-service (we'll stick to the easy name), you log onto the site and state your needs. Later, you check back and find responses from printers that expressed interest, formatted for easy comparison. The system, in fact, may analyze them for you, complete with options such as paper stock and turnaround times. You let the contract via the Web site; it tracks the project and manages any changes and generates a detailed invoice—to which it adds a couple of points to cover the service. And you may think it's worth the price because you don't have to live on the phone and the turnaround on the project was probably cut by a couple of days.

This is not e-commerce per se, but it assumes the use of e-commerce, not to mention full back-office computerization. Both the buyer and the vendor must have Web access. The vendor may need to have an accounting system that can be interfaced to the Web, but the details are usually handled (gratis) by the e-service at the time the vendor is enrolled.

If you worry that, as a vendor, e-services will turn you into a commodity and grind prices down until only a few nasty skinflints remain in business, that is because your sales are not based on any relationship with the customer. That's what they say, anyway. And early reports seem to bear them out, with e-services becoming a way to quickly identify the vendors that click with a buyer and fit the various needs of that buyer's projects. It also frees both buyers and sellers from a certain amount of clerical drudgery.

Services you can expect from such sites include one or more of the following:

- *Industrial exchanges.* Goods or services are sold as if on the stock exchange, with prices rising and falling according to demand. This works best with simple commodities, although that can include things such as electrical power and frozen squid.

- *Sales leads.* Buyers can post requests for quotations (RFQs) and requests for proposals (RFPs), and vendors can respond, often in formats designed to meet the information needs of that industry.
- *Industrial catalogue malls.* These sites aggregate the catalogues of the member vendors, letting the buyer do massive amounts of shopping and price comparisons in one sitting. They may impose a certain amount of (badly needed) classification uniformity.
- *Workflow services.* The site provides project management and progress tracking for multiparty or complex projects, from construction to trademark licensing.
- *Auctions and reverse auctions.* As the name implies, these sites let you sell surplus equipment, supplies, or raw materials, usually for more than you'd get from a liquidator. Reverse auction sites let you not only post your needs but also combine them with other small businesses, creating greater buying power.

(Forrester Research, the market research firm in Cambridge, Massachusetts, predicts that the use of e-services will mushroom, but any mystique of innovation they embody will quickly fall away. Those Net marketplaces—the name that Forrester uses—that are not one-stop shopping services by 2002 will fall by the wayside.)

Evidently, when it comes to e-commerce, the trick in the next few years will not be to just get online but to find where the online party is and join it. In other words, find the site where you can buy what you need to buy and join—and then find the site where you can sell what you need to sell and join it, too. (Even if you have nothing to sell through an e-service, your suppliers might be in one.) Finding the one best for you may be a simple matter of keeping your ear to the ground. Examples of e-services currently functioning include:

- AdAuction (www.adauction.com), media (advertising space and time slots) market.
- Altra (www.altra.com), energy market.

- Arbinet Global Clearing Network (www.arbinet.com), telecommunications bandwidth market.
- BidCom (www.bidcom.com), construction project workflow services. (Not to be confused with Bid.com, a Canadian auction site.)
- BizBuyer (www.bizbuyer.com), market for business products and services.
- Chemdex (www.chemdex.com), lab supplies and "life sciences chemicals" market.
- FreeMarkets (www.freemarkets.com), market for industrial parts, raw materials, commodities, and services.
- Gofish (www.gofish.com), bulk seafood market (*not* children's card games.)
- KillerBiz (www.killerbiz.com), business products and services market.
- PaperExchange (www.paperexchange.com), paper products market.
- Photonics Online (www.photonicsonline.com), industrial laser market and news site.
- PlasticsNet (www.plasticsnet.com), plastics industry market.
- QuestLink (www.questlink.com), electronic component design services market.
- SciQuest (www.sciquest.com), scientific, education, and industrial laboratory products and supplies market.
- SolidWaste.com (www.solidwaste.com), solid waste systems market and news site.
- TestMart (www.testmart.com), market for industrial test and measurement equipment.
- TradeOut.com (www.tradeout.com), surplus business equipment and supplies market.

Meanwhile, VerticalNet, Inc., (www.verticalnet.com) and Net Market Makers, Inc., (www.netmarketmakers.com) are two firms involved in the creation and management of net markets for various industries and could be a place to start when looking for an e-services site serving your own industry.

The Dark Side

Now we have to tell you that there are dangers ahead. With e-commerce, these appear to fall into two broad categories:

1. *Things people can do to you.* They can tax you and steal money from you. (But unlike the taxman, the thieves will be following policies that can be intuitively understood.)

2. *Ways you can foul up.* These include delivery foul-ups, false advertising, and if you are marketing to children, not paying attention to the specific rules that govern children's advertising and now govern children's data privacy as well. (And after reading the latter, you may resolve to never ask any child anything.)

Plus, this being business, the dangers you face include the usual fires, floods, market shifts, acts of God, wars, labor strikes, weird lawsuits, and your own ennui. But we'll stick to e-commerce issues.

■ TAXES

Of course, you'll have to pay taxes. (The sole disagreement about the old saying that the only thing certain in life is death and taxes has to do with who said it first.) Just what and how you pay depends on where you live.

➤ Income Taxes

First, if you are a U.S. citizen, the money you derive from your business is income and thus subject to income taxes. If your state has an income tax, the same is true there. The world of income tax as it relates to business is a large one, with plenty of detailed sources of information, so we will not get into it here.

If your business is a sole proprietorship without employees, then you can use your Social Security number for your tax ID, just as you do when filling out your personal income tax statements. If you have employees or partners or are incorporated, you need to get a federal tax identification number (TIN) for your business, otherwise known as an Employee Identification Number (TEIN.) You just need to fill out Form SS-4, downloadable from www.irs.ustreas.gov/prod/forms_pubs/forms.html.

➤ Local Taxes

Next, you need to get a resale certificate from your local tax authority. This is handled differently from place to place and state to state. But they are typically inexpensive and easy to get—check the government pages in the phone book. You'll need it for three reasons:

1. It lets you avoid paying sales taxes on items that you are buying for resale or for assembly into items you will resell.

2. You will learn about whatever municipal business taxes you will need to pay for the privilege of doing business in your city.

3. You will use it to submit your sales tax receipts to your state sales tax authority.

➤ Sales Taxes

This brings us to the confusing world of sales taxes. You are sitting in your town/state, filling orders through a Web site that is probably hosted in another town/state from a buyer in another town/state. (Or they could be in a different country, but we won't go into that.) Each of these may have a separate sales tax. You, the seller, are supposed to collect the tax. But which do you pay? And since there are more than thirty thousand taxing entities in the United States, many of them overlapping, how do you know what tax rate to use?

Thanks to various laws and court cases, the answer, at this writing, is that you collect the sale and use tax for the state or states in which you have a *nexus*—a physical presence. If you are in state X, you collect the sales tax of state X from buyers in state X. You'll be filled in on the details when you get your reseller certificate.

Meanwhile, you'll note that buyers in other states escape paying any sales tax on what you are selling. Because the tax is collected by the vendor, tacked onto the final sale total, that means that out-of-state buyers pay less for the same items, and you may automatically be at a competitive disadvantage to vendors located outside your state when it comes to selling to buyers inside your state.

This is why you see traditional vendors setting up subsidiaries to handle their e-commerce efforts. A company that has stores in 20 states will have to collect sales or use taxes from online buyers in those 20 states, because the company has an undeniable nexus in each. And that will put it at a disadvantage against a dot-com competitor that may have a presence in only one state. So the storefront firm sets up an e-commerce subsidiary that likewise has only one nexus. (Notice we are only talking about the collection of sales taxes. In theory, the buyer still owes it. And for taxes on cars, boats, planes, artwork, and furniture, states have been known to make collection efforts.)

When considering the nexus concept, keep in mind that:

- Your Web host is not considered to constitute a physical presence for your business and so does not create a nexus.
- Almost any other stationary physical presence can create a nexus, including warehouse space and even vacant storefronts whose leases have not run out. (Trucks in transit usually don't count.)

The sales tax situation may not sound like it is totally fair or thoroughly thought out. It's not and it wasn't—it is the result of the collision of various laws and court cases. As you'll see later, there is an ongoing effort to tinker with it, but so far these efforts appear to have satisfied no one.

One final issue before we go on: If you are selling software via downloads, you must find out from your state tax authority if your state considers such software to be "tangible personal property." If so, you will have to collect sales taxes from buyers in your state. Otherwise, maybe not.

➤ The Big Picture, Tax-Wise

Many issues were settled in 1996 when the city of Tacoma, Washington, decided to catch the Internet wave in terms of taxes. It declared that all ISPs and online services doing business within the city were telephone utilities and subject to the same 6 percent tax on total receipts generated within the city to which other phone utilities were subject. It also decided that any online vendor that sold anything to a Tacoma resident needed to pay the city's annual municipal business tax of $72.

On paper, the plan was hard to fault. However:

- The tax on telephone utilities was justified by the fact that the phone companies are regulated monopolies that are virtually guaranteed a profit. Although phone companies would love to see ISPs treated like themselves because of the competitive threat of voice-over-Internet software, the ISPs are clearly not regulated monopolies.
- If all 30,000 taxing entities in the United States started imposing Internet business taxes, the result would be chaos.

So Tacoma's action was greeted with gales of derision and was soon repealed. Reaction reached the national level with the passage of the U.S. Internet Tax Freedom Act (Public Law 105–277) in October 1998. It declared a three-year moratorium (until October 21, 2001) on three things:

1. *Special taxes on the Internet.* State and local governments are barred from taxing Internet access fees. Certain states that had already imposed such taxes before 1998 were grandfathered, meaning they could carry on as before.

2. *Multiple, discriminatory e-commerce taxes.* Local governments cannot impose taxes that would subject buyers and sellers of e-commerce to taxation in multiple states.

Neither can they impose special taxes on e-commerce or try to make funny interpretations of the nexus concept.

3. *Any taxation of Internet-only goods.* This provision protects from taxation, for the duration of the moratorium, goods or services with no comparable offline equivalents sold exclusively over the Internet.

The law also set up a commission to study the question of whether and how Internet sales should be taxed and declared that it was the sense of Congress that no federal taxes should be levied on Internet commerce or Internet access. It also called for the Internet to be made an international tariff-free zone, but of course no one government has the power to do that. And it asked the U.S. Department of Commerce to look into barriers hindering the competitiveness of U.S. businesses engaged in electronic commerce abroad.

The commission basically punted. Nevertheless, there may be changes in the sales tax picture. Of course, despite Congress's brave words, you can bet that there will be some kind of screwy sales tax structure. But it will probably not be a question of "every tax entity for itself." Tacoma saw to that.

---

(20)/(20)

Being located in Colorado, the Scrappin' Happy Web site at scrappinhappy.safeshopper.com has to charge a tax on the scrapbook supplies it sells to Colorado residents—but to them only, explains owner Carrie Hardy. As opposed to a sales tax, Colorado's use tax is based only on the taxes that both the buyer and the seller have in common in their jurisdictions. The tax is added to the order before shipping, and the buyer is sent the final price in the shipping notification, which is also the final invoice.

■ CREDIT CARD FRAUD

That someone places an order for what you are offering indicates they do indeed want it. Alas—and we may need to break this to you gently—that is not an indication that they intend to pay for it. They can use credit card fraud to steal it from you. Worse yet, you eagerly packed and shipped it to them with your best wishes.

That the credit card company gave authorization—in other words, said the card was valid—is no guarantee that you will get paid. The card could have fallen into the wrong hands and not been reported stolen yet. The number (rather than the physical card) could have been lifted, with the owner remaining unaware. Or it could have been issued under false pretenses (increasingly common under a scam called *identity theft*, where the thief applies for credit cards using the name and data of someone else) to someone who had no intention of paying.

Of course, most people are honest and do pay for what they buy—the system would collapse otherwise. The trick, then, is to spot the small percentage that is not honest. You can't look into the customer's soul, but there are surface manifestations of iniquity that you can look for.

➤ Funny Billing Addresses

If your merchant bank offers AVS, consider using it. AVS checks that the billing address given by the buyer matches the address on file for that card with the credit card company. If the card is stolen, the thief is unlikely to know the victim's address and is unlikely to give his own, so he will probably make up something. If you don't have that service, you can still manually check to see if the address is valid. For instance, you can go online at Yahoo! Maps (maps.yahoo.com) and see if it can map the address. Checking in phone books and the like may also reassure you.

➤ Ship-to Addresses in Certain Developing Countries

AVS does not work outside the United States. Meanwhile, fraud has proven to be a problem with customers who live in nations that are on the economic frontier, so to speak. Yahoo! Store has found that most fraudulent orders come from Romania, Macedonia, Belarus, Pakistan, Russia, Lithuania, Egypt, Nigeria, Colombia, Malaysia, and Indonesia. Orders from the first three are said to be nearly 100 percent fraudulent.

➤ Funny E-Mail Addresses

Anyone can immediately get an e-mail address at free services such as Hotmail under a made-up name and use it once—to place a fraudulent order. If you trace the address, you won't find anything useful.

➤ Expensive but Irrational Orders

A private individual orders a dozen Nintendo 64 video game players—but how many people have that many kids? Even if she did, how come she ordered none of the accessories and games?

➤ Overnight Shipping

Why should the thief have to wait for his stuff? Especially when he is not going to pay for express shipping any more than he is going to pay for the hardware?

➤ "Leave at Door"

Someone ordering a new set of bath towels might feel comfortable telling the shipper to just leave the box at the door. Someone ordering diamond jewelry probably would not—unless she doesn't live there anyway but knows that she needs to give you a valid shipping address and intends to scoop up the box before the real occupant gets home.

➤ Shipping and Billing Addresses Don't Match

In the business world, it is common to have items delivered to one place and the bill sent to another. With individuals, it is not common, and a policy of sending expensive items only to the billing address is entirely justified.

➤ Fresh Meat

Thieves are said to target new sites under the assumption that the newly minted merchants are babes in the woods who have not read the preceding material.

Okay, so you've gotten an order from motherteresa@ hotmail.com for three pearl necklaces for overnight delivery to an address that is different from the billing address. The addresses check out. You feel uncomfortable about the order, but that does not mean the order is fraudulent—someone could be having a big wedding.

What you can do is call the customer. Ask for verification of the billing information and then ask for home and office contact information on the pretense that it might be needed if there is a problem with delivery. Actually, you are just interested in seeing if the person is willing to talk to you. Do they sound suspicious, evasive, or forgetful of the order? If so, press on and say that because your system is down, you need the name and address of the bank that issued the card. (It's on the back of the card, but a thief won't have the card.) And for similar reasons, you need a different e-mail address.

If in the end you still feel uncomfortable, you can cancel the order or ask for payment in advance. Call back and refer to the policies of your "credit department." If the person is a thief, you will probably never hear from her again. If she is legitimate, she may try to meet your conditions.

If your customers are overseas, you may have to contact them by e-mail—or you may decide not to handle overseas orders. Many sites do not.

20/20

"I've only had two cases of bad credit card numbers," recalls Carrie Hardy. "Both came back 'denied.' I tried calling the buyers, but they had given bad phone numbers as well.

"In two other cases they gave me a bad credit card number, and I was able to call them and get the good number," she says.

EXPERTS SPEAK

"Don't ship just because you are too lazy to look into a red flag," warns John Schulte. "There are always people scamming, and you just have to accept that fact and do the best you can. It doesn't seem to be hurting that many people, though."

➤ AVS (Address Verification System)

A common way to protect yourself again fraud is AVS—the source of the red flag that Schulte mentions. It is (typically) an optional service offered by your merchant bank that checks the address given by the buyer with the address on file for that cardholder. The AVS data is included in the authorization code sent back to you by the merchant bank after the card number is initially processed.

Although AVS is said to reduce fraud drastically, it has gray areas, and you need to understand it to use it effectively. Basically, it works by including the numeric parts of the address given by the buyer (the street number and the zip code but not the apartment number and suite number) for comparison with the address on file. A code is then generated and returned with the authorization data, showing how close the match was.

But people move. They transpose numbers. They put down a five-digit zip code when the file shows the nine-digit version. Complicated addresses run afoul of the slightest sloppiness— was it 123 34th Street or 1233 4th Street? Therefore, an unfavorable code does not guarantee that fraud is being perpetrated. But it is up to you how to proceed: to be brave and take risks, to probe the matter further as explained in the previous section, or to back out.

Meanwhile, AVS does not work outside the United States. If you stick strictly to AVS codes, you will do no international business.

Typical AVS codes returned in the authorization process:

X (Exact) Both the address and the nine-digit zip code match.

Y (Yes) Both the address and the five-digit zip code match.

A (Address) The address matches, but the five-digit zip code does not.

W (Whole zip) The address does not match, but the nine-digit zip code does match.

Z (Zip) The address does not match, but the five-digit zip code does match.

N (No) Neither the address nor the five-digit zip code is a match.

U (Unavailable) No information was available, or the bank that issues the card does not support AVS.

S (Unsupported) The bank that issued the card does not support AVS.

R (Retry) The system of the bank that issued the card was not available.

E (Edit error) An editing error made the transaction ineligible for AVS.

_ AVS was not performed, probably because some other problem prevented authorization.

If the code is given in two or three characters, then the first character indicates whether the address number matched and the second indicates whether the zip code matched. **Y** indicates a match, **N** indicates no match, and **X** indicates no data. The third character, if present, is a card identifier.

➤ Other Measures

The ESP's control system for your site will often include facilities to block orders from particular credit card numbers, card holders, or even Internet addresses. You may have to input the information manually, or you may be able to put a block on the information of a particular order that proved to be fraudulent. But in such cases the horse is already out of the barn.

■ DELIVERY FOUL-UPS

There are rules specifying how goods should be delivered, and you break them—inadvertently or otherwise—at your peril. The FTC has its Mail or Telephone Order Merchandise Rule that applies to orders placed via phone, fax, or Internet.

Under this rule, the bottom line is that you must have a reasonable basis for claiming that a product can be shipped within the time stated by your advertising. If a shipping period is not stated, then the default time is 30 days, and you must have a reasonable basis for believing that you can ship the product in 30 days.

If you can't ship within the stated delivery time (or within 30 days), you must notify the customer of the delay, provide a revised shipping date, and explain that the customer has a right to cancel the order at this point and get a full and prompt refund.

If this notification states that there will definitely be a delay of up to 30 days and the customer does not respond, you can treat the silence as consent to the delay. You can make the notification by e-mail, fax, or phone. You should record what was sent, when and how, and the customer's response.

If your notification states that there will definitely be a delay of more than 30 days or that there will be an indefinite delay, you must get the customer's consent—silence no longer counts. That can be in written, e-mail, or verbal form.

The same is true for second or subsequent delay notifications—you must get the customer's consent.

If the customer does not consent, you must refund all the money paid by the customer. The customer does not have to specifically ask for a refund.

Meanwhile, you have the right to cancel an order that you can't fulfill in a timely manner, but you have to notify the customer and make a prompt refund.

Up to the moment an order is placed, you can change your stated shipment promises to whatever seems reasonable as the situation demands. Updated information given at the Web site at the time of the order overrides promises made in previous advertising.

But the FTC stresses that promised shipping times must have a reasonable basis. If you claim faster delivery than is possible, just for the sake of spicing up the ad, that's false advertising.

■ FALSE ADVERTISING

Of course, you are honest by habit. Certainly, you don't tell whopping lies to total strangers you meet on the street. But you do want total strangers to buy your stuff. When writing advertising copy, you may find a certain degree of puffery creeping into the prose. It may keep creeping. And you may need to read the rest of this section.

Section 5 of the Federal Trade Commission Act gives the FTC the power to act against deceptive or unfair acts or practices in any medium. *Deceptive* is taken to mean that the act both misleads consumers and affects consumers' behavior or decisions about the product or service. In addition, an act or practice is *unfair* if the injury it causes, or is likely to cause, is:

- Substantial.
- Not outweighed by other benefits.
- Not reasonably avoidable.

Advertising must tell the truth and not be misleading. Deception can be by commission or omission—you can't say something is free when there are handling charges, for instance. And you must be able to substantiate any claims you make, especially if they concern health, safety, or performance. There is no concrete standard for documentation, but if you say that "tests showed it was 25 percent faster," then there needs to have been a test showing that result. (If there were 100 other tests with sadly different results, that's another issue.)

Third parties involved in the act, such as ad agencies, Web designers, and catalogue promoters, are responsible for participation in any deception they knew about or should have been suspicious of. The FTC calls on them to get the advertiser to substantiate any claims and not simply rely on the advertiser's assurances that their product will help the buyer lose 30 pounds overnight.

Those who persist can face fines of up to $11,000 per violation plus injunctions and court orders that would, if violated, carry their own fines. Contempt of court violations, meanwhile, can mean jail time. Plus you can expect civil suits to swoop down on you like vultures on carrion.

To avoid these fates:

- Disclaimers and disclosures must be clear and conspicuous, meaning that a consumer must be able to notice, read or hear, and understand the information.
- Simply putting in a disclaimer or disclosure does not get you off the hook for making a false or deceptive claim.

- Demonstrations must involve product performance under normal use.
- Refunds must be made to dissatisfied consumers if you at any time promised to make such refunds.

Meanwhile, specific situations and associated rules apply to specific industries or product categories. Now we'll look at the ones likely to apply to a Web retailer (skipping, for instance, the fascinating telemarketing rules.)

➤ Business Opportunities

The FTC's Franchise and Business Opportunity Rule requires that vendors of franchise and business opportunities give buyers a detailed disclosure document at least 10 days before the buyer pays any money or legally commits to a purchase. This document must include:

- The names, addresses, and telephone numbers of other purchasers.
- A fully audited financial statement of the seller.
- The background and experience of the business's key executives.
- The cost of starting and maintaining the business.
- The responsibilities of the seller and the buyer once the purchase is made.
- The basis for any projected earnings that were represented, including the number and percentage of owners who have done at least as well.

➤ Multilevel Marketing (MLM)

Also known as *network* or *matrix marketing*, MLM involves selling goods or services through distributorships, with commissions paid both for the sale of goods by a participant and for goods sold by a person that the participant recruited into the program.

If commissions are paid only for recruiting new distributors, who have to pay dearly for their distributorships, it's called a *pyramid scheme.* Such schemes collapse when the participants exhaust their circle of friends and no new recruits are forthcoming. And they are illegal in most states. Typically, only the original organizers see any money, and everyone else loses their investment.

The FTC says that MLMs should pay commissions for the retail sales of goods or services but not for recruiting new distributors.

MLMs that involve the sale of business opportunities or franchises must comply with specific rules, including disclosing the number and percentage of existing franchisees who have achieved the claimed results.

➤ Lending

The Truth in Lending Act requires creditors who deal with consumers to disclose information in writing about finance charges and related aspects of credit transactions, including finance charges expressed as an annual percentage rate. In certain transactions involving the establishment of a security interest in the consumer's principal dwelling not involving its construction, the consumer has a three-day right of rescission.

➤ Credit Problems

The Fair Credit Billing Act requires that you acknowledge consumer billing complaints promptly in writing and that you investigate billing errors. You cannot take any action that would adversely affect the consumer's credit standing until the investigation is completed. You are also required to promptly post payments to the consumer's account and either refund overpayments or credit them to the consumer's account.

The act also requires that consumer reporting agencies (CRAs), such as credit bureaus and resellers of consumer reports, ensure the confidentiality, accuracy, and legitimate use of such data. When someone takes adverse action against a consumer on the basis of information in a credit report, they must identify the CRA that provided the report so that the consumer can learn how to get a copy to verify or contest its accuracy and completeness.

Creditors and others may not knowingly provide false information to CRAs, which are required to maintain reasonable procedures to ensure the maximum possible accuracy of their data.

The Equal Credit Opportunity Act prohibits lenders from discriminating on the basis of race, color, religion, national origin, sex, marital status, age, receipt of public assistance, or an applicant's good faith exercise of his or her rights under the Consumer Credit Protection Act. Creditors must provide an applicant with the reason for a denial of credit if the applicant asks.

The Consumer Leasing Act regulates personal property leases that exceed four months and are made to consumers for personal, family, or household purposes. The statute requires that certain lease costs and terms be disclosed, imposes limitations on the size of penalties for delinquency or default and on the size of residual liabilities, and requires certain disclosures in lease advertising.

➤ Environmental Claims

Your stuff is "good for the environment"? What does that mean? The FTC doesn't know, either, and says that it is deceptive to misrepresent, directly or indirectly, that a product offers a general environmental benefit. Your ads should qualify broad environmental claims or, better yet, avoid them altogether.

Meanwhile, the FTC says that your ads shouldn't imply significant environmental benefits if the benefit isn't significant. It uses the example of trash bags that are touted as recyclable yet are sold for the purpose of being filled with refuse and put out with the garbage, so in practice they are not recycled. Therefore, calling them recyclable is deceptive because doing so implies a significant environment benefit.

➤ "Free" Products

To say that one item will be free if another item is purchased—"buy one, get one free"—indicates that the consumer will pay nothing for the one item and no more than the regular price for the other. Such ads, says the FTC, should describe all the terms and conditions of the free offer clearly and prominently.

➤ Jewelry

Gemstone treatments refer to the way some stones are altered or treated to enhance their appearance and/or durability. Consumers need to be told if a gemstone has been treated, if the treatment is not permanent, or if the treated stone requires special care. Instructions should be provided if special care is required.

With synthetic or imitation gemstones, you should tell the consumer that the gemstone is not natural even if it has the same composition and properties as a natural stone. These gemstones can be described as "synthetic gemstones," "laboratory-created gemstones," or "(name of manufacturer)-created gemstones."

Imitation gemstones, meanwhile, only outwardly resemble natural stones and may be made of glass, plastic, or non-precious stones. The FTC says that you can describe them as "imitation gemstones," "simulated gemstones," or some similar word or phrase that lets consumers know that the stone is neither natural nor synthetic.

Pearls made spontaneously by oysters and other mollusks may be described as "natural." But if you sell cultured or imitation pearls, you must tell consumers that the pearl is not natural. Cultured pearls are made by mollusks with human intervention and should be advertised and described as "cultured." Imitation pearls are man-made and should be advertised and described as "imitation."

➤ Negative Option Offers

If you have a thing-of-the-month club that ships merchandise to subscribers who have not declined, that's a *negative option offer.* The FTC requires that you clearly and conspicuously disclose material information about the terms of the plan. Once consumers agree to enroll, you must notify them before shipping to allow them to decline the merchandise. But on any automatic shipment or continuity program, you should be careful to clearly disclose the terms and conditions of the plan before billing consumers or charging their credit cards.

➤ 900 Numbers

The FTC requires that ads for pay-per-call services disclose the cost of the call. Ads for services that promote sweepstakes or games of chance, provide information about a government program (but are not sponsored by a government agency), or target individuals younger than 18 years of age require additional disclosures.

Ads for 900 numbers cannot be directed at children under 12 unless the number concerns a bona fide education service.

➤ Testimonials and Endorsements

These must reflect typical experiences of consumers—unless the material clearly and conspicuously states otherwise. Stating that "your mileage may vary" or otherwise noting that not everyone will get the same result is not enough to qualify a claim. Additionally:

- Testimonials and endorsements can't be used to make a claim that the advertiser itself cannot substantiate.
- Nonobvious connections between an endorser and the company must be disclosed, whether they have to do with a financial arrangement for a favorable endorsement, a position with the company, or stock ownership.
- Expert endorsements must be based on appropriate tests or evaluations performed by people who have mastered the subject matter.

➤ Warranties

Warranties must be available before purchase for consumer products that cost more than $15. If your ad mentions a warranty on a product that can be purchased by mail, phone, or computer, it must tell consumers how to get a copy of the warranty.

➤ Guarantees

If your ad uses phrases such as "satisfaction guaranteed" or "money-back guarantee," you must be willing to give full refunds for any reason. If this offer involves terms, the consumer must be told of them.

➤ Wool and Textile Products

The Textile and Wool Acts require you to clearly and conspicuously disclose in each advertisement for a wool or textile product that the article is made in the United States, imported, or both. Just stating that all your products are either made domestically or imported is not enough. When touting fiber content, the generic names of the fibers (those names have been assigned by the FTC) must appear in their order of predominance by weight, but it is not necessary to include the percentage of each fiber.

Fibers present in amounts of less than 5 percent are to be listed as "other fiber(s)."

➤ **Made in the U.S.A.**

A product has to be "all or virtually all made in the United States" for it to be advertised or labeled as "Made in the U.S.A."

■ CHILDREN'S ISSUES

➤ **Advertising**

The FTC calls for extra care concerning advertising directed at children and points to rules issued by the Children's Advertising Review Unit (CARU) of the Council of Better Business Bureaus. The CARU rules contain provisions specific to the Internet, but the rules also state that these provisions must be interpreted in the context of the rest of the CARU rules.

General Rules

These are about what you would expect when the idea is to keep inexperienced, imaginative children from being exploited. A summation:

- Advertising must not mislead children about the product's features, benefits, and performance.
- Product claims must be factual and made clearly in age-appropriate language with age-appropriate child models.
- Demonstrations must be realistic and show safe use with appropriate protective equipment and adult supervision.
- Food, when shown being eaten, must be consumed in a healthy manner.
- The use of frightening material is forbidden.
- Targeting must be age appropriate.
- The advertiser must be able to substantiate any product claims, just as with adult advertising.
- There can be no use of peer pressure or promises of social success (or threats of social rejection.)
- *Only* or *just* cannot be used with the price.
- There must be clear, age-appropriate disclosures of any required notices, of any need for assembly or to supply

batteries, or of options or auxiliary items that must be purchased separately.

- Endorsements must represent the actual experience of the endorser. Celebrities may nonetheless endorse as long as their professions do not link them with the product.
- Cartoon characters may not pitch products in or adjacent to entertainment involving those characters. (But see the next section.)
- Premiums, if used, must be clearly distinguished from products.
- Club memberships must be clearly distinguished from product purchases, and there must be some interactive, ongoing activity exclusive to the club members before you can call it a club.
- The odds involved in any contests must be explained in age-appropriate language.
- Medications, drugs, and supplemental vitamins cannot be advertised to children.
- Children should not be urged to ask an adult to buy a product.

Finally, it is specifically forbidden to ask a child to hold a telephone receiver up to the TV to pick up dial tones played by the commercial and thus dial the phone. (The things you learn....)

Internet-Specific Rules
The rules say that advertisers who transact sales with children online should make reasonable efforts to provide the person responsible for the costs of the transaction with the means to exercise control over the transaction.

If there is no reasonable means provided to avoid unauthorized purchases of goods and services by children, the advertiser should enable the person responsible to cancel the order and receive full credit without incurring any charges. (Keep in mind that under existing state laws, parents may not be obligated to fulfill sales contracts entered into by their underage children anyway.) Additionally,

- Children should always be told when they are being targeted for a sale.
- If a site offers the opportunity to order or purchase any product or service either through the use of a Click Here to

Order button or other onscreen means, the ordering instructions must clearly and prominently state that a child must have a parent's permission to order.

- In the case of online ordering, there should be a clear mechanism after the order is placed allowing the child or parent to cancel the order.
- Web sites sponsored by advertisers must be clearly labeled as such.
- Cartoon character–driven Web sites may include ad pitches from those characters, but these must be clearly labeled as advertising.

➤ Data Collection

As of April 21, 2000, the U.S. Children's Online Privacy Protection Act began regulating the online collection of personal information from children under 13. The law will be enforced by the FTC against any Web site that:

- Is directed at children and collects information from children.
- Is directed at the general public but knowingly collects information from children.

The rule applies to all information collected from children after that date even if the site has previously collected data from the child or the child has already registered at the site. The FTC has to right to decide for itself based on content, whether a site is directed at children. Its rules apply to individually identifiable information about a child that is collected online, such as full name, home address, e-mail address, telephone number, or any other information that would allow someone to identify or contact the child. General information that is linked to the identifiable information is also covered, such as hobbies and interests plus information gathered by cookies or other tracking mechanisms.

Infraction invokes penalties similar to those of other FTC rules. Participation in an industry self-regulatory program, with guidelines that include independent monitoring and disciplinary procedures that have been approved by the FTC, can serve as a safe harbor against any enforcement actions under the rule.

The rule mandates:

- On-site disclosure notices.
- Parental notification.
- Verifiable parent consent.
- Exceptions where parental consent is not required.
- Situations where new consent is required.
- Data disclosure to parents on demand.
- Parental right to revoke consent and delete information.

On-site Disclosure Notices

An operator must post a link to a notice of its information practices on the home page of its Web site or online service and in each area where it collects personal information from children. An operator of a general audience site with a separate children's area must post a link to its notice on the home page of the children's area.

The link to the privacy notice must be clear and prominent. Operators may want to use a larger font size or a different color type on a contrasting background to make it so. A link in small print at the bottom of the page—or a link that is indistinguishable from other links on your site—is not considered clear and prominent. The notice must be clearly written and understandable; it should not include any unrelated or confusing materials. It must state the following information:

- The name and contact information (address, telephone number, and e-mail address) of all operators collecting or maintaining children's personal information through the Web site or online service.
- If more than one operator is collecting information at the site, the site may select and provide contact information for only one operator who will respond to all inquiries from parents about the site's privacy policies. Still, the names of all the operators must be listed in the notice.
- The kinds of personal information collected from children (for example, name, address, e-mail address, hobbies, etc.).
- How the information is collected—directly from the child or passively, say, through cookies.
- How the operator uses the personal information. For example, is it for marketing back to the child? Notifying contest

winners? Allowing the child to make the information publicly available through a chat room?

■ Whether the operator discloses information collected from children to third parties.

If the latter is true, the operator must disclose:

■ The kinds of businesses in which the third parties are engaged.
■ The general purposes for which the information is used.
■ Whether the third parties have agreed to maintain the confidentiality and security of the information.
■ That the parent has the option to agree to the collection and use of the child's information without consenting to the disclosure of the information to third parties.
■ That the operator may not require a child to disclose more information than is reasonably necessary to participate in an activity as a condition of participation.
■ That the parent can review the child's personal information, ask to have it deleted and refuse to allow any further collection or use of the child's information.
■ The notice also must state the procedures for the parent to follow.

Parental Notification
A notice must be sent to the parents containing the same information as at the Web site. The notice must also state that the operator wishes to collect personal information from the child and that the parent's consent is required for the collection, use, and disclosure of the information. It must explain how the parent can provide consent.

The notice to parents must be written clearly and understandably and must not contain any unrelated or confusing information. An operator may use any one of a number of methods to notify a parent, including sending an e-mail or surface mail.

Verifiable Parental Consent
Before collecting, using, or disclosing personal information from a child, an operator must obtain verifiable parental consent from the child's parent. Through April 2002, the FTC will

use a sliding scale to determine how rigorous the consent procedure needs to be. After that, details may change, subject to a review of its experience. The initial rule defines three levels of use:

Internal Use.   Operators may use e-mail to get parental consent for internal uses, such as marketing back to a child based on expressed preferences or sending promotional updates about site content, as long as they take additional steps to increase the likelihood that the parent has, in fact, provided the consent. For example, operators might seek confirmation from a parent in a follow-up e-mail or confirm the parent's consent by letter or phone call.

Public Disclosures.   When an operator wants to disclose a child's personal information to third parties or make it publicly available (for example, through a chat room or message board), they must use a more reliable method of consent, including:

- Getting a signed form from the parent via mail or fax.
- Accepting and verifying a credit card number.
- Taking calls from parents through a toll-free telephone number staffed by trained personnel.
- E-mail accompanied by digital signature.
- E-mail accompanied by a personal identification number (PIN) or password obtained through one of the verification methods just described.

But in the case of a monitored chat room, if all individually identifiable information is stripped from postings before they are made public—and the information is deleted from the operator's records—an operator does not have to get prior parental consent.

Limited Disclosure Option.   An operator must give a parent the option to agree to the collection and use of the child's personal information without agreeing to the disclosure of the information to third parties. That is, a parent can grant consent to allow his or her child to participate in activities on the site without consenting to the disclosure of the child's information to third parties.

Exceptions

The regulations include several exceptions that allow operators to collect a child's e-mail address without getting the parent's consent in advance. These exceptions cover many children's common online activities, including contests, online newsletters, homework help, and electronic postcards. Additionally, prior parental consent is not required when:

- An operator collects a child's or parent's e-mail address to provide notice and seek consent.
- An operator collects an e-mail address to respond to a one-time request from a child and then deletes it.
- An operator collects an e-mail address to respond more than once to a specific request—say, for a subscription to a newsletter. In this case, the operator must notify the parent that it is communicating regularly with the child and give the parent the opportunity to stop the communication before sending or delivering a second communication to a child.
- An operator collects a child's name or online contact information to protect the safety of a child who is participating on the site. In this case, the operator must notify the parent and give him or her the opportunity to prevent further use of the information.
- An operator collects a child's name or online contact information to protect the security or liability of the site or to respond to law enforcement, if necessary, and does not use it for any other purpose.

New Notice for Consent

An operator is required to send a new notice and request for consent to parents if there are material changes in the collection, use, or disclosure practices to which the parent had previously agreed. For instance, the operator may have gotten consent to disclose to a maker of stuffed animals, but with the passage of time she wants to sell the list to a maker of diet pills. That would require new notice and consent.

Data Disclosure to Parents

At a parent's request, operators must disclose the general kinds of personal information they collect from children (for example, name, address, telephone number, e-mail address, and hobbies) plus the specific information collected from the child.

Operators must ensure that they are dealing with the child's parent before they provide access to the child's specific information. They can use a variety of methods to verify the parent's identity, including:

- Getting a signed form from the parent via mail or fax.
- Accepting and verifying a credit card number.
- Taking calls from parents on a toll-free telephone number staffed by trained personnel.
- E-mail accompanied by digital signature.
- E-mail accompanied by a PIN or password obtained through one of the previous verification methods.

Revoking Consent and Deleting Information
At any time, a parent may revoke consent, refuse to allow an operator to collect further information or make further use of the information, and direct the operator to delete whatever information has been collected.

In turn, the operator may terminate any service provided to the child—but only if the information at issue is reasonably necessary for the child's participation. For example, an operator may require children to provide their e-mail addresses to participate in a chat room so that the operator can contact a youngster if he is misbehaving in the chat room. If, after giving consent, a parent asks the operator to delete the child's information, the operator may refuse to allow the child to participate in the chat room in the future. If other activities on the Web site do not require the child's e-mail address, the operator must allow the child access to those activities.

Chapter 16

Charting Your Results

The fact that money comes in is not enough. Well, admittedly, it's a good start, but you cannot sit on your hands. As soon as you do that, you'll find that some competitor has been staying up nights—and the results will be unpleasant for you.

In terms of e-commerce, that guy who is up at night is looking for ways to improve his operation by finding out what works and what does not and eliminating the latter. There are two principles to keep in mind:

1. *The Blitzkrieg Principle.* Reinforce success. Do not waste resources propping up failure. Make your major commitment to the sector where the breakout has occurred.

2. *The 80/20 Rule.* Eighty percent of your profit comes from 20 percent of your business. So identify that 20 percent and go after it.

Keep in mind, however, that you can take these metaphors too far. After all, you can't always just walk away from the line-holding 80 percent that was not involved in the breakout—the market could change tomorrow. But the situation is hopeless unless you know which is which.

The shopping-cart software of most ESPs will offer facilities (perhaps for an optional cost) that can help you figure out which is which.

■ HITS (PAGE VIEWS)

Hits indicates the number of times a file was transmitted by the server at the request of a browser. Notice that we said *file* and not *page*. A page might consist of the HTML file and 20 graphics files, and so accessing it would cause the server to log 21 hits. A hit on the HTML file itself is usually called a *page view* and is a more accurate measure of traffic. (Look around and you'll see large organizations calmly bragging about the total hits on their graphics-rich sites, comparing themselves favorably to sites that are measuring page views.)

Therefore, traffic reports should be restricted to the HTML files. Figure 16.1 shows such a report, which displays both hits on the home page and each internal page. Figure 16.2 shows details for an individual page over time.

Hits	Items Sold	Revenue	Page
215,130			Front Page
143,431			Shopping Basket
84,150			Info Page
26,275			Search
23,645	2,570	61619.67	Xenadrine RFA-1, 120 capsules, Cytodyne
14,788			Index
13,782			Creatine Monohydrate
11,132			Rate Us
10,946	6	124.70	Free Samples Drawing Win 6000 grams creatine monohydra
10,801	2,758	18641.44	Androstenedione 100 mg 60 capsules
10,168	379	18340.30	Creatine Monohydrate 2000 grams Value Nutrition
9,789			Androstenedione
9,657			Shop by 100s of Vitamin/Mineral/Sports Nutrition Companie
9,532	52	1216.80	Creatine Creatine Monohydrate 1000 grams Value Nutrition
7,053			TwinLab Products

Figure 16.1 This report generated by store.yahoo.com for an actual store shows the hits during the previous year for each page of the site. For item pages, it shows the number of items sold over that period as well as the revenue generated.

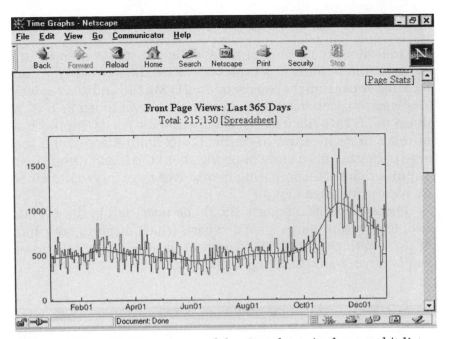

Figure 16.2 Clicking on one of the tiny charts in the page hit list in Figure 16.1 generates a full-screen version. This one is of the front page (the site's home page), with the jagged line showing the daily total and the smooth line showing the running average. Obviously, hits were generally stable for most of the year, with a modest surge in March followed by summer doldrums—until the Christmas buying season arrived like an earthquake.

Hits on the home page are usually a good indicator of how many total visitors you received, because people rarely jump directly to an internal page. (But there is, you should realize, nothing to stop them from doing that.) Tracked over time, the home-page hits figure is of great importance, because it indicates whether your marketing is having an impact—especially if the sales go up in proportion to the hits. But hits by themselves are meaningless—you are supposed to be selling something, not providing eye candy for Web surfers. You want buyers, not traffic.

The ratio between visitors and buyers is called the *conversion rate*. There is no average or standard conversion rate because every site's situation is different, but you should be happy if it is several percentage points.

Like the number of hits, the conversion rate, too, should be tracked over time. A sudden falloff can mean that your marketing is reaching the wrong audience. Figure 16.3 is a chart indicating the number of orders compared with the number of hits (the conversion rate) at an actual store (where, you'll note, the rate held steady).

Meanwhile, tracking the number of hits per internal page can also indicate what part of the site your visitors find genuinely interesting. But if there are no hits at all on a given page, the links to it may simply not be working.

Tracking the hits by time of day can also be illuminating. If they are heaviest during business hours or lunch, your visitors may be surfing from the office. That may indicate that radio would be a good advertising choice, because commuters and

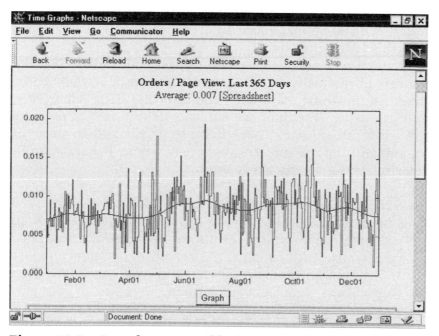

Figure 16.3 One of many possible time-series graphs that can be generated by store.yahoo.com, this one shows orders compared against page views (hits), a measure of the conversion rate, or how many visitors actually bought something. Trends in this rate over time can tell a site manager if serious buyers are being attracted. In this case the ratio held fairly steady at just under 1 percent—but there were dramatic spikes that the manager might want to investigate.

office workers listen to the radio. If hits predominate in the evening, your visitors may be coming from home, indicating that TV and newspapers might be better for that purpose. If there is a lot of traffic after midnight, they may be from overseas, something you can confirm by studying "referring URL" reports (see the next section.)

The hit numbers, incidentally, are never going to be scientifically accurate, as indicated in the discussion of Click Trails (also discussed in the next section). But since the source of inaccuracy is constant, you can still use the numbers as guides.

■ REFERRING URLS

Most browsers can tell a server what URL someone was at before they came to yours, and your shopping-cart software can often gather statistics from these. Figure 16.4 shows such a report, with additional information on how much revenue each referring URL generated.

But keep in mind that some visitors will have typed the address in manually or will have clicked on it in their bookmark list, meaning that there is no referring URL. Reportedly, you can expect that half of your site visitors will have come from a referring site. That, however, is enough to produce meaningful data. There are two areas where the tracking of referring URLs is particularly useful:

- *Search engines.* When the reference is a search engine, the system should also be able to record what the search word was (because the search results are on a specially generated page whose URL contains the search parameters). Figure 16.5 shows an example. In this way you can know what your visitors were looking for when they came to your site. You can know what descriptors are working and what search engines tend to generate traffic for your site (in case you were thinking of advertising).
- *Link exchanges.* If you have exchanged links with another site (as explained in Chapter 11), then you will want to track how many visitors came from that site and how much they spent. You may have to search through generic reports for

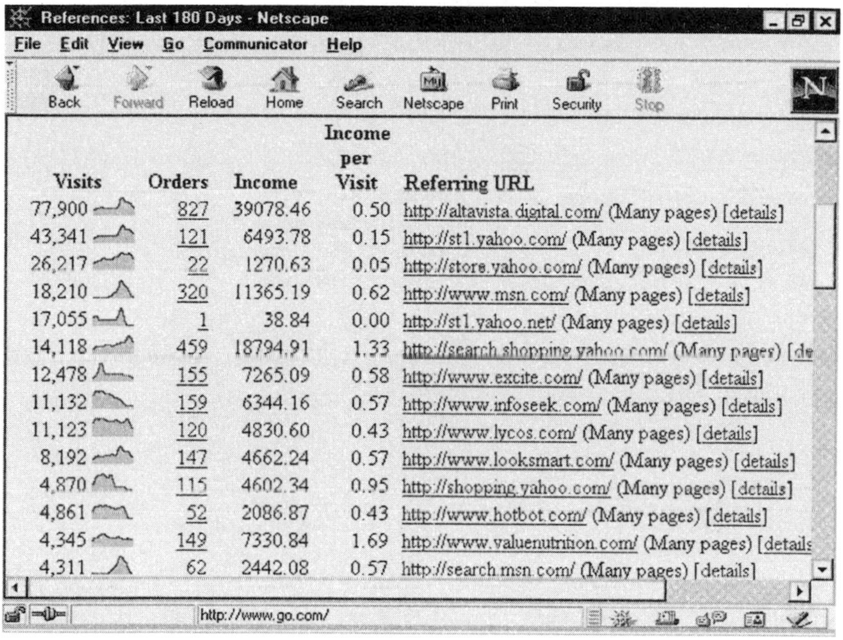

Visits	Orders	Income	Income per Visit	Referring URL
77,900	827	39078.46	0.50	http://altavista.digital.com/ (Many pages) [details]
43,341	121	6493.78	0.15	http://st1.yahoo.com/ (Many pages) [details]
26,217	22	1270.63	0.05	http://store.yahoo.com/ (Many pages) [details]
18,210	320	11365.19	0.62	http://www.msn.com/ (Many pages) [details]
17,055	1	38.84	0.00	http://st1.yahoo.net/ (Many pages) [details]
14,118	459	18794.91	1.33	http://search.shopping.yahoo.com/ (Many pages) [de
12,478	155	7265.09	0.58	http://www.excite.com/ (Many pages) [details]
11,132	159	6344.16	0.57	http://www.infoseek.com/ (Many pages) [details]
11,123	120	4830.60	0.43	http://www.lycos.com/ (Many pages) [details]
8,192	147	4662.24	0.57	http://www.looksmart.com/ (Many pages) [details]
4,870	115	4602.34	0.95	http://shopping.yahoo.com/ (Many pages) [details]
4,861	52	2086.87	0.43	http://www.hotbot.com/ (Many pages) [details]
4,345	149	7330.84	1.69	http://www.valuenutrition.com/ (Many pages) [details
4,311	62	2442.08	0.57	http://search.msn.com/ (Many pages) [details]

Figure 16.4 The References report generated by store.yahoo.com concerning an actual store, showing the Web addresses from which visitors came. The list, in this case, is ranked according to the number of visitors that came from a site, but the chart also shows how much income—and average income per visitor—was generated by each referring site. The full list showed more than sixteen hundred referring sites during the course of a year. Notice that some leading referring sites generated little revenue.

the site, or your system may give you a way to register a link so that traffic from there is specially tracked.

■ SEARCHES

The reports on referring URLs can tell you what search engines and search words led visitors to your site. But if your site has a search facility generated by the shopping cart, the system itself should likewise be able to track what search words your visitors

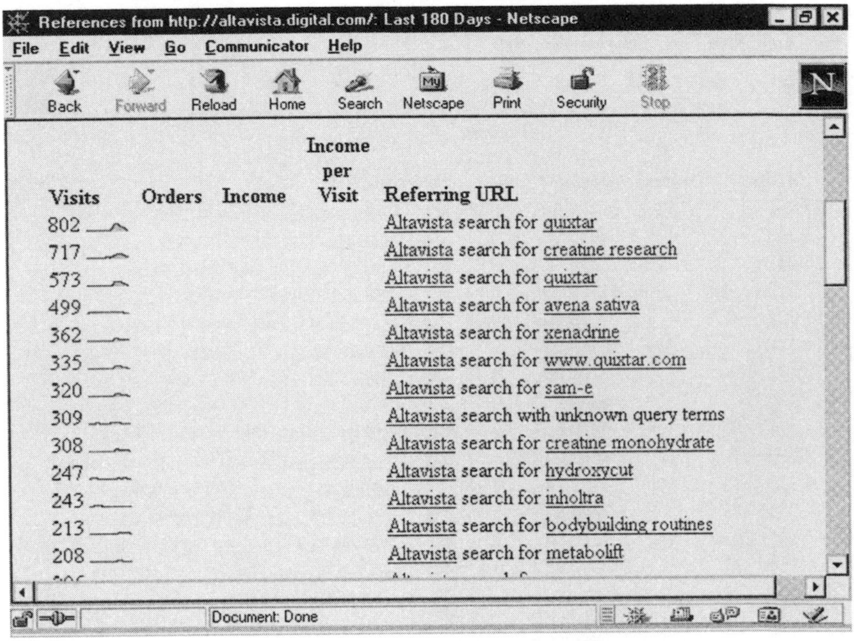

Visits	Orders	Income	Income per Visit	Referring URL
802				Altavista search for quixtar
717				Altavista search for creatine research
573				Altavista search for quixtar
499				Altavista search for avena sativa
362				Altavista search for xenadrine
335				Altavista search for www.quixtar.com
320				Altavista search for sam-e
309				Altavista search with unknown query terms
308				Altavista search for creatine monohydrate
247				Altavista search for hydroxycut
243				Altavista search for inholtra
213				Altavista search for bodybuilding routines
208				Altavista search for metabolift

Figure 16.5 Clicking the Details option for the first line of the chart in Figure 16.4 generated this chart, which shows what keyword the users were searching for when they came to the site from the referring URL, which happened to have been a search engine (AltaVista.)

used. Figure 16.6 shows an example report, including the ever-present most-popular search word.

Knowing what search words were used can give you a glimpse of the way your customers' minds are working (skipping the aforementioned most-popular search word). You might be surprised by the terminology they are using and decide to include it in your descriptor text, as explained in Chapter 8. You might realize that they are having a hard time finding something and choose to reorganize your site. Or you may discover that your site is missing something that they expect or that they have confused your site with something else.

■ CLICK TRAILS

A *click trail* is the path followed by an individual site visitor as he or she goes from one page to another. Figure 16.7 shows a

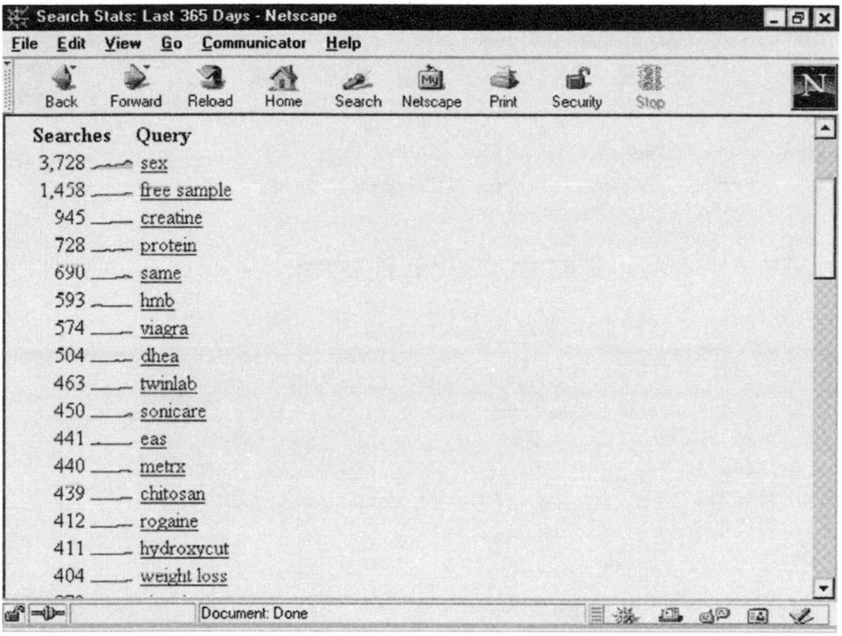

Figure 16.6 This is the Search report generated for an actual online store by store.yahoo.com, showing the words or phrases used by customers at the site's own search facility, ranked by the number of times each was used. You'll note that the first entry was used almost three times more often than the second and is also reportedly the most common word searched for on Web search engines.

report on one trail that culminated in a purchase. Following such trails can give you an idea of how your site looks to your visitors; following the paths of people who actually bought something can indicate what their decision process was like and where their interests lay. But following the paths of non-buyers can also be illuminating—if a lot of people put an item in their shopping cart and then abandoned it after looking at a certain page, you might want to ask why.

But be warned that you cannot take all click trails literally. Some will be garbage, and some will not tell the full tale. There are several reasons:

- *Caching.* If a visitor goes to a page and then returns to it later in that session, that person's browser will probably call

```
Trail of a Customer on Dec 30 - Netscape                                    _ 8 X
File   Edit   View   Go   Communicator   Help

  ◀        ▶        ⟳       ⌂        🔍        📧        🖨        🔒       🛑              N
 Back    Forward   Reload   Home    Search   Netscape   Print   Security   Stop


Time              Page
Dec 30 06:18:47   Fenu-Thyme Caps. 100 capsules, Nature's Way into shopping basket
Dec 30 06:18:47   Show shopping basket
Dec 30 06:19:04   Show shopping basket
Dec 30 06:19:28   Fenu-Thyme Caps. 100 capsules, Nature's Way
Dec 30 06:19:32
Dec 30 06:20:00   Vitanet Front Page
Dec 30 06:20:21   Search
Dec 30 06:20:28   Bee Pollen, 90 capsules, Health From the Sun/Bee Pollen into shopping basket
Dec 30 06:20:28   Show shopping basket
Dec 30 06:21:04   Bee Pollen 30 capsules Health From The Sun Bee Pollen
Dec 30 06:21:10   Bee Pollen CMP 1000MG 100 Capsules, American Health
Dec 30 06:21:21   Bee Pollen, 90 capsules, Health From the Sun/Bee Pollen
Dec 30 06:22:03   Place order vitanet-27664
Dec 30 06:23:06   Rate Us


              Document: Done
```

Figure 16.7 This screen shows an individual click trail report at an actual store. The customer initially added an item to the shopping cart, checked the shopping cart twice, browsed several other item pages, and ran a search that led to another item page, where he or she added a second item to the shopping cart. After looking at several more pages without selecting anything, the buyer went on to check out. (This is one of more than thirteen hundred click trails that day, of which 48 resulted in orders being placed.)

the page up for the second look from temporary storage (the *cache*) on the hard disk, rather than going back to the Web to ask for it again. So the visitor's second visit to that page will go unrecorded.

- *Proxy servers.* Some services perform intermediate storage (using what are called *proxy servers*) between your Web server and the user. This may make for faster connections, but the result can be that a page was fetched from the proxy rather than your Web server and therefore you do not know about it. When the proxy does come to your Web server for a fresh page, it may be for more than one user, or a single user may be handled by more than one proxy, making hash of the click trail.

- *Search engines.* These will visit a site periodically and leave click trails that may appear nonsensical.

■ REPEAT CUSTOMERS

Some systems will have a *repeat customer detector* that lets you know that you have achieved that Holy Grail, customer retention. It does this by examining orders as they come to see if the buyer's information matches the information on any previous orders.

You could, of course, do this manually with the customer database you are supposed to be maintaining. Loyalty should certainly be rewarded, perhaps by offering repeat customers discounts on further purchases.

Note that we are talking about repeat customers, not return visitors. No system can check to see if the latest site visitor has been there before—there is no way for the Web server to do that because today's browsers do not give away the identity of the user. You can only learn the domain that the visitor came through. This is, however, enough information to allow the authorities to catch those who engage in abusive behavior because the domain usually represents the perpetrator's ISP, and by using a subpoena, an investigator can learn who was online at the moment in question.

Chapter 17

Summing Things

The GartnerGroup of Stamford, Connecticut, one of the leading market research firms in information technology, issued findings in late 1999 that looked startling. It announced (at a conference in Cannes, France, of all places) that sometime around the years 2006 to 2008, e-commerce would cease to exist.

What it meant was that e-commerce as a separate and distinct way of doing business would fade away. In its place would be business, just business, some of which would be conducted online.

In the meantime, though, it predicted a roller coaster of failed expectations. The craze of Web-only dot-com start-ups that got going in the late 1990s would peak by 2002 with a steep crest of inflated expectations. Then, as it became clear that about 75 percent of e-business projects were failing to match their aspirations, the trend would crash into a "trough of disillusionment." The downward slope would be littered with investor abandonment, dot-com shakeouts, and heavily publicized failures.

But it would be the expectations that were at fault, not e-commerce itself. The participants had sought a magic road into the new digital economy without any regard for sound business models, strategies, and implementation.

In the meantime, those organizations that had sought to ignore what was happening on the Web would also feel considerable pain with their own waves of business failures.

But then true e-business based on reality rather than hype would slowly but steadily rise from the ashes. Steady experience would lead to optimized e-business until the year 2008, when the distinction between e-business and business will have faded away, predicted the analysts.

So if e-commence is fated to merge with commerce, let's look at the future of commerce. What the pundits see is a steady crescendo of noise—not the noise made by pushier and pushier advertising but the noise made by an avalanche of new products.

Mercer Management Consulting says that recent history points to a near future dominated by a glut of what it calls *value propositions*—a product or service (or combination of products, services, or both) offered at a set price. Today, a typical supermarket carries 50,000 SKUs, the firm complains. The number in 1970 was 20,000. About 25,000 new consumer SKUs were added in 1998 alone, compared with 4,414 introduced in 1980. Warehouse stores were adding SKUs at an annual compounded rate of 17 percent between 1986 and 1998. The total number of consumer packaged goods available in the United States today amounts to about 350,000 SKUs, or seven times the capacity of an average supermarket.

And the situation is not confined to the supermarket. In 1960, there were 161 mutual funds available to U.S. investors. The number rose to 361 by 1970 and to 564 by 1980. The total then mushroomed to 3,105 in 1990, and about 7,300 in the year 2000. Figuring in population growth, the number of funds per capita has grown by a factor of more than 27.

In the same period, the number of different credit cards available grew from a handful to about a hundred thousand, and the market was showing signs of saturation. In 1980, there were only a handful of sport utility vehicle models, whereas there are now more than 40 basic models. The total number of basic car models on the market was about two hundred sixty. And there were more than eighteen thousand consumer magazine titles published in 1998.

This is all well and good, but the flipside is that the populations of the Western developed countries are stable or declining. The U.S. population is growing at less than 1 percent a year, France and most Scandinavian countries are at almost zero population growth, Italy's and Portugal's populations are expected to begin declining soon, and the population of Russia has been in decline since 1990. Countries in other parts of the world can be expected to experience similar trends as they develop to the point where they can adopt a Western lifestyle and no longer need children as unpaid farmhands. But until they reach that point, they cannot be counted as full-fledged markets.

Therefore, more and more products are going to be pressed into the hands of about the same number of buyers. At some point in the foreseeable future, consumers will have an effectively infinite number of products from which to choose, in the sense that they could never get to them all. And they can never get to them all because (alas) the amount of spare time that individuals enjoy is not growing and could not keep up with the growth of SKUs even if it were.

So, says Mercer, what businesses will be competing for in the future will not be primarily revenue or profits or market share or shelf space but *mindshare*. If the buying public is mindful of you, those other things will follow. (And keep in mind that this means positive mindshare, where people know about you and like you. They can also know about you and dislike you—a lot of people knew what an Edsel was and nevertheless did not buy one.)

How to get their mindshare? Pumping money into advertising is not enough and just puts you with the rest of the herd anyway. (Mercer notes that total advertising spending in the United States rose from $19 billion in 1975 to $77 billion in 1996, adjusted for inflation. And we may see a point of diminishing returns with advertising, with consumers coming to resent heavy advertising as a waste of time.) The resulting advice is usually aimed at Fortune 1000 companies, but for small businesses it can be reformulated like this:

- *Reinforce success.* Find your strong point, be it ownership of a technical standard, a popular brand name, a good distribution channel, a loyal cadre of users, or your own industry experience, and work from it.
- *Focus on the buyer.* It's a greater marketing cliché. What it really means is that you need to find out not only what sells but also why it sells and why the other stuff does not. Get into the mind of the buyer.
- *Target the buyer.* Having identified the buyer and found out how he or she thinks, promote your product to that buyer. Don't worry about the growing mass of SKUs out there

competing for, if nothing else, the buyer's attention. Just get your message in front of your buyer.

- *Develop a relationship with that buyer.* Personalize your pitches as much as you can. Offer customer service as if everything depended on it. And that means a handsome, informative, easy-to-use Web site.

In the end, the buyers who matter will know about you and trust you and your product, making you the vendor of choice in your field, and they will regard the marketing efforts of the competitors as mere noise.

The point of this book is to put the tools of e-commerce into your hands for that purpose, especially since e-commerce, as we have shown, is on its way to becoming commerce, period. We hope we have also shown that:

- Setting up e-commerce sites can be done inexpensively and quickly through many specialized ESPs.
- Anyone with a browser can set up a site, but getting a merchant account to take credit card orders may be a bigger hurdle.
- Although you are not faced with the cost of setting up a store, you are still faced with the cost of customer acquisition. And that by itself makes customer retention worth the effort.
- Online marketing must respect the users (no spam or other reliance on unsolicited e-mail, in other words).
- There are marketing channels specific to the online world, such as search engines and Usenet newsgroups plus affiliate programs, virtual malls, auctions, and so on.
- Effective customer retention and marketing efforts require the creation of some kind of database of customers and prospects. The best way to create a list of prospects is through an opt-in page.
- You must respect the users' privacy concerns.
- There are specific rules to follow if you are marketing to children.

It's a new world, but it's one you should be taking into account if you are planning to start a business. The beauty of it is that in some cases, it may be the *only* world you need to take into account.

Appendix **A**

Sources
of Information

Note: Some of these sources are market research firms, and the information they put out is typically embodied in bound reports that cost hundreds or even thousands of dollars. However, to promote the sale of these reports, they announce the gist of them, often in press releases that you can find on their Web sites.

Disclaimer: Among the sources listed below, Wood has written for multiple Ziff Davis and CMP publications

2-Tier Affiliate Program Directory
www.2-tier.com/

Synergy Internet Marketing
5012 E. Roberts Lane
Nampa, ID 83687
phone (208) 461-2202

This site lists affiliate programs and includes background material that stresses the advantages of joining or producing an affiliate program—but it is honest about the pros and cons and the steps necessary to be successful.

ActivMedia Research
www.activmedia.com

> 46 Concord Street
> Peterborough, NH 03458
> phone (603) 924-9100, (800) 639-9481
> fax (603) 924-2184

This market research firm does ongoing studies of e-commerce.

American Express Small Business Exchange
home3.americanexpress.com/smallbusiness/

> American Express Company
> 200 Vesey Street
> New York, NY 10285
> phone (212) 640-2000
> fax (212) 619-9802

This site tries to be a sort of encyclopedia for small business, with material covering a broad range of business topics, including e-commerce and how to get an American Express card.

AssociatePrograms.com
www.associateprograms.com

> Lot 12, Esplanade
> Tuan, Queensland
> Australia 4650
> (No phone listed)

This site actually deals with affiliate programs and includes numerous links, both to affiliate programs and information about affiliates and a discussion board.

Bizreference.com
www.bizreference.com

> (no address given)

This site is an advertising-supported portal to sites containing information of interest to small businesses, including e-commerce.

Boston Consulting Group
www.bcg.com

> Exchange Place, 31st Floor
> Boston, MA 02109
> phone (617) 973-1200
> fax (617) 973-1339

This consulting firm has become very active in the field of e-commerce and posts synopses of its research on its Web site.

CashPile
cashpile.com

> (No address listed)

This site is devoted to affiliate programs and contains numerous links, listings, and background information on the topic.

Clickz
www.clickz.com

> 401 Andover Street
> North Andover, MA 01845
> phone (978) 681-4100
> fax (978) 681-0088

This ad-supported online magazine covers electronic business mostly from the advertising and marketing angle. If you are able to visit only one site when doing e-commerce background research, this one will suffice.

CommerceNet
www.commercenet.com

> 10050 N. Wolfe Road, Suite SW2-255
> Cupertino, CA 95014
> phone (408) 446-1260
> fax (408) 446-1268

CommerceNet is an industry association for firms involved in e-commerce, and its Web site has background material on a wide variety of e-commerce topics.

Computer Industry Almanac Inc.
www.c-i-a.com

> 1013 S. Belmont Avenue
> Arlington Heights, IL 60005
> phone (847) 718-0423, (800) 377-6810
> fax (847) 758-1927

The almanac covers the Internet as well as the computer industry.

Cyber Dialogue
www.cyberdialogue.com

> 304 Hudson Street
> New York, NY 10013
> phone (212) 255-6655

This market research firm studies online consumers.

Datamonitor
www.datamonitor.com

> 106 Baker Street
> London, W1M 1LA, United Kingdom
> phone 44 (0) 171 316 0001
> fax 44 (0) 171 316 0002

Among other things, this research firm tracks market dynamics concerning the Internet and telecommunications.

Dow Jones Business Directory
bd.dowjones.com

> Dow Jones & Company, Inc.
> 200 Liberty Street
> New York, NY 10281

phone (212) 416-2000

fax (212) 416-4348

This site lists itself as a directory of high-quality business information sites. And it does appear to live up to that billing, with links in categories from careers to public records.

E-commerce Guide
e-comm.internet.com

internet.com Corp.

501 Fifth Avenue, 3rd Floor

New York, NY 10017

phone (212) 547-7900

fax (212) 953-1733

This advertising-supported site is rich in articles and discussion groups concerning e-commerce and what it calls *e-tailing* (electronic retailing).

E-commerce Research Room
www.wilsonweb.com/research/intro.htm

Wilson Internet Services

P.O. Box 308, Rocklin, CA 95677

phone (916) 652-4659

Advertising-supported site run by a e-commerce consulting firm, with a long list of introductory and general e-commerce article that can be reached through online links.

E-commerce Tax News
www.ecommercetax.com

Markle Stuckey Hardesty & Bott, Certified Public Accountants, APC

22 Battery Street, Suite 700

San Francisco, CA 94111

phone (415) 925-1120

fax (415) 925-1140

This online newsletter covers the moving target of Internet taxes in the United States and abroad.

eMarketer
www.emarketer.com

> e-land inc.
> 821 Broadway, 3rd Floor
> New York, NY 10003
> phone (212) 677-6300
> fax (212) 777-1172

This site not only offers the usual news and information on doing business online, but it also has a special emphasis on Internet and e-commerce statistics and any news that contains such statistics.

eRetail.Net
www.eretail.net

> Solutions East Inc.
> 6312 Seven Corners Center #263
> Falls Church, VA 22044
> (no phone given)

This site presents daily news of interest to the Internet retailing scene, mostly in the form of links to other news sites.

FlashCommerce
flashcommerce.com

> (no address given)
> phone (415) 642-3510
> fax (603) 375-8019

This site is an online community based on the idea of small business owners talking about the latest e-commerce news and developments. For the sake of sparking discussions, the site ends up compiling a lot of basic e-commerce news.

Forrester Research
www.forrester.com

400 Technology Square

Cambridge, MA 02139

phone (617) 497-7090

fax (617) 613-5000

Forrester is the granddaddy of information technology market research firms.

GartnerGroup Dataquest
www.gartner.com

www.dataquest.com

56 Top Gallant Road

Stamford, CT 06904

phone (203) 316-1111

This market research firm is a combination of Dataquest (in San Jose, California) and the GartnerGroup (in Stamford, Connecticut) Both were leading firms even before the merger. The firm began the year 2000 by hiring 20 e-commerce experts, pushing its e-commerce staff to more than 250 people.

Greenfield Online, Inc.
www.greenfieldcentral.com

15 River Road, Suite 310

Wilton, CT 06897

phone (203) 834-8585

fax (203) 834-6413

This market research firm specializes in Internet-based consumer research.

Intermarket Group
www.intermktgrp.com

P.O. Box 500126

San Diego, CA 92150-0126

phone (619) 675-0311

fax (619) 675-9245

The market research firm produces, among other things, the semiannual *eCommerce Almanac* reference directory.

International Data Corporation (IDC)
www.idc.com

5 Speen Street

Framingham, MA 01701

phone (508) 872-8200

This market research firm produces numerous reports on numerous technology-related topics and is truly international.

J.D. Power and Associates
www.jdpower.com

30401 Agoura Road, Suite 200

Agoura Hills, CA 91301

phone (818) 889-6330

fax (818) 889-3719

This market research firm covers all aspects of the automobile market—including car sales over the Internet.

Jupiter Communications
www.jup.com

627 Broadway

New York, NY 10012

phone (212) 780-6060

fax (212) 780-6075

This market research firm covers consumer e-commerce, and it is probably the leading voice in that field.

Mercer Management Consulting
www.mercermc.com

2300 N Street, NW

Washington, DC 20037

phone (202) 778-7000

fax (202) 778-7997

This group has produced some interesting studies on the economics of e-commerce and trends among users.

Mediamark Research
www.mediamark.com

650 Avenue of the Americas, 3rd Floor

New York, NY 10011

phone (212) 884-9200

This market research firm studies the effect of advertising.

National Mail Order Association, LLC
www.nmoa.org

2807 Polk Street NE

Minneapolis, MN 55418-2954

phone (612) 788-1673

fax (612) 788-1147

If e-commerce boils down to mail order with electronic order entry, then this organization has a lot to offer. The site includes numerous tips and warnings plus pointers on writing direct-mail ad copy.

Navidec Inc.
www.navidec.com

6399 South Fiddler's Green Circle

Greenwood Village, CO 80111

phone (303) 222-1000

fax (303) 222-1002

This consulting and market research firm performs "Cybershopper" surveys to examine the buying habits of the U.S. online population.

NetBusiness
www.techweb.com/netbiz/

CMP Media Inc.
600 Community Drive
Manhasset, NY 11030
phone (516) 562-5000

This online magazine covers not only e-commerce but also the issues involved in running intranets, extranets, and so on.

Net Market Makers Inc.
www.netmarketmakers.com

2140 Shattuck Avenue, Suite 1110
Berkeley, CA 94704
phone (510) 647-3799
fax (510) 647-3553

This consulting company sets up *net markets* (also known as *e-services* or *e-markets*) that serve as business-to-business Web hubs for specific industries. Its Web site carries news and information about net markets, making it a place to start looking for one in your industry.

Net Profit Center
www.net-profit-center.net

Planet Computer Services
(no address or phone given)

Online compilation of material on e-commerce backed up by links to other sites (that contain the original data or news stories).

Nielsen Media Research
www.nielsenmedia.com

299 Park Avenue
New York, New York 10171
phone (212) 708-7500
fax (212) 708-7795

You've heard of the Nielsen Ratings for broadcast media audience estimates? The firm also does advertising research, which these days includes the Internet.

Nua Ltd.
www.nua.ie

> Merrion House, Merrion Road
> Dublin 4, Ireland
> phone 353 1 2187600
> fax 353 1 283 9988

Yes, this Internet service firm is in Ireland. Its Web site has an extensive bibliography of e-commerce research.

PC Data, Inc.
www.pcdata.com

> 11260 Roger Bacon Drive
> Reston, VA 20190
> phone (703) 435-1025
> fax (703) 478-0484

This market research firm covers computer sales and, recently, Internet usage.

Planet IT E-Business
www.planetit.com/techcenters/e-commerce

> CMP Media Inc.
> 600 Community Drive
> Manhasset, NY 11030
> phone (516) 562-5000

This is the e-commerce branch of Planet IT, an online community for information technology executives, with news, analysis, and feature stories.

Roper Starch Worldwide
www.roper.inter.net

> 205 East 42nd Street, 17th Floor
> New York, NY 10017

phone (212) 599-0700
fax (212) 867-7008

This market research firm covers consumer spending.

Charles Schwab & Co., Inc.
www.schwab.com

101 Montgomery Street
San Francisco, CA 94104
phone (415) 627-7000
fax (415) 627-8840

This brokerage firm also publishes (or sponsors and then publishes) economic research of various kinds.

Sell It! On the Web
www.sellitontheweb.com

Netsavvy Communications
United Kingdom (no address listed)
fax 44 171 691 7568

This advertising-supported site lists a great deal of general information about e-commerce and related topics, like picking shopping-basket software and marketing tips. Operated out of the United Kingdom, it appears to embody the point made in Chapter 11—newsletters are a great marketing tool.

Small Business Taxes and Management
www.smbiz.com

The A/N Group
(no address given)

The title says it all. There is also a collection of links of interest to small businesses.

SmartAge Knowledge Center
www.smartage.com/knowledge_center/

3450 California Street
San Francisco, CA 94118
phone (415) 674-3787
fax (415) 674-3782

SmartAge is an e-commerce consulting and services firm (including e-commerce hosting), and its site contains general information about e-commerce.

TopHosts.Com
www.tophosts.com

TopHosts International Inc.
46 Metcalfe Road, Suite 100
Regina, SK S4V 0H8 Canada
phone (306) 546-3778
fax (306) 546-3779

This site amounts to an online magazine concerning Web-hosting business and technology, with lists of reviewed Web-hosting firms. It's a good place to start looking for an e-commerce service provider.

UPS Library of E-commerce Information
www.ec.ups.com/ecommerce/library/library.html

(no address given)

Yes, this is the United Parcel Service of America, Inc., and yes, it has a Web site promoting the use of e-commerce, containing mostly general pointers.

Useit.Com
www.useit.com

Jakob Nielsen's Website
(no address given)

This site is devoted to Web site layout and design issues. The layout of the site itself is spartan, with almost no graphics. Go thou and do likewise.

Usenet

Discussions of e-commerce can show up in nearly any newsgroup (one surfaced in soc.culture.malaysia), but the best bets appear to be alt.ecommerce and alt.business. You never know when you are going to stumble on gold—any thread with more than one message may be worth reading.

ZDNet E-business
www.zdnet.com/icom/e-business

> ZD, Inc.
>
> 28 East 28th Street
>
> New York, NY 10016-7930
>
> phone (212) 503-3500

This is an online magazine in the Ziff Davis chain (hence the name) devoted to e-commerce, with a steady offering of news, features, reviews, and links.

ZdNet E-business Best Practices
www.zdnet.com/enterprise/e-business/bphome/

> ZD, Inc.
>
> 28 East 28th Street
>
> New York, NY 10016-7930
>
> phone (212) 503-3500

A page in the ZDNet system (the online version of the Ziff Davis family of technical magazines), this is a fascinating collection of good and bad examples of e-commerce sites. Try not to show up on the second list.

Appendix B

Representative
E-commerce
Service Providers

This list is thought to be representative of ESPs (ISPs with tailored packages that include shopping-cart functions) but is not claimed to be exhaustive. Inclusion does not imply an endorsement. When available, toll numbers were included in preference to toll-free numbers because the former are not subject to abuse and provide geographical pointers. Services that did not display any phone numbers were skipped.

1-800-Hosting.com, Inc.
www.1-800-HOSTING.com
(214) 720-1442

1 Stop Web Site E-commerce
www.1stopwebsiteecommerce.
   com
(323) 462-2962

4e-commerce.com
www.bhcom.com
(760) 360-4600

9NetAvenue
www.9netavc.com
(201) 902-9300

Advanced Internet Technologies, Inc.
www.aitcom.com
(910) 485-2382

Affinity Hosting
www.affinity.net
(310) 354-2626

Alta Host
www.altahost.com
(760) 726-3678

Amazon.com Zshops
www.amazon.com
(206) 622-2335

America's Host
www.americashost.com
(810) 790-2257

Apollo Hosting, Inc.
www.123besthost.com
(757) 898-8666

Bell Atlantic
www.baweb.com
(800) 509-0764

Bigstep.com
www.bigstep.com
(415) 229-8500

Burlee Networks
www.burlee.com
(877) 428-7533

BuyItOnline
www.buyitonline.com
(888) 266-1117

Catalog.com, Inc.
www.catalog.com
(972) 380-2202

C I Host
www.cihost.com
(817) 868-6999

CommuniTech.Net
www.communitech.net
(816) 300-4678

Concentric Network Corp.
www.concentric.com
(408) 817-2800

Coollink
www.coollink.net
(214) 576-3000

DataRealm Internet Services, Inc.
www.datarealm.com
(877) 227-3783

digitalNATION
www.digitalnation.net
(703) 642-2800

EarthLink
www.earthlink.net
(408) 815-0770

E-commerce Technology Austin
www.ectaustin.com
(512) 477-0929

eCongo.com, Inc.
www.econgo.com
(408) 871-7980

Freemerchant
www.freemerchant.com
(510) 595-2500

GoBizGo
www.gobizgo.com
(858) 455-4685

Henshaw Consulting & Internet Services
henshaw.net
(303) 512-0402

Host Depot
www.hostdepot.com
(954) 723-0762

HostPro, Micron Internet Services
www.hostpro.com
(888) 638-5831

Hostway.com
www.hostway.com
(312) 236-2132

IBM Small Business Center
www.ibm.com/smallbusiness/
webconnections
888-IBM-5800, code WC326

iCat
www.icat.com
(206) 505-8800

IE Internet.Com
ieinternet.com
353 (0) 1 667 7244 (Ireland)

INetU
www.inetu.com
(610) 266-7441

Infinities Online
www.infinities.com
(803) 750-7500

Interactive Multimedia Corp (IMC)
www.imconline.com
(404) 252-2972

Interland, Inc.
www.interland.com
(404) 586-9999

iTOOL
www.itool.com
(877) 464-8665

Jumpline.Com
www.jumpline.net (sic)
(614) 421-9401

JustWebIt.Com, Inc.
www.justwebit.com
(801) 222-0202

Kurant storesense.com
www.storesense.com
(415) 241-9150

LiteSpeed Technologies
www.litespeed.net
(561) 832-3929

Mal's E-Commerce
www.ait2000.com
0034 971 192306 (Spain)

Media3 Technologies
www.media3.net
(781) 826-1213

MindSpring
www.mindspring.com
(404) 815-0770

Mini-Host Domain Hosting Services
www.minihost.com
(334) 821-5940

NetNation Communications, Inc.
www.netnation.com
(604) 688-8946 (Canada)

OLM
olm.net
(203) 878-8637

Pegasus Web Technologies
www.pwebtech.com
(888) 734-9320

**PowerSurge
Technologies, Inc.**
www.powersurge.net
(319) 266-3337

Radka Hosting
www.radka.com
(815) 444-1100

**Sage Networks
(Interliant, Inc.)**
webhosting.interliant.com
(914) 640-9000

SiteHosting.net
www.sitehosting.net
(562) 699-6400

SmartAge
www.smartage.com
(415) 674-3787

SpeedyWeb.com
www.speedyweb.com
(888) 416-4678

Stores Online
www.storesonline.com
(800) 233-0669

Superb Internet Corp.
www.superb.net
(604) 638-2525 (Canada)

ValueWeb
www.valueweb.net
(954) 334-3449

Verio
www.verio.com
(303) 645-1900

Vservers
www.vservers.com
(425) 897-1991

Web 2010
www.web2010.com
(407) 445-2427

WebAxxs.net
www.webaxxs.net
(203) 878-8637

Webhosting.com, Inc.
www.webhosting.com
(416) 260-5411 (Canada)

WebIntellects, Inc.
www.webintellects.com
(760) 727-4449

WebXess, Inc.
www.webxess.net
(512) 918-3288

**Worldwide Internet
Publishing, Inc.**
www.worldwideinternet.net
(561) 994-3600

Yahoo! Stores
store.yahoo.com
(408) 616-3801

$\mathcal{A}ppendix$ C

Useful HTML Tags

The Web is founded on HTML files. But as you may have noticed in Chapters 8 and 9, when building an e-commerce site through a shopping-cart site-creation system, you don't have to worry about creating HTML files. You just input the text that will be displayed, and the system generates the files.

But typically, if the text contains HTML tags, then they will be acted on. And you might want to include HTML tags with your text, because doing so will give you far greater control over the appearance of the text, letting you add emphasis and tweak the formatting.

First, some background: Formatting commands in the HTML language—the tags we've been talking about—are inserted into the text, and they pass on instructions to the user's browser. The HTML tag syntax is quite simple, with codes placed between angle brackets: <center> would tell the browser to center the material that comes after the code.

If the tag sets a condition that can be turned off, another tag that includes the slash character is used to do so. For instance, the tag </center> would turn off the centering.

Anything between angle brackets that the browser does not understand, it ignores.

The thing to remember about designing Web sites is that the users are spread around the globe, with equipment that varies wildly and is beyond your control. Because their screen widths and fonts will vary, there is no way to totally control how a particular page will appear on the screen of a given user (unless each page is sent as a graphic image, a painfully slow proposition.) So although HTML tags can add snap to your pages, there is, on the other hand, no point trying to be too fancy.

HTML tags include codes for:

- Text appearance (typefaces, color, size, font).
- Text formatting.
- Hyperlinks.
- Page setup.
- Images.
- Page layout (frames, tables/columns, image/text alignment).

In this section we will be concerned mostly with the text appearance and formatting tags and also with hyperlinks. The other considerations can be handled for you by the ESP's site-creation system. If you are in a position where you do need to create complete HTML files, there is now a range of excellent authoring tools available, and word processors such as Microsoft Word 2000 will save word processing files in HTML format.

Some services assume the use of Microsoft FrontPage, an HTML authoring tool that will handle the coding details for you.

■ A NOTE CONCERNING PARAGRAPHS

When interpreting standard HTML, the browser will ignore line breaks and even blank lines between paragraphs and spaces between words, and it will run all text it encounters into one paragraph until it sees either an end-of-paragraph tag or a line break tag: <p> or <br>, respectively. When inputting text through a site-creation system, the system will know to interpret line breaks as, well, line breaks. But when testing the appearance of your text before site creation, you will need to use the <p> and <br> codes to get coherent results. Leaving these in when cutting and pasting the text to the site-creation system, explained in Chapter 9, should have no effect.

Text-formatting tags such as <center> trigger an end of paragraph because formatting cannot change inside a paragraph.

■ CONTROLLING TEXT APPEARANCE

➤ Typefaces

Almost two dozen tags control text appearance, many of which are limited to niche uses. The tags for the main ones, and their common combinations, are shown in the following list. Figure C.1 shows how they look on the screen.

```
<b>boldface</b>
<i>italic</i>
<u>underlined</u>
<tt>typewriter (or teletype) style</tt>
<b><i>boldface italic</i></b>
<b><u>boldface underline</u></b>
<b><i><u>boldface underline italic</u></i></b>
<i><u>underline italic</u></i>
```

Of course, no tag is needed for normal text. (The technical term for a normal typeface, incidentally, is *roman*.)

➤ Color

For changing font color, the syntax is similar, with a tag before and an end tag after the text in question:

```
<font color = "colorname">text to be colored</font>
```

Note that the color name should be in quotation marks. The color names that you can use depend, in the end, on the browser software and the available display hardware. But it is safe to use the following color names because they are supported by both Microsoft Internet Explorer and Netscape Navigator:

- Aqua.
- Black.

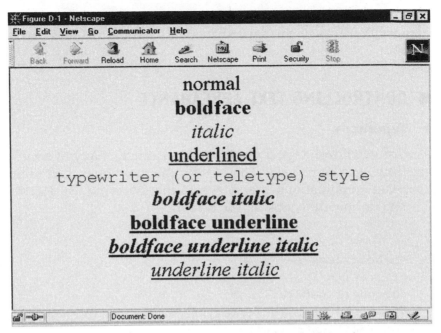

Figure C.1 How the typical HTML typefaces look on the screen, using large type for clarity.

- Blue.
- Gray.
- Green.
- Lime.
- Maroon.
- Navy.
- Olive.
- Purple.
- Red.
- Silver.
- Teal.
- White.
- Yellow.

Figure C.2 shows some in use. Now, at this point, purists would go on and lecture you about how you can specify the exact shade you want using RGB hexadecimal values. Yes, with considerably more effort, you can generate custom colors that

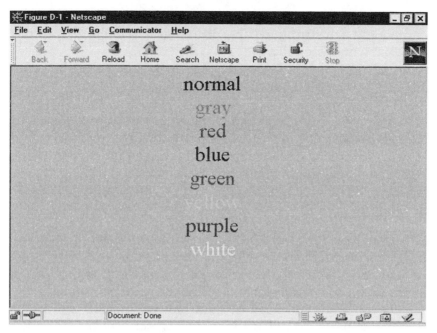

Figure C.2 Representative screen colors in use—as rendered in black and white, of course.

will look almost exactly like the ones listed previously. If you are not heavily into color schemes, skip the next section. Otherwise, take a deep breath and read on.

RGB refers to red, green, and blue, and the idea is to break the desired color into its red, green, and blue components and then assign the intensity of each component a value of 0 to 255 (i.e., 1 of 256 intensity levels). Each of these values is then rendered in the base 16 (i.e., hexadecimal) number system. To let the world know you are using a hexadecimal number, you place a # symbol in front of it. In hexadecimal, you count to 15 and then start over with #10—as opposed to the old-fashioned decimal system, where you count to 9 and start over with 10. You use letters for the numbers between 9 and 15 so that #A is the same as 10, #F is the same as 15, #10 is the same as 16, and #FF is the same as 255. Taking purple as an example, we remember from kindergarten that purple is half red and half blue, with no green. So on a scale of 256, red would be 128, blue would be 128, and green would be 0. In hexadecimal, 128 is #80. To create the color name, the two-digit hexadecimal numbers for each component are strung together in red-green-blue order, so our example would look like

```
<font color="#800080">text to be colored</font>
```

Obviously, there is no end to fiddling with color values. Our advice: using color sparingly will give it more meaning. And sticking to the big-name colors will make the process go faster, and no one will think any less of you.

➤ Type Size

Sitting at a modern word processor with a modern printer, you have almost total control over the size of your text. With a few mouse clicks you can size it by *points*. Seventy-two points is about an inch; a comfortable reading size is 10 or 12 points.

On the Web, you have no such power. Instead, the user's browser will have a default font size, which can be set by the user. You have to scale up or down from whatever that default size is.

The way HTML approaches it, each font has sizes 1 to 7, and the default size is 3. If the default text size of the user's browser is 12 points (a good bet, that being the factory setting for most browsers), then the seven sizes are equivalent to 8, 10, 12, 14, 18, 24, and 36 points.

The syntax for putting text in 36 points—size 7—would be:

```
<font size=7>text to be resized</font>
```

Figure C.3 shows a browser screen with the seven sizes in use. But before we leave the subject, there are two points we need to make:

1. You may come across an alternate syntax that adds or subtracts numbers to or from 3 so that our example would change to <font size=+4>. Either method should work.

2. As font sizes go, 36 points is not that big, which is why banner headlines and titles are typically created with graphics rather than with sized text.

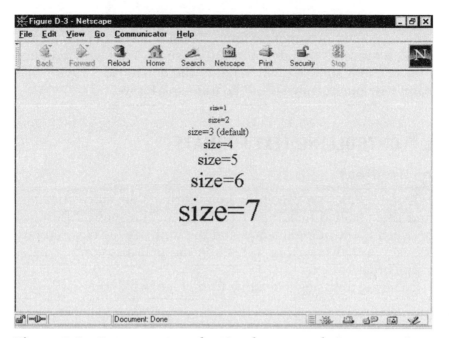

Figure C.3 Browser screen showing the seven relative screen sizes that HTML allows you. The size is relative to the default text size as set by the user. But most users can be expected to have left it at the "factory setting"—12 points, as shown here.

➤ Fonts

A syntax similar to the color and size control can be used to control the text font. The tag to display some text in a font called Playbill would look like this:

```
<font face="Playbill">text to be in the new font</font>
```

But this assumes that the user has, in the font control panel of his or her machine, a font whose name exactly matches whatever is in quotes in the tag and that its characteristics exactly match those of the font you are using. And you have no control over this. So now we have to back up and suggest that you not use the font control tag because the results are unpredictable. (If the named font is not found, the browser reverts to its default font, so you are safe in that respect.)

However, with your ESP's site-creation system, you may be able to specify ornamental fonts. These will be placed on the page as graphics and downloaded as such. They will produce predictable results but will magnify the download time for that page. Obviously, they should be used sparingly.

■ CONTROLLING TEXT FORMATS

➤ Headings

HTML includes six predefined text formats for use as headers and titles, called headings 1 through 6. The main difference between the heading formats and the font size tag covered previously is that inserting a heading tag will also force a paragraph break.

The tag for using a heading format looks like this:

```
<h1>Header Text</h1>
```

The tags for the other formats would, of course, be h2 through h6. As with the font-size tag, the size of the text is relative to the default size used by the browser. If it is 12 points, the size of h1 through h6 would be 24, 18, 14, 12, 10, and 8 points, respectively.

But your site-creation system may have specific ideas of how headers should be displayed, so you may not need the heading formats at all, or their use may cause unneeded complications, especially as they introduce a paragraph break. And 24 points really is not that big when it comes to titles and banners.

➤ Preformatting

As noted previously, HTML does not preserve the spacing and line breaks that it finds in text. Suppose you have a preexisting financial chart, with the fiscal quarters on separate lines and the figures spaced into nice vertical columns. Cutting and pasting it into a Web page will produce an incoherent solid block of text. To get it to look good in HTML will require major surgery—the lines will have to end in paragraph tags, and you may have to set up a table to show the columns as you want them.

Admittedly, there are authoring tools these days that will help you. Your ESP's site-creation tool may be able to help. (It should at least preserve the line breaks on the text that you input.)

But an extremely simple solution (as shown in Chapter 8) is to use the HTML preformat tag. The syntax looks like this:

```
<pre>Existing text whose formatting is to be preserved</pre>
```

The results that can be archived with the `<pre>` tag are shown in Figure C.4. Notice that the text is displayed in a fixed-width typewriter-style font, which will allow columns to line up

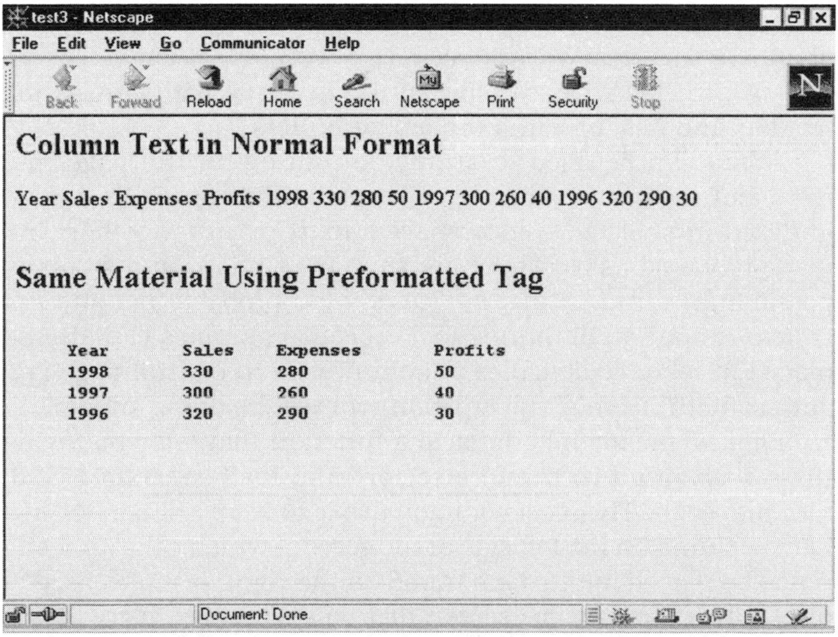

Figure C.4   The material at the top of this browser screen is chart text that was lined up by rows and columns and was then pasted directly into a Web page. HTML ignores the line breaks and multiple spaces, reducing the chart to hash. Below, the chart's formatting is restored by simply using the `<pre>` tag.

but will not look as fancy as the variable-width fonts that most browsers use by default and that make the output resemble a page from a printed book. However, size, typeface, and color tags can still be applied.

■ OTHER FORMATTING AND LAYOUT CONTROLS

The handiest of the remaining HTML tags is undoubtedly the previously mentioned `<center>` tag. Everything—both text and graphics—after the tag is centered on the screen. Centering continues until an end tag is encountered. So the syntax would look like this:

`<center>`Everything to be centered.`</center>`

Beyond that, there are other formatting controls that, for various reasons, would not be appropriate for use in the context of an ESP site-creation system.

Lists, for instance, can format the material with alternating headers and data or with numbers or bullets.

Tables can be used to arrange anything on the page into rows and columns or just rows or just columns. Cells can be outlined in selected colors, spaced apart or run together, and made to vary in size. There are so many options and so many possibilities for error that novices should probably not attempt tables without an authoring tool. Because graphics can also be placed in table cells, tables are often used to control page layout—something your site-creation tool will be doing anyway.

Frames, meanwhile, refer to a function that lets you divide the screen into two or more sectors and load separate HTML files into each. The most common use is to keep a site index in a narrow frame on the left side of the screen, which calls up material to be placed in the main frame on the right. It is also used to place advertising on the screen that will remain in place as the user goes to other pages in the site. Using frames is not appropriate with an ESP site-creation system, which will have its own page layout controls. If you are in the situation where a site is being created using frames, keep in mind that the opening page of most such sites includes a link to a no-frames version of the opening page. This is because there are still users out there with browsers that do not support frames and also because search engines typically cannot follow frame links.

■ HYPERLINKS

Although adding links may be handled by your site-creation tool, there may be situations where you want to add links manually, such as when you want to link a certain word in the text. There are two forms of links: external (to another file, perhaps at another site anywhere on the Web) and internal (to a different spot in the same file). And you can combine the two. We'll cover these approaches separately. There are other wrinkles involving the use of frames that we won't get into.

➤ External Hyperlinks

The way you designate a hyperlink is with an *anchor tag.* It precedes the items to be linked and contains A (for *anchor*) and HREF (for *HTTP reference*) and the Web address of the link. Following the item to be linked, you put an anchor end tag, with the slash character.

For instance, beneath the copyright notice of your site information page you may have the words *Privacy Notice,* which are linked to a page with a full explanation of your privacy policy that carries the file name privacy.html. The link would look like this:

```
<A HREF="http://privacy.html">Privacy Notice</A>
```

On the users' screen, the words *Privacy Notice* will be underlined to designate the linkage. Putting the cursor over the linkage will cause the destination to appear in the URL field at the bottom of most browser screens. Clicking the link will access the target file.

Notice that the file name is in quotes. The http:// prefix does not need to be there if you are addressing a local file, that is, a file in the same subdirectory of the same server. For files that are part of the same site, this is usually the case. But you will need it if you link to a remote site. For instance, you may already have a privacy notice at another site and want to reuse it. We'll assume that the file is again named privacy.html and located at a site named www.yourfirm.com. So the link would look like this:

```
<A HREF=
"http://www.yourfirm.com/privacy.html">Privacy
Notice</A>
```

► Internal Links

It is possible to link to a selected spot in the same file. But first you have to select that spot and give it a name. You do that by inserting a *name tag* at the spot. For instance, if you put your privacy policy at the end of the information page instead of on another page, you could link to it from any other spot on the page. To do that, you would attach a name tag to the initial text of the statement. We'll assume you used the name *privacy* and that the first word of the statement was *Our.* The name tag would look like this:

```
<A NAME="privacy">Our</A> privacy policy is simple...
```

Notice that this, too, is an anchor tag and needs an end tag. There will be no indication on the browser screen that the text has been tagged with a name except that you will jump to this point after clicking the associated hyperlink.

To link to this point, you use an anchor tag that includes the # symbol to indicate that the link is local. In our case it would look like this:

```
<A HREF="#privacy">Privacy Notice</A>
```

The linked text will be underlined just like any other link. But as noted, the target will be invisible to the user.

Note that although named links look quite useful for setting up virtual footnotes, they should be employed sparingly because their use implies that your material runs beyond the bottom of the screen, and every time you go there, you will lose some readers.

➤ External, Named Links

It is possible to link to a named target in an external file. If we have the target #privacy in the file policy.html at the site www.ourfirm.com, we could link to it with a tag that looks like this:

```
<A HREF=
"http://www.ourfirm.com/policy.html#privacy">
Privacy Notice</A>
```

■ TESTING

Before incorporating text with HTML tags into a page, you might want to test its appearance. You can do this by creating a simple text file with the material and saving it, using .htm as the file extension instead of .txt. Then you load it into our browser using the File Open (or in Netscape, File Open-Page) command. In this case you do not need the file setup tags that HTML uses on the Web—the text and the appearance tags are enough.

If you are using an authoring tool, it will have a Preview facility to load the material into a browser.

The more complicated your tagging, the more convenient (and wiser) it will be to test the code before attempting to use it.

All links must also be tested, and they should be tested after the files are loaded on the server. That links work or don't work while the files are on your desktop machine is not a true indication of what will happen online, because you could be tripped by subtleties in the way files are named. For instance, you may be using the name file.htm when the server expects file.html, or you assumed the file is named file.html when it ended up on the server as FILE.HTML.

Glossary

A Classification of Residential Neighborhoods (ACORN)
A marketing segmentation system that classifies consumers according to the type of area in which they live.

Acquiring bank A bank that issues merchant accounts to businesses that want to accept credit card payments. The name derives from the fact that such banks acquire a merchant's sales tickets and then credit the order value to the merchant's account. (American Express and Discover sign up merchants directly and thus act as acquiring banks. They also issue cards directly and therefore act as issuing banks.)

Active server pages (ASP) Occasionally you will notice that the Web page you have been given has an extension of .asp instead of .html or .htm. That is because it is a product of Active Server Pages, a Windows NT script language intended to link Web pages to the contents of databases.

Address verification service (AVS) A fraud protection service created by Visa and MasterCard that compares the address given by a buyer with the address on file for that buyer, on the theory that a card thief would not know the address of his victim. The AVS system returns a code indicating how well the address matches. The merchant can then decide whether to proceed, contact the buyer for clarification, or cancel the order.

Advertising schedule A price listing of the advertisements that can be placed in a particular magazine, newspaper, Web page, and the like, showing production details as well.

Affiliate   A Web site linked to your own under an agreement that pays a commission to the remote site for any purchases by referred customers.

Affinity group   The demographic or psychographic classification assigned to a group of (usually) targeted consumers.

Affinity rewards program   A program that rewards shoppers for making purchases.

AIDA   The acronym for a popular advertising formula: get Attention, arouse Interest, stimulate Desire, and incite Action.

Alphanumeric   Refers to data that can be represented by keys on the keyboard and transmitted as a character code, such as **ASCII**, which see.

America Online (AOL)   This service amounts to a subset of the Internet with commercial features and a centrally managed network plus a flashy, proprietary interface. It can be used for Internet e-mail and for access to the Internet and to the Web, but it can be problematic when used to access Web sites that are subject to constant change. To speed throughput, the AOL system stores the image of popular Web pages so that it does not have to repeat the process of fetching them the next time a user accesses that address. This means that you may be looking at an earlier version of the file.

American Standard Code for Information Interchange (ASCII)   The computer character code in common use except in IBM mainframes. Similar versions exist for various European languages.

Analog   Describes how information in one medium is converted into analogous information in another medium—as opposed to digital, whereby the information is encoded into digital form. A standard phone is analog, a computer is digital, and you need a modem to bridge the gap.

Animation   The GIF file format—one of the formats used for graphics files on the Web—allows multiple images to be basically stacked one atop another in the file. If layers are present, the browser will automatically display one after another, allowing a small (and silent) animation to be added to the page without any programming—everything is built into the graphics file. To keep down total file size, the data in a layer can be limited to the sector of the image where the change actually takes place so that those logos with a whirling globe in the corner do not take up exorbitant space or download time. But they still take more bytes than static images and should be used sparingly.

Anonymous FTP (file transfer protocol)   The procedure for accessing files posted for public use on the Internet in an FTP site. You use the word *anonymous* as your log-in name and your e-mail address as your password. After that, you have full access to the contents of the subdirectory.

Applet   A small program, usually in a language called Java, which can be embedded in the HTML code of a Web page and run by the users' browser when the page loads. They are not full-fledged programs in that they are not allowed to take over your computer, change files, print things, send nasty e-mail to your boss, and so on. They are allowed to make a connection back to the host that sent them.

Application service provider (ASP)   A vendor that provides a specific application, chiefly over the Internet, such as an auction service or project management facility.

Archive   Backup copies of disk material kept for security or audit purposes.

Assembler   A highly complicated programming language that directly controls the inner workings of a computer. Used mostly by professionals on projects where high-speed execution is essential.

Asynchronous (also **Asynch**)   In data communications, this term describes signals that are not synchronized to any timing signal but instead consist of discrete bytes whose spacing may be random.

Audio streaming   The process of broadcasting audio clips from a Web page.

Authorization   The process of checking for adequate funds (or credit limit) in a cardholder's account with the credit card issuer. A positive authorization reserves funds to cover the purchase (or lowers the credit limit). The money is actually deducted at the time of settlement, defined later. Usually, authorization is followed by capture, which see.

Automatic call distributor (ACD)   A system that routs incoming calls to idle telephone agents or, if no one is idle, plays messages begging the callers not to hang up.

Backbone   The high-speed line, or collection of connections, that forms a network's major trunk or arterial pathway. The term is completely relative.

Back-end systems   Systems that perform back-office functions, such as general ledger, inventory management, receivables, payables, and so on. The front end would be the desktop or Web interface.

Bandwidth The volume of material that you can move through a connection. This is usually controlled by the speed of your modem. The term is borrowed from radio frequency broadcasting, where you have the use of a band of the electromagnetic spectrum, and the width of that band determines your capacity. On the Internet you are, of course, typically using the whole capacity of your modem, so the term is misleading. Bandwidth is usually measured in bits per second—which can also be misleading because what you are transmitting is bytes, not bits.

Banner ads Advertisements that are usually rectangular and placed at the top of a Web page. Their placement is typically paid for by a third party, and clicking them jumps the user to the advertiser's Web site.

Binary A base-2 number system that uses only the integers 1 and 0.

Bit A single binary integer—a single 1 or a single 0. Not to be confused with a byte.

Bits per second (bps) The speed rating of a data communications connection, referring to how many bits—including data and framing bits—that can be moved in a second. It is not the same as the *baud rate,* which is the rate at which signals are introduced into the line.

Browser The software on a user's machine that interprets the HTML formatting codes in a Web file for display on the screen and executes the hypertext links, thus giving the user access to the World Wide Web when connected (directly or via a modem) to a Web host.

Browser wars The struggle for market share between Microsoft (with Internet Explorer) and Netscape (with Navigator, later Communicator) by giving away the product. Netscape faded after an early lead.

B2B Business to business.

Buffer Special computer memory used to hold data that is in transit from one place to another.

Byte Eight binary integers, used to represent one alphanumeric character. When transmitted, a byte may take up 10 bits, thanks to the need to insert *framing bits* between bytes.

C A programming language commonly used by professionals for commercial projects. Variants (just so you'll know they're not typographical errors if you ever see them) are C+ and C++.

Capture The process whereby a merchant converts an authorized transaction into a transaction that can be deposited into his or her merchant's account. It amounts to a merchant's request for settlement and can be done only with authorized transactions and *should* be done only when the order is shipped.

Card association   A company such as Visa or MasterCard that supplies credit cards and related services (including authorization and settlement systems) to banks. The banks then issue the credit cards to consumers and merchant accounts to businesses.

Cardholder   A buyer who has a credit card and intends to use it or has already used it to buy something from you.

Card Not Present (CNP) account See **Mail Order/Telephone Order (MOTO) account.**

Catalogue aggregation   The gathering of product data from multiple vendors for display at one site, standardized and displayed so it can be easily compared.

Channel conflict   If you sell your products through the retail channel and then set up a Web site selling the same products at a price competitive with that offered by the retailers, you will have annoyed the retailers and have created what is called *channel conflict.* Firms as diverse as Compaq Computer Corporation and Levi Strauss have experienced it.

Chargeback   A request by the cardholder or the card issuer to reverse a disputed charge. The acquiring bank will typically charge the merchant a fee for each chargeback.

Chat   A conversational connection with one or more members of a network, where the messages of each can be seen and responded to immediately in real time.

Chat room   An online site displaying the chat messages between anyone who has logged in there. Chat rooms usually have a declared topic, oft more honored in the breach than in the observance.

Churn   A term used to denote the endless treadmill that characterizes some consumer e-commerce efforts, which are dominated by a nonstop need to acquire new customers, there being no mechanism to build customer loyalty.

Cliquer   A term used by Forrester Research for someone who uses the Internet in such a fashion that it is integrated with other daily activities and is not the focus of his or her day.

Colocation   Typically, this term refers to the practice of installing a server you own on the premises of a host provider to enjoy the high-speed backbone line available there. There are also security and maintenance advantages.

Common gateway interface (CGI)   A set of rules that describes how a Web server communicates with other software. Using CGI, a programmer can write a Web program (such as a shopping-cart function, a log-in procedure, or even a simple page hit counter) in any language that he or she is familiar with as long as it can run on the server. When you notice that the URL contains cgi-bin, you know that the server is running a CGI program.

Compatibility   Refers to the ability of hardware and software to work together regardless of their origins.

Compression   Owing to the redundancy that exists in most grassroots communication frameworks (such as the English language) plus the duplication patterns that often appear in text, most material can be compressed by a factor of 2. Today's modems depend on compression to reach high speeds. Material that is already compressed cannot, however, be recompressed. On the other hand, some material, especially video, can be compressed to much higher ratios (such as factors of 80) depending on content.

Conversion rate   The percentage of potential customers, interested parties, or Web site visitors that you turn into buyers.

Cookie   Think of the phrase *strangers with candy* and you'll understand why the concept of Internet cookies has been controversial in some circles. A cookie is a line of identifying data that the server gives to a browser upon its first visit, which the browser is expected to store and give back to the server when it visits again or asks for another page. Cookies do not turn the Internet into Big Brother because no browser currently in circulation will identify the user by name to a server. Cookies are used by shopping-cart software to track what pages and selections the user has made. They may expire after you log off or after a set amount of time. Your browser can usually be set so that it refuses cookies or asks your permission before accepting one.

Copy   When used as a noun, this term refers to written material for use in a project, such as an ad or a Web site.

Cost per inquiry (CPI)   The total cost of a marketing campaign divided by the number of inquiries it generated.

Cost per order (CPO)   The total cost of a marketing campaign divided by the number of orders it generated

Cost per thousand (CPM)   In advertising, CPM refers to the cost per thousand *impressions,* an impression being the act of being seen by someone. (*M* means "thousand" in advertising, from the Roman numeral.)

Counter   A number, often placed on the bottom of the page, showing how many times the page has been viewed. This feature is not automatic and must be rigged through HTML coding whose nature depends on the server software.

Crash   The complete failure of a computer system; symptoms include locking up and ignoring further input. A software crash (the most common kind) can usually be rectified by rebooting. A disk crash may require the replacement of hardware.

Credit card   A card that replaces cash or checks, such as Visa, MasterCard, American Express, Diners Club, or Discover, with purchases batched and billed monthly to the cardholder for partial or complete payment. It can be a debit card or a charge card as well.

Critical mass   The volume of commerce needed to make a market efficient or, better yet, trigger the so-called network effect (which see.) There appears to be no reliable way to calculate this volume.

Cross-promotion   The practice of promoting a site or product in more than one medium, such as the Web, radio, TV, newspapers, and so on.

CSV (comma-separated value or variable) Format   A simple file format used for transferring data between two applications. (It is also called **comma-delimited format,** and there is a similar **tab- delimited format**.) In e-commerce, CSV is often used to upload inventory information to a store's site (and download order information.) Most spreadsheets and database programs can export data into the CSV format. Therefore, you can extract the needed data from an existing application or assemble it in some handy form such as a spreadsheet before exporting it and uploading it. Similarly, downloaded CVS files can be fed into many spreadsheet, database, or accounting applications.

   CSV sees data as records divided into fields. For a widget inventory file, you might want to include model, size, color, price, and a comment. A CSV file that would impart this information, written on a spreadsheet and exported in the CSV format, would look like this:

```
model,color,size,price,comment
Widget2000, red,medium,349,"""Slightly"""
dented
Widget2001,red,medium,349,Left-handed
model
```

> Widgetaire,,large,449,Available only in
> mauve.

The first line shows the names of the fields in use. (These may be specified by the ESP service's shopping-cart software, or you may be asked to define them.) Each of the following lines contains the data for one of the inventory items, broken into data fields, which must appear in the same order as they do in the first line. (This makes spreadsheets handy for organizing the data, because you can arrange the fields in columns.) Notice that fields in a record can be left blank—there is a color given for the last one. There are three sets of quotation marks bracketing the word *slightly* in the first comment because the word was in quotation marks in the original comment, and commas and quotation marks that are to appear in the text of a data field must themselves be set between quotation marks.

Cursor   The flashing spot on the screen where any impending screen activity will take place. Its hypnotic affect is easy to exaggerate, but there are office furniture makers who offer desks with built-in alarms to remind users to flex their bodies every few minutes.

Cyberspace   The sum total and effect of everything that happens online. Increasingly, this means the Internet. The term comes from the 1984 novel *Neuromancer* by William Gibson.

Database   A collection of data configured for easy access and analysis by specialized software.

Data transfer   An ISP or ESP will generally have some limit of how much data your site is allowed to send out to the Internet over a given day, week, or month. (Even if there is no stated limit, you can bet that they will be prepared to act if you start clogging up their connection.) Unless you are sending out video streams, it will probably never be an issue.

Digital   A communication method whereby data is encoded in binary form, as opposed to analog, where the signal changes media (such as from sound to electricity) without any encoding.

Discount rate   Bank jargon for the transaction fee that an acquiring bank charges a merchant for handling credit card transactions.

Disintermediation   The use of the Web to buy directly from the manufacturer, circumventing the intermediaries. The idea has ruined the digestion of many marketing executives, but it has not proven a factor in the consumer market, where there is too much friction. (In other words, people are not going to go online to buy their favorite cold cream from the manufacturer. Even if they could remember who makes that brand, it is just as easy to pick it up while they are at the store.)

Distribution channel   The succession of intermediaries through whose hands a product passes from the maker to the end user. These fall into categories, such as retail, distribution, and OEM.

Domain name   At www.wiley.com, the domain name is wiley.com. The .com means "commercial." There is also .net (used by ISPs and other net enterprises), .gov (for government sites), .mil (for military sites), .edu (for colleges and universities), and .org (for nonprofit organizations). Overseas, a suffix is added to identify the country, so www.ourplace.com.ca would be a Canadian (not Californian) site. Thousands of names have been registered by people who are not using them but just sitting on them, hoping to eventually sell them to a real user. Already, the authorities are looking for ways of dealing with such so-called cyber squatters.

Drop shipping   The practice whereby a manufacturer ships an item directly from its warehouse with your label on it after you receive an order for it at your Web site (or wherever.) The manufacturer gets more sales, and you don't have to keep an inventory or have a shipping department. Management, however, can be a nightmare.

Duplex   Refers to the ability of a telecommunications connection to carry data in both directions. *Full duplex* means data is traveling in both directions at once; *half duplex* means it can go in either direction but in only one direction at a time. (*Simplex* means it can go only in one direction, period.) However, *duplex* is often used to describe whether data is echoed locally or remotely, regardless of the actual nature of the connection. *Full duplex* means a remote echo, and *half duplex* means a local echo.

E-commerce   Commerce that takes place over the Internet. (But strictly speaking, it would also include EDI.) Business-to-business e-commerce implies bulk sales in a supply chain. Consumer e-commerce implies people buying things from retail Web sites.

Electronic commerce provider   An ISP that provides e-commerce Web sites, with shopping-cart software and (typically) credit card processing services. Also called a **commerce service provider (CSP).**

Electronic data interchange (EDI)   Automated electronic mail between business systems, using formats set by industrial organizations, for things such as automatic invoicing, ordering, and shipping notification.

Electronic software distribution (ESD)   The sale of software through downloads.

Encryption   The process of turning text or other data into what appears to be random gibberish to anyone who does not have the decryption key.

Enterprise resource planning (ERP)   The last word in corporate software, ERP integrates most corporate functions to plan what is needed tomorrow on the basis of what is being manufactured today and what was sold yesterday.

Exponential market   Also called a **circular market,** this term refers to any market where participants can be both buyers and sellers, thus speeding up the arrival of critical mass and the network effect (which see.) An example would be electrical utilities, which both buy and sell to each other. (The opposite of an exponential market is a *linear market.*)

File transfer   The sending of files in such a fashion that the file that arrives at the remote computer is identical to the one on the sending computer.

File transfer protocol (FTP)   The most common method of moving files between two Internet sites, especially now that Telnet has fallen into disfavor. With FTP you can log in and send, retrieve, delete, and rename files. You can also use FTP to transmit files too large for an e-mail system to handle. Meanwhile, in a practice predating the advent of HTTP and the Web, many sites publish files by placing them in a subdirectory that can be reached using *anonymous* as the password. These are called *anonymous ftp servers* (which see), but in fact they have names, remain in contact with their families, and so on.

File uploading   To transmit a file of any description using a file transfer protocol, as opposed to auto-typing a text file.

Finger   An Internet software tool used mostly by Net experts to see if a given person has an account at a given site. Fingers from the outside are barred by many sites for security reasons.

Flames   Online messages, usually in discussion conferences, that constitute a heated exchange, quarrel, or feud between two or more users.

Flamers   Online users engaged in producing flames. Self-conscious flamers often begin and end their flames with <flame on> and <flame off>, but most are blind to their own sins.

Fragmentation   (1) Describes the state of having the files on your hard disk scattered in pieces throughout its internal tracking system, thus slowing down the process of file retrieval. Later versions of Windows include a defragmenter to fight the problem. (2) The condition of a market in which there is no one dominant participant, just a lot of small buyers and sellers chasing each other. This situation is deemed inefficient but is beloved of e-services or netmarkets, which hope to profit by imposing order.

Frames   An HTML feature whereby a Web page can display contents from other Web pages, allowing for more sophisticated organization. Typically, pages with frames have the site contents in a narrow column on the left side of the screen and the file being read in a wide column on the right. Older browsers cannot display frames, and not all search engines can follow links from a frame deeper into the site, so sites based on frames often include a link to a no-frames version of the site.

Framing bits   Bits used in asynch connections to separate bytes from each other.

Fraud protection   For merchants concerning credit card transactions, this includes AVS (which see), scanning for credit cards known to be stolen, and checking for buyer behavior common among thieves. Fraud protection is usually offered by an ESP's online payment service.

Frequently asked questions (FAQ)   An FAQ list is often included in a Web site to explain what the organizers are up to, using a question-and-answer format—regardless of whether that format is the best under the circumstances. Because FAQ files are often written before any questions have actually been asked, a better name might be RAQ (readily answered questions).

FTC notification   A notice sent to a customer concerning an order that cannot be shipped within 30 days, fulfilling the requirements of the Federal Trade Commission (FTC).

FUD   Fear, uncertainty, and doubt, the hot buttons of choice among computer and high-tech marketers. Sex has only recently been discovered. Not to be confused with Elmer Fudd, a cartoon character who has never known FUD.

Fulfillment   The process of shipping something after the order for it has been received.

Gateway   Connection between an e-mail service and some other service or mode of transmission, such as to the Internet, a fax number, the telex network, or even surface mail via hardcopy printouts.

Graphics   Refers to a computer's ability (if present) to plot individual pixels on the screen, rather than simply displaying alphanumeric text as if it were a glass typewriter.

Graphics interchange format (GIF)   Probably the most common file format used on the Web for graphics files. GIF allows animations by stacking images as layers in the file, which the browser can show automatically. It also permits the use of transparent colors so that the background of an image will not stand out from the background of the page.

Headers   In e-mail, the date, sender's name, subject, recipient's name, and routing details. To see full details, you need to find a View Full Header or Page Source command. And you may need to do that with spoofed spam to get an idea of where the e-mail really came from.

Hexadecimal   A base-16 number system that programmers use to represent binary numbers. The hexadecimal numbers run 1 through F (15), and 16 is 10.

Hit   In Web parlance, a hit is the act of a server sending a file from a site to a browser. But any given page may contain multiple files, and the sending of each file will be counted as a hit. Therefore, the hits that count are *page views*—the hits on the page's underlying HTML file. Someone who brags of total hits should be given a wide berth.

Home page or **homepage**   The opening page of a site, the first one a visitor normally sees, also called the *index page.*

Horizontal market   A horizontal market involves selling items to companies in more than one industry, typically for internal use by those companies, rather than as raw material for production. The opposite is a *vertical market.*

Host   A computer that performs an ongoing service, such as running a Web site.

Hosting provider   An enterprise that provides web space to third parties, usually for money. Typically they do not provide dial-in Web access, such as an ISP does, so the customer of a hosting provider will still need an ISP account to see his/her own site.

Hypermedia   Material on a Web page that links to another page or to other material elsewhere on the same page.

Hypertext   Text that, when invoked, triggers the display of something else. Typically, it is text on a Web page linked to another page or other material on the same page.

Hypertext markup language (HTML)   The formatting language used to create Web pages. Note that we said *formatting,* not *programming.* HTML controls the layout of the material, using control codes placed inside < angle brackets > called *tags* to which a Web browser is programmed to respond. Tags unknown to a browser are ignored, making it easy to create new generations or flavors of HTML. Such tags are often used to for so-called server side includes or to trigger CGI scripts (which see) to link the page back to a program on the server.

Hypertext transport protocol (HTTP) The protocol for moving Web files across the Internet. The servers that use HTTP comprise the subset of the Internet called the World Wide Web. Web pages were originally distinct because of their uses of hypertext to link one to another and thus make Internet navigation easier. A graphical interface—dubbed a *browser*—made seeing the links easier, and the use of graphics was found to offer far more advantages than just hypertext. But today's graphical browsers still rely on HTTP.

Image map A way of indexing a site from a single graphic that has been segmented so that clicking on different parts of it will invoke a link to different files. A map may have a different link for each state, for instance. (Formerly, it was necessary to differentiate between server-side and client-side maps, but now client-side maps are the norm, meaning that all intelligence is handled by your browser.) Some search engines cannot follow image-map links, and older browsers will not follow them properly, so many sites include text-based versions of the same links at the bottom of the page.

Integrated circuit (IC) A computer chip.

Integrated services digital networks (ISDN) Basically a digital telephone system that is, in urban areas, being added to the PSTN, which see. It gives you a 128,000-bps connection, which sounds pretty good unless cable modem connections are available.

Internet merchant account A merchant account that lets you accept payments over the Internet. Individual acquiring banks may impose rules and requirements over and above that of a MO/TO or CNP account (which see), so if you already have such an account, you must still ensure that it can be used as an Internet account. Different rates may apply.

Internet protocol (IP) number A unique number, in four parts, separated by periods, such as 206.208.4.16. It's sometimes called a *dotted quad*. Every computer on the Internet has an IP number as part of the addressing scheme.

Internet relay chat (IRC)   The Internet version of a chat room.

Internet service provider (ISP)   An enterprise that provides third parties with access to the Internet, usually for a fee. Typically, an ISP also provides hosting and may be called an **Internet Presence Provider (IPP).**

InterNIC   This is an obsolete name for the service that handled domain registrations in the United States. It remains in use for the generic concept, and the name is now used as an information portal concerning domain registration. Actual registration is now handled by a number of accredited registrars, which you can find at www.internic.net. To find out who is in charge of a site, use the Whois function at InterNIC to find the registrar that registered the site; then go to that registrar (InterNIC has a list of links) and use the Whois function there.

Issuing bank   A bank that issues a credit card to the cardholder. In credit card jargon, this is also referred to as the cardholder's bank, although the cardholder probably thinks of his or her bank as the place where he or she has a checking or savings account—but that is another matter altogether. (American Express and Discover issue cards directly to consumers, thus acting as an issuing bank.)

Java   Programming language used for applets.

JavaScript   Programming language similar to intent to Java but much simpler.

Keyword   A word input by a user to search the text of a database or Web search engine to locate a document or Web site that contains it. Search engine keywords can often be reserved by advertisers so that their ads will be displayed when a reserved word is searched for.

Kilobytes   Bytes measured in increments of 1,024 (that being two raised to the tenth power.)

Lifetime value of a customer   The amount a customer spends during the time he, she, or it does business with a vendor, minus the cost of acquiring that customer. Being able to claim *ownership* of the customer (become the default buying channel) is a big deal in the B2B market because it sets the B2B market apart from the ever-churning mass consumer market. However, the need to make the claim tends to set various B2B markets against each other.

Linear market   A market where products move from one end of the supply chain to the other, as with traditional manufactured goods. The opposite is an exponential or circular market.

Local area network (LAN) An arrangement whereby computers can share each other's disk files and other peripherals, usually through coaxial cables or some other method of direct connection.

Log off To issue the necessary commands to end a connection with a remote host in a controlled fashion, as opposed to simply hanging up.

Log on To complete the necessary steps to connect with and use a remote computer.

M When talking about computers, **M** means "million," not "thousand."

Macro A simple program that (usually) plays back a series of keystrokes and thus automates a chore or task, such as setting up a word processing document or drawing a screen particle. Many application programs include some sort of macro language for this purpose, varying from simple keystroke playback utilities to elaborate programming facilities.

Mail bomb Vast quantities of e-mail sent to a particular address to crash the account, sometimes done to take revenge on spammers.

Mail list A sort of inverted conference. Items mailed to the list's e-mail address are automatically forwarded to everyone on its subscriber list. Some lists are moderated, which means that someone gathers the postings, culls and edits them, and sends them out in one batch in basically the same fashion as a newsletter.

Mail-order/telephone-order (MOTO) account A merchant account that lets the merchant take credit card orders over the phone or through the mail; also called a CNP account, which see. MOTO transactions involve more risks than face-to-face transactions where the card is presented, and so a merchant account may not cover MOTO transactions without additional requirements being met. Meanwhile, a MOTO account will not necessarily cover Internet transactions.

Maintenance, repair, operating (MRO) equipment General items sold in horizontal markets to companies for their internal use.

Manual authorization Under this system, the shopping-cart software sends you the data concerning a credit card order by e-mail or fax, and you manually enter it into a transaction-processing system. You'll need the card type, card number, cardholder name, expiration date, and AVS data. Under manual authorization there is increased risk of data entry errors.

Market makers   E-services or net markets call themselves market makers because they bring together buyers and sellers. But they are not market makers in the stricter sense of stock brokerages, which take ownership of shares while acting as intermediaries and make or lose money on price fluctuations.

Megabyte   A million bytes. Well, technically, it's 1,024 (two to the tenth power) kilobytes (or 1,048,576 actual bytes) because computers use the binary system. The trick is to note the difference between megabytes and megabits, because a byte is eight bits. Megabytes are usually used to measure memory, and megabits are usually used to measure transmission speed.

Megahertz   One million cycles per second. In references to radio, this term refers to transmission frequency, but in computer science it refers to the speed of the computer's internal clock—the original PC ran slightly under 5 million cycles per second, and the latest Pentium machines run at about 600. In the first microcomputers it took multiple cycles to accomplish any meaningful operation, but the latest machines are down to 1 cycle or so per operation.

Merchandising   The creative display of products for potential customers, typically based on the brand.

Merchant   An entity that offers goods (or services or software) in exchange for payment.

Merchant account   A bank account that lets you accept credit card payments. The bank that issues it is the acquiring bank (which see), because it acquires the merchant's sales authorization slips. A MOTO or CNP account lets you accept credit card payments without a signed authorization slip. An Internet account will let you accept credit card payments over the Internet.

Merchant account independent service organization (ISO) A third-party company that sells and supports merchant accounts, as opposed to an acquiring bank.

Merchant bank   See **acquiring bank.**

Merchant Identification (MID)   A number that identifies a merchant account to a payment-processing network and to the shopping cart software.

Meta tags   A *tag* is data in an HTML file (i.e., the kind of file used on the Web) to give formatting information to the browser. All HTML tags are text set between angle brackets.

A meta tag is in HTML format but does not contain information of use to the browser, which ignores it. Although also used for programming purposes, meta tags are of interest in e-commerce because they are seen by search engines when they examine the contents of a site. By using special keyword and description meta tags, you can insert the keywords you want the search engine to associate with your site and the description to use when it lists your site on a search results page. (Otherwise, it typically lists the initial text in the file.) Examples:

```
<META NAME="Keywords" CONTENT="Widgets,
Gadgets, Gizmos, Gimcracks, Stuff">
<META NAME="Description" CONTENT=
"Conglomerated Gadget. Click here for the
finest in unidentified stationary objects.">
```

Note the use of angle brackets and quotation marks. (The use of upper- or lowercase is optional.) A web site called Meta Tag Builder at http://Vancouver.webpages.com/VWbot/mk-metas.html will convert text into the proper format. Within an HTML file, the meta tags should be placed between the <HEAD> and </HEAD> tags.

Metcalfe's Law (from Robert Metcalfe). The value of a network grows by the square of the number of participants so that having four fax machines is four times more useful than having two. See **network effect.**

Modem The interface device between a computer and the phone line (or cable TV network, etc.).

Moderator Someone who monitors the traffic in a particular conference or newsgroup, settling quarrels and keeping discussion on track.

Multitasking The ability to run multiple programs at the same time, as opposed to loading multiple programs but running only one.

Multiuser The ability of a computer—through a sophisticated operating system and multiple terminal connections—to serve more than one user at more than one terminal at a time. Examples are Unix and Windows NT.

National Security Agency (NSA) A U.S. government agency involved in cryptography.

Netizen Term used by Forrester Research for someone whose life seems dominated by the Web, spending at least 10 hours a week on-line.

Network effect   The more entities that participate in something, the more there is to be gained by an entity through participation. One fax machine is useless. Two fax machines can perform a valuable but limited task. But when there are millions of fax machines out there, having one gives you the potential of communicating with millions of other users, making it tremendously useful. (See **Metcalfe's law.**)

Node   A computer that is a participating member of an established network.

Normalization technology   The translation routines used by a catalogue aggregator to convert the product terminology used by the various vendors in question into one standard set of terms.

Page impression/view   A hit involving a Web page, without regard to the number of files it may contain.

Parallel   Data connection in which each bit in a byte has its own line. Used for printers and similar peripherals.

Parity   Error-checking bit optionally added to each asynch or serial byte.

Payment Card   Bank jargon for credit card.

Payment-processing network   A system that connects a site's shopping-cart software credit card networks (of Visa, MasterCard, etc.). The credit card networks then connect to acquiring banks (which hold the merchant accounts) and issuing banks (which issued the credit cards to the buyers). Payment-processing networks are also known as **third-party processors** or **front-end processors**—or just **processors.**

Personal identification number (PIN)   The form of password protection used primarily by automatic teller machines, security tokens, and smartcards.

Pixel   One dot on the display screen.

Platform   The combination of hardware and operating system that defines a particular, standardized, computing environment.

Point of presence (POP)   The place (usually downtown) where your carrier's network can be connected. For ordinary users, this means the dial-in number.

Point-to-point protocol (PPP)   Extends TCP/IP connectivity over high-speed modems directly to a desktop computer, giving it full Internet participation. Similar to SLIP (which see), but slower because it offers more error detection and correction features.

Portal   A Web site listing other Web sites and online services; a source of information and chat rooms; of interest to a particular segment of users, be it doctors or asthma sufferers. The promoter typically seeks to sell advertising on the page to someone hoping to reach the target audience.

Post office protocol (POP)   The protocol that your e-mail software uses to fetch e-mail from your host's mail system. It lets people get e-mail from any host anywhere as long as they have the e-mail address and password.

Privacy seals   Logos granted by a certifying organization for placement on a Web site, showing that the site meets the organization's standards for the protection of personal identification (or, if the site does distribute/sell personal information, that it openly states this fact).

Privacy statement   A statement on a Web site concerning the site's policy regarding the use of any personal data gathered by the site from users. If it states that data is not kept confidential, there is often an opt-out feature that lets users specify that their name be removed from the database.

Protocol   The codified rule for doing something technical, such as interfacing a server to the Web.

Pseudo SICs   The addition of a fifth (and eventually, a sixth) character to the standard four-digit SIC code.

Psychographics   Descriptors of a consumer's lifestyle and attitudes.

Public switched telephone network (PSTN)   If you can pick up a phone and dial another phone that is outside your organization, then your phone is attached to the PSTN.

Pyramid scheme   A scam constantly being rediscovered by get-rich-quick spammers in which returns on an investment are actually derived from the input of later investors rather than any commercial activity. It can be a Ponzi scheme (where fantastic interest rates are promised), a chain letter whose recipients are supposed to send money to the sender of the letter and pass it on, or a top-heavy multilevel marketing scheme in which income is generated by the recruitment of dealers rather than the sale of products.

QWERTY   The standard U.S.-style keyboard, so named because of the arrangement of the left-side keys in the second row. The layout was intended to make certain letter combinations difficult and thus prevent jamming and also to put an anagram of the word *typewriter* in the top row to facilitate sales demos. The main variant is the Dvorak keyboard, named after its inventor.

Random access memory (RAM)   The memory embodied in the chips inside the computer, as opposed to the data stored on the hard disk or the diskettes. The name refers to the fact that you can address one byte without scanning through all the others first, as you would have to with magnetic tape. Data stored in RAM is *volatile,* meaning it goes away when the power is turned off.

Read the friendly (yes!) manual (RTFM)   Sometimes rendered **RYFM.** It's the eternal prayer of customer support personnel.

Real-time authorization   A facility that lets a site's shopping-cart software authorize a credit card number while the shopper completes the checkout process. A positive authorization lets the checkout proceed. A negative outcome generates an error message to the buyer, and checkout cannot be completed until an approved number is entered.

Request for proposal (RFP)   A buyer publicly requests that vendors bid on a complicated project

Request for quotation (RFQ)   A buyer publicly requests that vendors bid on supplying a commodity or easily described product.

Scaling   Wall Street is fascinated with Internet companies because they can scale, meaning they can handle huge volumes of sales as easily as small volumes. Unfortunately, problems also scale.

Script file   A record of the commands necessary to (usually) log on to a remote system, used with a modem software package to automate the procedure.

Scripting language   A programming language of ordinary functions, intended for simple jobs such as automating repetitive procedures (for example, setting up the formatting and addressing of a business letter). Also, any language used in a script file.

Search engine   A web site tied to a database that catalogues the text of all accessible files on the Web. The sites are searched periodically, not all files are accessible, and many files (i.e., databases, graphics) contain no useable text. Hence, no search engine can offer comprehensive, real-time coverage.

Secure sockets layer (SSL)   An Internet protocol (originated by Netscape) designed to ease the public's jitters about giving out credit card numbers over the Web. Basically, it encrypts the connection between the browser and the server using a security certificate that both possess (without requiring any knowledge or involvement from you, the user.) The encryption also serves to ensure message authentication and integrity, because a message that was tampered with en route won't decrypt correctly. If you see that the URL begins with https//:, that means that SSL will be used. If you have an up-to-date browser, it will switch into SSL mode automatically.

Settlement   The process of transferring funds between the cardholder's issuing bank (to whom the cardholder has paid his or her credit card bill) and the seller's merchant account at the acquiring bank (or the reverse, for a refund). Settlement is used by Visa and MasterCard. American Express and Discover also settle transactions, but they own both the cardholder and the merchant account.

Serial   A data connection in which all the bits of every byte are sent sequentially and serially down the same line, used for modem connections and for certain peripherals.

Serial line internet protocol (SLIP)   Extends TCP/IP connectivity over high-speed modems directly to a desktop computer, giving it full Internet participation. Similar to PPP but faster while less reliable.

Serial port   An input/output connection on a computer designed to be used with a modem or modem-like device (such as certain printers or scanners).

Server   Strictly speaking, a server is just a computer that provides a specific service to another computer, called the *client*. On the Internet, a server is a computer that transmits files to clients who request them or runs certain programs. On the Web, the clients are users at their desktops running browsers. The computer that hosts your site, the computer that forwards your e-mail, and the computer that runs the multiuser game you're addicted to are all servers.

Server side includes   These are commands embedded in a Web page that trigger commands to its server when the page is accessed. When you call up a page and see that it is displaying the correct date and time, that trick was probably performed using a server side include (meaning that code on the page included action on the server side). Because it is part of an HTML tag, you don't see the command, only its results. However, you can see the commands if you use your browser's Page Source function. They look like `<!—#include virtual="/path/to/file"—>`.

Shopping-cart (or -basket) software   Software, running on a server of an ISP or ESP, that captures what purchase selections that site visitors make and then walks them through the checkout and purchase procedure.

Signature-required account   The type of merchant account used in physical stores, where the user of a credit card must present the card and sign the sales ticket for the transaction to be valid. This is also called a **card present** or **card swiped account.**

Simple mail transport protocol (SMTP)   The protocol used to send e-mail over the Internet. When setting up your e-mail software, you'll need your host's SMTP address. Hopefully, that is the only time you'll ever need to be aware of it.

Site   A set of linked Web pages accessible through a single address, typically devoted to one purpose and maintained by one party.

Spam   Bulk, unsolicited promotional e-mail of an annoying nature. Typically, the less targeted the e-mail is, the more moronic (and persistent) the come-on, with the crowded nadir belonging to pyramid schemes and get-rich-quick scams. The latter often involve the sale of (believe it or not) bulk e-mail software. The term *spam* is said to come not from a brand name for canned spiced ham but from a Monty Python sketch about a Spam restaurant. (The original online meaning of *spam* meant that you were expressing annoyance by filling the screen with reams of meaningless text, electronically shouting down the other person.)

Special interest group (SIG)   Another name for a conference.

Spoof   In reference to e-mail, to send a message with a false return address so as to cover the source of spam.

Standard industrial classification (SIC)   A system used to classify businesses, defined (in its basic form) by the U.S. Department of Commerce.

Stock keeping unit (SKU)   An individual inventory item, including variations of a product, such as those of size and color.

Store and forward   The mode that most e-mail uses, whereby messages are stored until forwarded to the receiver, usually when the receiver eventually logs in, or immediately to a fax machine or to a hardcopy printer for surface mail.

Strange attractor   A silly name, borrowed from quantum physics, for whatever deciding factor attracts a user to e-commerce, such as convenience, lower price, faster delivery, and so on.

Strategy   In the world of corporate e-commerce, the accepted wisdom is that you go ahead and pay whatever it takes to get customers today, hoping that tomorrow—when you've

achieved the economies of scale that e-commerce allows—
they will still be around and amount to a profitable customer
base. As a reason for spending millions of investors' dollars,
you can't beat it.

Surfing   The act of casually looking around on the Internet.

T1   A leased line that can carry 1.544 megabits per second. T1
lines are often described as having the capacity of 24 phone
lines but costing much less. T1 lines are often used to connect large customers to an ISP or to connect smaller ISPs to
main trunks.

T3   A leased line that runs at 44.736 megabits per second.
Although more than enough to run full-motion, full-screen
video (which takes about 10 megabits), it is typically not used
for that but for interhost trunk lines.

Telnet   An Internet function that lets you log onto one Internet computer from another one anywhere on the Internet
and, basically, use it as if you were sitting at one of its
directly attached terminals. It is handy for file management,
but the abuse potential is self-evident, and many hosts have
disabled it. These days you have to use FTP to accomplish
some of the same things.

Terminal Identification (TID)   The number that identifies
to the credit card payment-processing network the terminal
where a transaction took place. An online store would have a
virtual terminal with a TID.

Ticket size   Bank jargon for the monetary value of an order
placed with a credit card.

Tool Bar   An on-screen arrangement of icons that will call up
functions pertinent to the task at hand.

Transaction   An exchange of goods for payment. In terms of
online credit card processing, a transaction begins when a
credit card order is placed with your store. Each attempt to
authorize a credit card is an order attempt and therefore a
transaction. A refund to a buyer is also a transaction.

Transparent   In a market, transparency implies that the price
is known by both the buyer and the seller. In bidding, it
implies that the outcome can be predicted by anyone who
knows all the facts and was not rigged to favor a crony.

Transport Control Protocol/Internet Protocol (TCP/IP)
The data communications method used over the Internet.

Uniform resource locator (URL)   This is the Web address
as used by your browser. When accessing yourplace, it will
use http:// www.yourplace.com/index.html. Of course, in
your marketing literature you can leave off the http://,

which simply tells the browser that it will use hypertext protocol at this site. You can also leave off /index.html (or index.htm if it's a Windows NT site), which tells it to carry out the default procedure and find the HTML file named *index*.

Unix   Also rendered as UNIX. An operating system originated by AT&T and designed for multiuser systems, with built-in telecommunications functions. It is popular mostly in the academic and scientific communities. There are versions that will run on the PC, but it is rarely used for that purpose. The name is a play on Multics, a prior operating system. For users from the PC world, the thing about Unix is that the file names are case sensitive, so that read.me and Read.Me are separate files. Unix is probably a common operating system for Web servers—but tinkering with it should strictly be left to the staff of your ISP or ESP. (Yes, it is pronounced like *eunuchs*. Every possible joke this fact could possibly engender was made long ago. So let's move on.)

Upload   To transmit a file from a user to a host computer or Internet address—the opposite of *download*.

Usenet   A semiformal set of discussion conferences associated with the Internet. Individual conferences are called *newsgroups*. There are, in worldwide distribution, tens of thousands of newsgroups.

Vaporware   Any software product that has been announced and perhaps even reviewed in the press but has yet to appear on the shelves. There have been products that existed in no other form.

Video streaming   The process of broadcasting video from a Web page. Your ISP or ESP will need special hardware for this to work well, and the recipient needs a high-speed connection if the results are going to be worth watching.

Virtual   Something that exists in computer terms but will not be found in the real world. Virtual memory, for instance, is RAM that the computer thinks exists but is really part of the hard disk.

Virus   In the computer world, a self-replicating program that attaches itself to a legitimate program (such as an operating system utility) and seeks to attach copies of itself to other programs. May also cause damage to the system, intentionally or otherwise.

Web page   What you see on the screen when you go to a specific Web address, being the sum total of the contents of the

HTML file at that address and any graphic files to which it links, as formatted on the screen by your browser.

World Wide Web   That part of the Internet using HTTP and HTML, whose users depend on graphical browsers. It is officially three words, not two.

Worm   (1) A self-replicating program that attempts to take over the computer it is resident in and also propagate copies of itself through whatever network it is attached to. (2) Someone who tries to make unauthorized use of a system. This term is preferred over *hacker* by many insiders.

Index

ActivMedia Research, 16, 40, 252
AdAuction, 209
Address Verification System,
 219–220
Advertising
 online, 158–159
 spending, growth of, 248
 through affiliate programs,
  199–203
 to children, 228–230
 via affinity programs, 179
 via e-mail, 163–165
 via link exchanges, 170–171
 via newsletters, 165–166
 via Online Communities,
  166–170
Affiliate programs, 177, 179,
 199–205
Affinia, 203
Airborne Express, 198
AltaVista, 162
Altra, 209
Amazon.com, 6–7, 205
America Online, 13
American Express Small Business Exchange, 252
Arbinet Global Clearing Network, 210

Artwork
 acquiring, 85–92
 cropping, 89
 example, 93
 logos, 91–92
 thumbnails, 90
 transparent colors, 89–90
AssociatePrograms.com, 252
Auctions, online, 187–195
Autoresponder, 38

Banner ads, 158, 172
Banner farms, 201
Banner, adding to example site,
 118–119
BBBonline, 173
BBBonline, use of, 175
BBS. See Online Communities
Bedbug letter, 181
BidCom, 210
Bigstep.com, 32
BizBuyer, 210
Bizreference.com, 252
Boston Consulting Group, 4, 253
Business plan
 creating, 61–67
 example, 67–71
 formal version, 71–73

Business plan *(continued)*
  need for, 51
  pointers for formal version, 74
Buy.com, 7

Carpetbagger, defined, 169
CashPile, 253
CDNow Online Inc., 7
Celebration, need for, 151
Channel conflict, 50
Charles Schwab & Co., Inc., 17, 262
Chat rooms. *See* Online Communities
Chemdex, 210
Children's Advertising Review Unit, Council of Better Business Bureaus, 228
Children's data privacy, rules governing, 230–235
Click trails, charting, 242–245
Click-through programs, 201
Clickz, 253
Cliquers, 18
CommerceNet, 253
Commissions, via affiliate programs, 201
Common Gateway Interface (CGI), 38
Competing sites, analysis of, 57–60
CompuServe, 13
Computer Industry Almanac Inc., 13
Computer Industry Almanac Inc., 254
Concentric Network, 30, 41
Consumer Credit Protection Act, 225
Consumer Leasing Act, 225
Consumers
  concerns about on-line shopping, 10
  on-line demographics, 12–20
  reasons for using e-commerce, 10
Convenience, as e-commerce advantage, 9
Conversion rate, 9, 238
Copy writing, examples
  index page, 105–107
  information page, 111–112
  item page, 108
  product data page, 109–111
Cost overruns, 103
CPA WebTrust Program, 173, 174
Creative Design Group, 94
Credit card fraud, 215–220
CSV data files, use to create site, 141–142
Customer
  acquisition cost, 176
  reassurance programs, 172–174
  retention, 176–177
Customer service
  e-commerce failure rate, 182
  meeting expectations, 183–185
  multi-channel approach, 183, 186
  via e-mail, 186
Customer value, 177
Cyber Dialogue, 40, 254

D & M Escrow Service, 195
Data privacy, children's, 230–235
Database retrieval, from test site, 148–150
Datamonitor, 13, 254
de Haaf, Brian, 41
Deja.com, 167
Delivery problems, 220–221
Descriptors
  adding to example site, 135–137

deciding, 95–97
    example, 97
    need for, 51
Direct mail and Web marketing,
    157, 158
Disintermediation, 20
Domain registration, 36
Dow Jones Business Directory,
    254
Drop shipping, defined, 11
Dutch auctions, 190

EarthLink, 27
eBay, 187
E-commerce Guide, 255
E-Commerce Research Room,
    255
E-commerce service providers
    (ESPs)
    defined, 27
    desirable features, 77–80
    examples of, 27–33, 265–268
    features to look for, 34–40
    finding, 77
    free, 32–33, 42
    free vs. paid, 33–34
E-Commerce Tax News, 255
E-commerce
    business-to-business, defined,
        22
    defined, 21–22
    paralysis as barrier to entry, 41
    questions to ask before pro-
        ceeding, 43–49
    small business use of, 40
    to cease to exist, 246
    volume, projections of, 3–6
eCongo.com, 32
Electronic Data Interchange
    (EDI), defined, 23
EMarketer, 256
Equal Credit Opportunity Act,
    224
eRetail.Net. 256

Escrow services, 195
Escrow.com, 195
E-services, 207–210
Excite, 162

Fair Credit Billing Act, 224
False advertising, 221–222
Federal Trade Commission
    and 900 numbers, 226–227
    and children's advertising
        issues, 228–235
    and children's data privacy,
        230–235
    and deceptive advertising,
        222–228
    and Fair Credit Billing Act,
        224
    and jewelry, 225–226
    and multilevel marketing,
        223–224
    and pyramid schemes, 223
    Business Opportunity Rule,
        223
    Mail or Telephone Order Mer-
        chandise Rule, 220–221
FedEx, 197
File access, desirability, 34
File transfer protocol (FTP), 38
Fixed width text, defined, 110
FlashCommerce, 256
Forrester Research, 3, 17, 18, 19,
    40, 183, 209, 257
Forumone Communications
    Corp, 168
FreeMarkets, 210
Freemerchant, 33, 42
Friday morning, 143
Futzing, 34
Futzing and industrial produc-
    tivity, 142

GartnerGroup Dataquest, 4, 14,
    20, 246, 257
Get rich quick schemes, 46–48

Gofish, 210
Gold rush
  examples, 6–8
  Klondike, 24
Good Housekeeping, 173
Graphics file attributes, 86–87
Green, David, 94, 97, 103, 165, 175
Greenfield Online, Inc. 15, 17, 257

Hardy, Carrie 42, 60, 83, 94, 171, 180, 186, 196, 199, 205, 215, 218
Hits. *See* Page Views
Hobby sites, advertising on, 159
Home page, defined, 99
HotBot, 162
Hoyle, Harry, 20
HTML
  and e-mail, 164
  fonts, setting, 275
  forcing paragraphs, 270
  headings, 276
  hyperlinks, setting, 279–281
  page formatting, 278
  preformatting tag, 276–277
  templates, 34
  testing, 281
  text color, setting, 271–274
  text size, setting, 274
  typefaces, setting 271

iCat, 28, 42
IDC (International Data Corporation), 3, 14, 258
I-Escrow, 195
Information page
  adding to example site, 132–134
  defined, 100
InfoSeek, 162

Intermarket Group, 19, 173, 257
Internet Clearing Corporation, 196
Internet Service Provider (ISP), defined, 26
Internet tax moratorium, 214
InterNIC, 171
iShip.com, 198
Item page, adding to example site, 125–128
Item pages, defined, 99

J.D. Power and Associates, 25, 258
Jewelry, Federal Trade Commission rules, 225–226
Jupiter Communications, 3, 10, 15, 18, 182, 186, 258
Jurassic Park, rejoinder from, 43

Keyboard conversations, 185
KillerBiz, 210
Klondike gold rush, 24
Knowledge, as e-commerce advantage, 9

Layout tips, Web pages, 113–114
Link exchanges
  and referring URLs, 240–241
  used for advertising, 170–171
Links page, adding to example site, 139–140
Liszt, 168
Little Moonjumper Inc., 42
Logos, 91–92
Lycos, 162

Magazines, and Web marketing, 157
Magic bullet, none, 162
Mail Lists. *See* Online Communities
Mallpark, 207

Malls, online, 205–207
Marketing
  to children, 228–230
  Web sites, new methods, 156
  Web sites, overview, 155–157
  via affiliate programs, 199–203
  via affinity programs, 179
Mary Jo M, 49
Matsumoto, Mary Jo, 49
Mediamark Research Inc., 13, 259
Mercer Management Consulting, 10, 176, 247, 248, 258
Merchant account, applying for, 81–83
Merchant status, and ESPs, 35
Meta tags, 106, 107, 137, 161
Mindshare, need for, 248
Mindspring, 28
Monday afternoon, 81
Monday morning, 76
Multilevel marketing, and Federal Trade Commission, 223–224

National Mail Order Association, LLC, 11, 259
Navidec, 14, 19, 259
Net Market Makers Inc., 210, 260
Net Markets, 207–210
Net Profit Center, 260
Net Rules, 18–19
NetBusiness, 260
Netizens, 18
NetMall, 207
Network effect, 4
Newsletters
  advertising, compared, 166
  used in marketing, 165–166
Newspapers, for Web marketing, 157
Nexchange, 203
Nielsen Media Research, 13, 260

900 numbers, Federal Trade Commission rules, 226–227
1999 Christmas buying season, results of, 10
Nua Ltd., 12, 261

Online auctions, 187–195
Online Communities
  correct use, 168
  feuds, 169
  incorrect use, 169
  and spam, 169
  use for marketing, 166–170
Online Malls, 205–207
Operational factors, setting for example site, 137–139
Opt-in page
  adding to example site, 134
  defined, 100–101
Order Page, settings on example site, 137
Order retrieval, from test site, 148–150

Page views
  charting, 237–240
  defined, 237
PaperExchange, 210
Patience, need for, 151, 174
PC Data, Inc., 261
Peniston, Lyerly, 42
Personalization
  desirability, 178
  methods, 178–179
Photonics Online, 210
Pixel, defined, 92–93
Planet IT E-Business, 261
PlasticsNet, 210
Population, trends, 247–248
Preformatting tag, in HTML, 109–110
Price, as e-commerce advantage, 8

Privacy seals, 172–174
Prodigy, 13
Product data page
  adding to example site,
    128–132
  defined, 99
Product family pages, defined,
    99
Product, as e-commerce advan-
    tage, 9
Pyramid schemes, and Federal
    Trade Commission, 223

QuestLink, 210

Radio, and Web marketing, 157
Referring URLs, tracking,
    240–241
Repeat customers, detecting,
    245
Resource Marketing Inc., 174
Roper Starch Worldwide, 13,
    261

Scanner, advantage of, 94
Schulte, John, 11, 12, 24, 25, 49,
    80, 83, 103, 158, 218
SciQuest, 210
Scrappin' Happy, 42
Search engines
  drawbacks to using, 165
  ranking methods, 162
  ranking tips, 159, 162
  and referring URLs, 240
Search words, buying 159, 162
Searches, on-site, charting
    results, 241–242
Section page, adding to example
    site, 123–125
SecureTrades.com, 196
Sell It! On The Web, 262
Shipment tracking, 196
Shipping Services, 196–198

Shipping tips, 198–199
ShopNow.com, 206
Shopping cart software, defined,
    25
Shopping cart, off-site support,
    39
Site layout example, 102–103
Site layout, 98–103
Site map, desirability, 103, 113
Sitematic, 31
SKUs, growth of, 247
Small Business Taxes and Man-
    agement, 262
Small business, common mis-
    takes, 74–75
SmartAge Knowledge Center,
    263
SmartAge, 31
SolidWaste.com, 210
Spam (e-mail abuse), 163
Stores Online, 31
Sunday afternoon, 61
Sunday morning, 57
Swainhart, Christopher, 174

Tacoma, WA, 214
Taxes
  income, 212
  local 212
  sales, 212–215
  sales, and Tacoma, WA, 214
  sales, nexus, 213
Telephone, dialing via TV, for-
    bidden, 229
Testing, example site, 143–146
TestMart, 210
Text
  adding to example site, 120
  adjusting size in example site,
    121–122
  writing, for site, 104–111
Thursday afternoon, 134
Thursday morning, 115

TopHosts.Com, 263
Tracking, of affiliate programs,
202
TradeOut.com, 210
Traffic allowances, 27
Transparent colors, 89–90
TRUSTe, 174
Tuesday afternoon, 95
Tuesday morning, 85
Tulips, financial bubble in 1634,
23
TV, and Web marketing, 157
2-Tier Affiliate Program Direc-
tory, 251
Two-tiered affiliate programs,
202

U.S. Children's Online Privacy
Protection Act, 230
U.S. gross national product, 6
U.S. Internet Tax Freedom Act,
214
U.S. Postal Service, 197
United Parcel Service, 197
UPS Library of E-Commerce
Information, 263

Useit.Com, 263
Usenet, 264

Value America Inc., 7
Value propositions, glut of, 247
Variable width text, defined, 110
Verio, 30
VerticalNet Inc., 210
Vstore, 203

Wal-Marting of America, 40
Web pages, layout tips, 113–114
WebCrawler, 162
Wednesday afternoon, 104
Wednesday, morning, 98

Yahoo! Store
charting examples, 237–245
defined, 29
use to create example site,
115–142
Yahoo!, 162

ZdNet E-Business Best Practices,
264
ZDNet E-Business, 264